Study Gu[ide]

James Buckley
Black Diamond Group

Understanding Psychology
NINTH EDITION

CHARLES G. MORRIS

ALBERT A. MAISTO

Prentice Hall

Boston   Columbus   Indianapolis   New York   San Francisco   Upper Saddle River
Amsterdam   Cape Town   Dubai   London   Madrid   Milan   Munich   Paris   Montreal   Toronto
Delhi   Mexico City   Sao Paulo   Sydney   Hong Kong   Seoul   Singapore   Taipei   Tokyo

Prentice Hall
is an imprint of

© 2010 by PEARSON EDUCATION, INC.
Upper Saddle River, New Jersey 07458

10 9 8 7 6 5 4 3 2 1

ISBN 10: 0-205-79011-9
ISBN 13: 978-0-205-79011-1

Contents

How to Use This Study Guide

Preface

Your Time Is Valuable

Invest your study time so you get the greatest benefit!

The following techniques have been shown to increase a student's mastery of new information:

- Use as many of your senses and abilities as possible—writing, reading, hearing, speaking, drawing, etc.

- Organize information so it is meaningful to you.

- Study with other people whenever possible.

- Have FUN. We remember what we enjoy.

This study guide has been designed to provide you with ideas and resources in all of these areas. This preface explains how to effectively use the sections in each chapter.

Chapter Overview

This section provides you with a summary of the key topics covered in the chapter, including all Key Terms highlighted in bold. You should read this section after reading the entire chapter in your text. Practice exams are an important way to check your progress.

Learning Objectives Exercise

After you have read and studied each chapter, you should be able to answer the learning objectives. Your exams are written based on the learning objectives so it is important to practice writing them.

Chapter Outline

Using an outline is a good way to organize your notes taken from the lecture and the text. This section should help you determine which concepts will be emphasized on an exam.

Key Terms

This section lists the key terms found in the chapter, along with their definitions. If you need to go back and review any key terms, they are page referenced to the section in your textbook where the terms are discussed.

Vocabulary Flashcards

Most students have trouble finding enough time to study. Try cutting out and carrying these flashcards with you so if you ever have to wait you can pull out a couple of cards and make good use of your time. Flashcards can also serve a very useful function during times of stress. Stress is much worse when we feel overwhelmed; in fact, we tend to shut down and do nothing. At those times divide up what you have to do and do a small portion every day. Studying 10 flashcards today is less overwhelming than thinking about the 100 pages on your next exam.

Posttest

The questions in "Check Your Understanding" and "Applying Your Understanding" after each section in your textbook measure your starting point. The questions in the Posttest in this Study Guide measure how far you have progressed toward your goal of mastering the material.

Study Tips

Improving Your Memory

1. Learn general information first and then specific.

2. Make material meaningful to you.

3. Create associations with what you already know.

4. Learn it actively.

5. Imagine vivid pictures.

6. Recite out loud.

7. Reduce noise and interruptions.

8. Overlearn the material.

9. Be aware of your attitude toward information.

10. Space out learning over several days.

11. Remember related information when you are having trouble recalling something.

12. Use mnemonic devices (rhymes or words created from material).

13. Combine several of these techniques at once.

Memorizing Complex Information

There are memory techniques that make learning easier and faster. One technique, known as the "loci memory system," involves picturing yourself in a familiar setting and associating it with something you need to learn. Let's assume that you needed to memorize the function and structure of a neuron. Begin by picturing yourself walking into the entry hall of your home. At the same time pretend that you are walking through a dendrite. As you walk down the hall toward the living room, imagine that you are traveling in the dendrite to the cell body. As you exit the living room and walk down the hall toward the bedrooms, think of traveling down an axon toward the terminal button that contains the neurotransmitter. In this example you are connecting new information with something very familiar. We recall information much better when we involve our imagination. An even better way to perform this exercise would be to actually walk through your home while you visualize the parts of a neuron. In this situation you would not only be using your imagination but at the same time doing something physically. It is important to realize that we have strong memories for what we do physically. Just think how long you have remembered how to ride a bike even though you may not have ridden a bike for years.

When and How to Study

1. Plan two hours of study time for every hour you spend in class.
2. Study difficult or boring subjects first.
3. Avoid long study sessions.
4. Be aware of your best time of day.
5. Use waiting time by studying flash cards.
6. Use a regular study area.
7. Don't get too comfortable.
8. Use a library.
9. Take frequent breaks.
10. Avoid noise distractions.

Study in Groups

Research has shown that one of the most effective ways to learn is to study with other students. Your grades on exams will be better and you will have a lot more fun doing it!

How to Form a Group

1. Look for dedicated students who share some of your academic goals and challenges.
2. You could write a note on the blackboard asking interested students to contact you, or pass around a sign-up sheet before class.
3. Limit groups to five or six people.
4. Test the group by planning a one-time-only session. If that session works, plan another.

Some Activities for a Study Group

1. Compare notes.
2. Have discussions and debates about the material.
3. Test each other with questions brought to the group meeting by each member.
4. Practice teaching each other.
5. Brainstorm possible test questions.
6. Share suggestions for problems in the areas of finances, transportation, child care, time scheduling, or other barriers.
7. Develop a plan at the beginning of each meeting from the list above or any ideas you have.

Better Test Taking

1. Predict the test questions. Ask your instructor to describe the test format—how long it will be, and what kind of questions to expect (essay, multiple choice, problems, etc.).
2. Have a section in your notebook labeled "Test Questions" and add several questions to this section after every lecture and after reading the text. Record topics that the instructor repeats several times or goes back to in subsequent lectures. Write down questions the instructor poses to students.

3. Arrive early so you can do a relaxation exercise.

4. Ask about procedure for asking questions during the test.

5. Know the rules for taking the test so you do not create the impression of cheating.

6. Scan the whole test immediately. Budget your time based on how many points each section is worth.

7. Read the directions slowly. Then reread them.

8. Answer easiest, shortest questions first. This gives you the experience of success and stimulates associations. This prepares your mind for more difficult questions.

9. Next answer multiple-choice, true-false, and fill-in-the-blank questions.

10. Use memory techniques when you're stuck.
    - If your recall on something is blocked, remember something else that's related.
    - Start from the general and go to   specific.

11. Look for answers in other test questions. A term, name, date, or other fact that you can't remember might appear in the test itself.

12. Don't change an answer unless you are sure because your first instinct is usually best.

Tips on Test Taking

Multiple-choice questions

1. Check the directions to see if the questions call for more than one answer.

2. Answer each question in your head before you look at the possible answers, otherwise you may be confused by the choices.

3. Mark questions you can't answer immediately and come back to them if you have time.

4. If incorrect answers are not deducted from your score, use the following guidelines to guess:
   - If two answers are similar, except for one or two words, choose one of these answers.
   - If two answers have similar sounding or looking words, choose one of these answers.
   - If the answer calls for a sentence completion, eliminate the answers that would not form grammatically correct sentences.

   - If answers cover a numerical range, choose one in the middle.
   - If all else fails, close your eyes and pick one.

True-False Questions

1. Answer these questions quickly.

2. Don't invest a lot of time unless they are worth many points.

3. If any part of the true-false statement is false, the whole statement is false.

4. Absolute qualifiers such as "always" or "never" generally indicate a false statement.

Machine-Graded Tests

1. Check the test against the answer sheet often.

2. Watch for stray marks that look like answers.

Open-Book and Notes Tests

1. Write down key points on a separate sheet.

2. Tape flags onto important pages of the book.

3. Number your notes, write a table of contents.

4. Prepare thoroughly because they are usually the most difficult tests.

Essay Questions

1. Find out precisely what the question is asking. Don't explain when asked to compare.

2. Make an outline before writing. (Mindmaps work well.)

3. Be brief, write clearly, use a pen, get to the point, and use examples.

Reading for Remembering

1. **Skim**
   Skim the entire chapter.

2. **Outline**
   Read the outline at the front of the chapter in the text.

3. **Questions**
   Write out several questions that come to your mind that you think will be answered in the chapter.

4. **Read**

   Read material with the purpose of answering your questions, critical evaluation, comprehension, and practical application.

5. **Highlight**

   While reading highlight the most important information (no more than 10 percent).

6. **Answers**

   As you read, get the answers to your questions.

7. **Recite**

   When you finish reading an assignment, make a speech about it. Recite the key points.

8. **Review**

   Plan your first review within 24 hours.

9. **Review again**

   Weekly reviews are important—perhaps only four or five minutes per assignment. Go over your notes. Read the highlighted parts of your text. Recite the more complicated points.

More About Review

You can do short reviews anytime, anywhere, if you are prepared. Take your text to the dentist's office, and if you don't have time to read a whole assignment, review last week's assignment. Conduct five-minute reviews when you are waiting for water to boil. Three-by-five cards work well for review. Write ideas and facts on cards and carry them with you. These short review periods can be effortless and fun.

Anxiety Interferes with Performance

Do you freeze up on exams, worry that you won't do well? We can turn one exam into a "do or die" catastrophic situation. Yes, we should try our best but we are not doomed for life if we fail at something. Perhaps the following examples will help you see a failure for what it is, just one more step in the process of life.

- Einstein was four years old before he could speak and seven before he could read.
- Isaac Newton did poorly in grade school.
- Beethoven's music teacher once said of him, "As a composer he is hopeless."
- When Thomas Edison was a boy, his teachers told him he was too stupid to learn anything.
- Woolworth got a job in a dry goods store when he was 21, but his employers would not let him wait on a customer because he "didn't have enough sense."
- A newspaper editor fired Walt Disney because he had "no good ideas."
- Leo Tolstoy flunked out of college.
- Louis Pasteur was rated as "mediocre" in chemistry when he attended college.
- Abraham Lincoln entered the Black Hawk War as a captain and came out as a private.
- Winston Churchill failed the sixth grade.

Failures mean very little in the big picture of our life. It is just important that we keep trying.

Effective Note-Taking During Class

1. **Review the textbook chapter before class.**
   Instructors often design a lecture based on the assumption that you have read the chapter before class. You can take notes more easily if you already have some idea of the material.

2. **Bring your favorite note-taking tools to class.**
Make sure you have pencils, pens, highlighter,
markers, paper, note cards, or whatever materials
you find useful.

3. **Sit as close to the instructor as possible.** You will
have fewer distractions while taking your notes.

4. **Arrive to class early.**
Relax and get your brain "tuned-up" to the subject
by reviewing your notes from the previous class.

5. **Picture yourself up front with the instructor.**
The more connected you feel to the material and
the instructor, the more you will understand and
remember the topic.

6. **Let go of judgments and debates.**
Focus on understanding what the instructor is
saying because that is what you will find on the
test. Do not get distracted by evaluating the
instructor's lecture style, appearance, or strange
habits. When you hear something you disagree
with, make a quick note of it and then let it go.

7. **Be active in class.**
It is the best way to stay awake in class! Volunteer
for demonstrations. Join in class discussions.

8. **Relate the topic to an interest of yours.**
We remember things we are most interested in.

9. **Watch for clues of what is important.**

- repetition
- summary statements
- information written on the board
- information the instructor takes directly from
his or her notes
- notice what interests the instructor

When Instructors Talk Too Fast

1. Read the material before class.

2. Review notes with classmates.

3. Leave large empty spaces in your notes.

4. Have a symbol that indicates to you that you have
missed something.

5. Write down key points only and revise your notes
right after class to add details.

6. Choose to focus on what you believe to be key
information.

7. See the instructor after class and fill in what you
missed.

8. Ask the instructor to slow down if you think that
is appropriate.

CHAPTER 1

The Science of Psychology

CHAPTER OVERVIEW

The chapter begins with an inspirational vignette on the life story of Oprah Winfrey, which the authors use as a springboard to raise fascinating questions about human beings, their motivations, and personality traits—the same kinds of questions psychologists ask.

Psychology is the scientific study of behavior and mental processes. Through its many subdivisions its proponents seek to describe and explain human thought, feelings, perceptions, and actions.

Developmental psychologists are concerned with processes of growth and change over the life course, from the prenatal period through old age and death. *Neuropsychologists* and *physiological psychologists* focus on the body's neural and chemical systems, studying how these affect thought and behavior. *Behavioral geneticists* explore how genetics influence behavior. *Experimental psychologists* investigate basic psychological processes, such as learning, memory, sensation, perception, cognition, motivation, and emotion. *Personality psychologists* look at the differences among people in such traits as sociability, anxiety, aggressiveness, and self-esteem. *Clinical* and *counseling psychologists* specialize in the diagnoses and treatment of psychological disorders, whereas *social psychologists* focus on how people influence one another's thoughts and actions. *Industrial* and *organizational psychologists* study problems in the workplace and other settings.

Despite a broad range of careers and interests, the subfields of psychology are held together as a distinct scientific discipline by five enduring issues or fundamental themes:

Person–Situation: Is behavior caused more by inner traits or by external situations?

Nature–Nurture: How do genes and experiences interact to influence people?

Stability–Change: How much do we stay the same as we develop and how much do we change?

Diversity–Universality: In what ways do people differ in how they think and act?

Mind–Body: What is the relationship between our internal experiences and our biological processes?

Psychology has much in common with other sciences. Like the other sciences, psychology relies on the **scientific method** to find answers to questions. This method involves careful observation and collection of data, the development of **theories** about relationships and causes, and the systematic testing of **hypotheses** (or predictions) to disprove invalid theories.

Psychology has a long tradition because humans have wondered about behavior and mental processes since ancient times. As a scientific discipline, however, psychology's history is short, dating back only to the late 19th century.

Wilhelm Wundt established the first psychology laboratory in 1879 at the University of Leipzig in Germany. His use of experiment and measurement marked the beginnings of psychology as a science. One of his students, Edward Titchener, established a perspective called **structuralism**, which was based on the belief that psychology's role was to identify the basic elements of experience and how they combine.

In his perspective known as **functionalism**, American psychologist William James criticized structuralism, arguing that sensations cannot be separated from the mental associations that allow us to benefit from past experiences. James believed that our rich storehouse of ideas and memories is what enables us to function in our environment.

The **psychodynamic theories** of Sigmund Freud, his colleagues, and successors added another new dimension to psychology: the idea that much of our behavior is governed by unconscious conflicts, motives, and desires.

Championing an approach that differed from Freud's, John B. Watson, a spokesman for **behaviorism**, argued that psychology should concern itself only with observable, measurable behavior. Watson based much of his work on the conditioning experiments of Ivan Pavlov.

B. F. Skinner's beliefs were similar to those of Watson, but he added the concept of reinforcement or reward. In this way, he made the learner an active agent in the learning process.

Gestalt psychologists influenced the way we think about perception. According to **Gestalt psychology**, perception depends on the human tendency to see patterns, to distinguish objects from their backgrounds, and to complete pictures from a few clues. In this emphasis on wholeness, the Gestalt school differed radically from structuralism.

Humanistic psychology, with its focus on meaning, values, and ethics, emphasizes the goal of reaching one's fullest potential. **Cognitive psychology** is the study of mental processes in the broadest sense, focusing on how people perceive, interpret, store, and retrieve information. Unlike behaviorists, cognitive psychologists believe that mental processes can and should be studied scientifically. This view has dramatically changed American psychology from its previous behaviorist focus.

Evolutionary psychology focuses on the functions and adaptive value of various human behaviors and the study of how those behaviors have evolved. **Positive psychology** studies subjective feelings of happiness and well-being; the development of individual traits such as integrity and leadership; and the settings that encourage individuals to flourish. In this way, it seeks to add a new dimension to psychological research. Most contemporary psychologists do not adhere to a single school of thought. They believe that different theories can often complement one another and together enrich our understanding of human behavior.

The chapter next delves into obstacles faced by women in the early years of psychology. Although psychology has profited from the contributions of women from its beginnings, women often faced discrimination: Some colleges and universities did not grant degrees to women, professional journals were often reluctant to publish their work, and teaching positions were often closed to them.

As the chapter's subject turns to human diversity, the material examines how a rich diversity of behavior and thought exists in the human species, among individuals and groups. Being attuned to this diversity can help reduce the tensions that arise when people misunderstand one another. It can also help us to define what humans have in common.

Feminist theory explores the differences and similarities in thought and behavior between the two sexes or **genders**. Culturally generated beliefs regarding these differences are called *gender stereotypes*. Psychologists are trying to determine the hereditary and cultural causes of gender differences as well as the origins of **sexual orientation**.

Race, a biological term, refers to subpopulations who are genetically similar. **Ethnicity** involves a shared cultural heritage based on common ancestry, which can affect norms of behavior.

The intangible aspects of **culture**—the beliefs, values, traditions, and norms of behavior that a particular people share—make an important contribution to human diversity. Because many subcultural groups exist, psychology must take both inter- and cross-cultural influences into account. In **cross-cultural research**, psychologists examine the way these influences affect behavior.

The chapter next moves into a discussion of the various research methods used in psychology. Psychologists use naturalistic observation, case studies, surveys, correlational research, and experiments to study behavior and mental processes.

Psychologists use **naturalistic observation** to study behavior in natural settings. Because there is minimal interference from the researcher, the behavior observed is likely to be more accurate, spontaneous, and varied than behavior studied in a laboratory. Researchers using this method must be careful to avoid **observer bias**.

Researchers conduct a **case study** to investigate in depth the behavior of one person or a few persons. This method can yield a great deal of detailed, descriptive information that is useful for forming hypotheses, but is vulnerable to observer bias and overgeneralization of results.

Survey research generates a large amount of data quickly and inexpensively by asking a standard set of questions of a large number of people. Great care must be taken, however, in the wording of questions and in the selection of respondents.

Correlational research investigates the relation, or correlation, between two or more variables. Although two variables may be *related* to each other, that does not imply that one *causes* the other.

An **experiment** is called for when a researcher wants to draw conclusions about cause and effect. In an experiment, the impact of one factor can be studied while all other factors are held constant. The factor whose effects are being studied is called the **independent variable**, since the researcher is free to manipulate it at will. The factor on which there is apt to be an impact is called the **dependent variable**. Usually an experiment includes both an **experimental group** of **participants** and a **control group** for comparison purposes. Often a neutral person records data and scores results, so **experimenter bias** doesn't creep in.

Many psychologists overcome the limitations of using a single research method by using multiple methods to study a single problem.

Regardless of the research method used, psychologists usually study a small **sample** of subjects and then generalize their results to larger populations. Proper sampling is critical to ensure that results have broader application. **Random samples**, in which each potential participant has an equal chance of being chosen, and **representative samples**, in which subjects are chosen to reflect the general characteristics of the population as a whole, are two ways of doing this.

Because of differences among people based on age, sex, ethnic background, culture, and so forth, findings from studies that use White, male, American college students as participants cannot always be generalized to other groups. In addition, the gender, race, and ethnic background of a psychologist can have a biasing impact on the outcome of research.

The chapter's focus turns next to ethics and psychology, specifically research on humans and animals, along with a look at related guidelines and objections.

The APA has a code of ethics for conducting research involving human participants or animal subjects. Researchers must obtain informed consent from study participants. Participants must be told in advance about the nature and possible risks of the research. People should not be pressured to participate.

Although much of what we know about certain areas of psychology has come from animal research, the practice of experimenting on animals has strong opponents because of the pain and suffering that are sometimes involved. Although APA and the federal government have issued guidelines for the humane treatment of laboratory animals, many animal rights advocates argue that the only ethical research on animals is naturalistic observation.

The chapter concludes with the question of careers in psychology, and asks what can be done with a background in psychology or an advanced degree. A background in psychology is useful in a wide array of fields because so many jobs involve a basic understanding of people. Careers for those with advanced degrees in psychology include teaching, research, jobs in government and private business, and occupations in the mental health field. Opportunities in the mental health field depend on one's degree of training. Practice in psychiatry requires medical training; practice in clinical psychology requires a doctoral degree. Positions in counseling psychology and social work are additional career options.

LEARNING OBJECTIVES EXERCISE

After you have read and studied the chapter, you should be able to answer the following learning objectives.

WHAT IS PSYCHOLOGY?

- Define *psychology* and describe the major subfields within psychology.

- Describe the five enduring issues that cut across the subfields of psychology.

- Explain what psychology has in common with other sciences, how psychologists use the scientific method, and the difference between theories and hypotheses.

- Apply critical thinking to an article in a magazine or newspaper.

THE GROWTH OF PSYCHOLOGY

- Describe the emergence of scientific psychology in the late 19th and early 20th centuries.

- Explain the differences between psychodynamic, behavioral, humanistic, cognitive, evolutionary, and positive psychology.

- Describe the role of women in the history of psychology.

HUMAN DIVERSITY

- Explain the importance of understanding human diversity and describe psychology's increasing attention to human diversity.

RESEARCH METHODS IN PSYCHOLOGY

- Describe the characteristics of case studies, surveys, correlational research and experimental research, and the strengths and weaknesses of each research method.

- Describe the differences between independent and dependent variables and between control groups and experimental groups.

- Explain the importance of sampling in psychological research. Differentiate between random and representative samples.

- Explain how unintended biases can affect the results of research.

- Identify key ethical issues in psychological research with humans and nonhumans.

ETHICS AND PSYCHOLOGY: RESEARCH ON HUMANS AND ANIMALS

- Identify key ethical issues in psychological research with humans and nonhumans.

CAREERS IN PSYCHOLOGY

- Describe some of the career paths that are available to people who have studied psychology. Distinguish between psychiatrists, psychoanalysts, clinical psychologists, counseling psychologists, and social workers.

The following is an outline conveying the main concepts of this chapter.

I.   What Is Psychology? (page 3)
   A.   The Fields of Psychology
      i.   Developmental Psychology
      ii.   Physiological Psychology
      iii. Experimental Psychology
      iv.   Personality Psychology
      v.   Clinical and Counseling Psychology
      vi.   Social Psychology
      vii. Industrial and Organizational (I/O) Psychology
   B.   Enduring Issues
      i.   Person–Situation
      ii.   Nature–Nurture
      iii. Stability–Change
      iv.   Diversity–Universality
      v.   Mind–Body
   C.   Psychology as Science
      i.   Scientific Method
      ii.   Theory
      iii. Hypotheses
   D.   Critical Thinking: Thinking Like a Scientist
      i.   Define Problem
      ii.   Suggest Theory
      iii. Collect and Examine Evidence
      iv.   Analyze Assumptions
      v.   Avoid Oversimplifying
      vi.   Draw Conclusions Carefully
      vii. Consider Alternative Interpretations
      viii. Recognize Relevance of Research
   E.   APPLYING PSYCHOLOGY: THE BENEFITS OF STUDYING PSYCHOLOGY
      i.   Self-understanding
      ii.   Critical Thinking Skills
      iii. Skill in the Application of the Scientific Method
      iv.   Study Skills
      v.   Job Skills

II.   The Growth of Psychology (page 11)

Indicate A, B, C, D, or E and write the correct name of each psychologist below his picture.

A.   Wilhelm Wundt
B.   William James
C.   Sigmund Freud
D.   John B. Watson
E.   B. F. Skinner

1. _____   2. _____   3. _____   4. _____   5. _____

    A.   The "New Psychology": A Science of the Mind
        i.   Wilhelm Wundt and Edward Bradford Titchener: Voluntarism and Structuralism
        ii.   William James: Functionalism
        iii.   Sigmund Freud: Psychodynamic Psychology
    B.   Redefining Psychology: The Study of Behavior
        i.   John B. Watson: Behaviorism
        ii.   B. F. Skinner: Behaviorism Revisited
    C.   The Cognitive Revolution
        i.   The Precursors: Gestalt and Humanistic Psychology
        ii.   The Rise of Cognitive Psychology
    D.   New Directions
        i.   Evolutionary Psychology
        ii.   Positive Psychology
        iii.   Multiple Perspectives of Psychology Today
    E.   Where Are the Women?
        i.   Women Have Contributed to Psychology Since Beginning
        ii.   Margaret Floy Washburn
        iii.   Christine Ladd-Franklin
        iv.   Mary Whiton Calkins
        v.   Women PhDs Continue to Increase

III.   Human Diversity (page 20)
    A.   Gender
        i.   Gender Stereotypes
        ii.   Feminist Psychology
        iii.   Sexual Orientation
    B.   Race and Ethnicity
        i.   Racial and Ethnic Minorities in Psychology
    C.   Culture
        i.   Cross-Cultural Research

KEY TERMS

Behaviorism	School of psychology that studies only observable and measurable behavior. (p. 14)
Case study	Intensive description and analysis of a single individual or just a few individuals. (p. 24)
Cognitive psychology	School of psychology devoted to the study of mental processes in the broadest sense. (p. 16)
Control group	In a controlled experiment, the group not subjected to a change in the independent variable; used for comparison with the experimental group. (p. 28)
Correlational research	Research technique based on the naturally occurring relationship between two or more variables. (p. 26)
Cross-cultural research	Research involving the exploration of the extent to which people differ from one culture to another. (p. 23)
Culture	The tangible goods and the values, attitudes, behaviors, and beliefs that are passed from one generation to another. (p. 23)
Dependent variable	In an experiment, the variable that is measured to see how it is changed by manipulations in the independent variable. (p. 28)
Ethnicity	A common cultural heritage—including religion, language, or ancestry— that is shared by a group of individuals. (p. 22)
Evolutionary psychology	An approach to, and subfield of, psychology that is concerned with the evolutionary origins of behaviors and mental processes, their adaptive value, and the purposes they continue to serve. (p. 17)
Experimental group	In a controlled experiment, the group subjected to a change in the independent variable. (p. 28)
Experimental method	Research technique in which an investigator deliberately manipulates selected events or circumstances and then measures the effects of those manipulations on subsequent behavior. (p. 27)
Experimenter bias	Expectations by the experimenter that might influence the results of an experiment or its interpretation. (p. 28)
Feminist theory	Feminist theories offer a wide variety of views on the social roles of women and men, the problems and rewards of those roles, and prescriptions for changing those roles. (p. 21)
Functionalist theory	Theory of mental life and behavior that is concerned with how an organism uses its perceptual abilities to function in its environment. (p. 12)
Gender	The psychological and social meanings attached to being biologically male or female. (p. 21)
Gestalt psychology	School of psychology that studies how people perceive and experience objects as whole patterns. (p. 15)
Humanistic psychology	School of psychology that emphasizes nonverbal experience and altered states of consciousness as a means of realizing one's full human potential. (p. 15)
Hypotheses	Specific, testable predictions derived from a theory. (p. 8)
Independent variable	In an experiment, the variable that is manipulated to test its effects on the other, dependent variables. (p. 28)
Naturalistic observation	Research method involving the systematic study of animal or human behavior in natural settings rather than in the laboratory. (p. 24)
Observer bias	Expectations or biases of the observer that might distort or influence his or her interpretation of what was actually observed. (p. 24)
Participants	Individuals whose reactions or responses are observed in an experiment. (p. 27)

Positive psychology	An emerging field of psychology that focuses on positive experiences, including subjective well-being, self-determination, the relationship between positive emotions and physical health, and the factors that allow individuals, communities, and societies to flourish. (p. 17)
Psychodynamic theories	Personality theories contending that behavior results from psychological factors that interact within the individual, often outside conscious awareness. (p. 13)
Psychology	The scientific study of behavior and mental processes. (p. 3)
Race	A subpopulation of a species, defined according to an identifiable characteristic (that is, geographic location, skin color, hair texture, genes, facial features, and so forth). (p. 22)
Random sample	Sample in which each potential participant has an equal chance of being selected. (p. 30)
Representative sample	Sample carefully chosen so that the characteristics of the participants correspond closely to the characteristics of the larger population. (p. 30)
Sample	A subgroup of a population. (p. 29)
Scientific method	An approach to knowledge that relies on collecting data, generating a theory to explain the data, producing testable hypotheses based on the theory, and testing those hypotheses empirically. (p. 8)
Sexual orientation	Refers to the direction of one's sexual interest toward members of the same sex, the other sex, or both sexes. (p. 21)
Structuralism	School of psychology that stresses the basic units of experience and the combinations in which they occur. (p. 12)
Survey research	Research technique in which questionnaires or interviews are administered to a selected group of people. (p. 26)
Theory	Systematic explanation of a phenomenon; it organizes known facts, allows us to predict new facts, and permits us to exercise a degree of control over the phenomenon. (p. 8)

After studying the text and completing the Study Guide activities, answer these questions to determine if you need to review any areas before the course exam.

MULTIPLE CHOICE

1. Psychology is the science of _____.
    a. behavior and mental processes
    b. objective introspection
    c. inductive reasoning
    d. emotions

2. The scientific method has been applied to psychological issues for about the last _____ years.
    a. 100
    b. 200
    c. 300
    d. 400

3. A specific, testable prediction about a phenomenon, usually derived from a theory, is a _____.
    a. thesis
    b. hypothesis
    c. principle
    d. prognosis

4. The basic atoms or units of experience and their combinations were the foundation of _____.
    a. functionalism
    b. structuralism
    c. behaviorism
    d. psychoanalysis

5. Consciousness as a continuous flow is an important concept to _____.
    a. structuralism
    b. functionalism
    c. objective introspection
    d. behaviorism

6. Freud's theories differed radically from the views of American psychologists of the time because of _____.
    a. its extensive use of laboratory research to support its claims
    b. the emphasis it placed on Eastern philosophies and culture
    c. the emphasis it placed on unconscious processes
    d. its emphasis on environmental learning as the source for most personality characteristics

7. The idea that psychology should be based only on observable, measurable behaviors is central to _____.
    a. behaviorism
    b. cognitive theory
    c. structuralism
    d. psychodynamic theory

8. Gestalt theory emphasizes _____.
    a. flow of consciousness
    b. the atoms of thought
    c. environmental stimuli
    d. our tendency to see patterns

9. The scientific study of the ways in which people perceive, interpret, store, and retrieve information is central to _____ psychology.
    a. humanistic
    b. behavioral
    c. existential
    d. cognitive

10. Research that observes behavior in its actual setting without controlling anything is called _____.
    a. correlational method
    b. naturalistic observation
    c. survey research
    d. case study method

11. The _____ is a detailed description and analysis of a single individual or a few individuals and may include a variety of information gathering methods.
    a. correlational method
    b. naturalistic observation
    c. survey research
    d. case study method

12. The degree of relationship between two or more variables is _____.
    a. correlation
    b. naturalistic observation
    c. reliability
    d. synchronicity

13. The only research method that can demonstrate a cause-and-effect relationship between variables is the _____ method.
    a. correlational
    b. naturalistic observation
    c. survey research
    d. experimental

14. A researcher manipulates the _____ variable to see how it affects a second variable.
    a. placebo
    b. independent
    c. dependent
    d. correlational

15. A sample carefully chosen so that the characteristics of the subjects correspond closely to the characteristics of the general population is known as a _____ sample.
    a. random
    b. controlled
    c. biased
    d. representative

16. Subjects in Milgram's studies were told they were taking part in studies on ____ but were really being tested on _____.
    a. learning, biofeedback
    b. pain thresholds, biofeedback
    c. learning, obedience
    d. obedience, learning

17. Milgram's studies on obedience raised significant controversy regarding _____.
    a. the quality of laboratory equipment used in psychological research
    b. laboratory research on human sexuality
    c. the use of placebo techniques to treat severe psychological disorders
    d. ethics and the use of deception in research

18. Which of the following mental health professionals is the only one who can prescribe medicine?
    a. a psychologist
    b. a social worker
    c. a counselor
    d. a psychiatrist

19. Critical thinking involves all of the following EXCEPT _____.
    a. examining evidence
    b. considering alternatives
    c. accepting common knowledge
    d. analyzing assumptions

20. Wundt used the term _____ to convey the concept of attention as a selective process actively controlled by intentions and motives.
    a. experimentation
    b. voluntarism
    c. stream of consciousness
    d. introspection

21. Genetic or evolutionary influences were largely unexplored in the psychology of the 1960s. Rather, behaviors were explained as a result of learning and experience. This tendency is conveyed by the term _____.
    a. environmental bias
    b. deception
    c. observer bias
    d. experimenter bias

22. Susan gives students a word list to memorize, then she tests the number of words remembered from the list and how long the students retain certain words in memory. Susan is most likely a _____ psychologist.
    a. behavioral
    b. developmental
    c. evolutionary
    d. cognitive

23. Which of the following statements concerning women in psychology is NOT true?
    a. The number of women enrolled in psychology graduate programs has increased steadily over the last 50 years.
    b. Women receive approximately 75 percent of the bachelor's degrees awarded in psychology.
    c. In the early years of psychology, females were openly invited to participate in the field, but few accepted, opting instead for more traditional occupational roles.
    d. The absence of females in the early years of psychology may reflect a larger problem—the inattention to human diversity.

24. Which of the following statements supports the case for including studies on human diversity in the field of psychology?
    a. It is important to recognize and understand the similarities and differences found in people of diverse backgrounds.
    b. Interpersonal tensions such as prejudice and conflict may be better understood.
    c. Comprehension of human diversity may lead to appreciation of different values, behaviors, and approaches to situations used by others.
    d. All of the above.

25. _____ is based on genetic similarity while _____ is based on cultural characteristics.
    a. Race; ethnicity
    b. Ethnicity; race
    c. Gender; sex
    d. Diversity; feminism

SHORT ESSAY QUESTIONS

1. Describe the importance of sampling related to issues of gender, race, and culture in research.

2. Explain Milgram's study, why it was so controversial, how it affected the APA's ethical guidelines, and the issue of deception and punishment in psychological research.

3. Discuss the differences between structuralism and functionalism; behaviorism and cognitive psychology, and how Freud's psychoanalytic differed from these schools.

4. Discuss the design of an experiment studying the effects of alcohol on aggressive behavior. Label the hypothesis, independent variable, dependent variable, control and experimental group, and the measures taken to avoid experimental bias.

5. Define the terms: sample, population, random sample, and representative sample. Explain how researchers can overcome obstacles to obtaining a good sample.

6. Explain the goals and interests of evolutionary psychologists and give two examples of the types of findings they have uncovered.

7. Describe the role played by women in the history of psychology, some obstacles that have prevented women from achieving equal status with men, and the current status of women in psychology.

8. Define and discuss the emerging field of positi psychology and its unique perspective on me wellness as opposed to mental illness.

ANSWERS AND EXPLANATIONS TO MULTIPLE CHOICE POSTTEST

1. a. Psychology is the science of behavior and mental processes. p. 3

2. a. It was in the late 1800s that the scientific method was applied to questions about human behavior and mental processes. p. 11

3. b. A hypothesis is a testable prediction about the phenomenon in question. p. 8

4. b. Structuralism focuses on basic units or atoms of experiences and their combinations. p. 12

5. b. Consciousness as a continuous flow is important to functionalism. p. 12

6. c. Freud believed that people are motivated by unconscious instincts and urges. p. 13

7. a. Behaviorists believed that psychology was the study of observable, measurable behavior—and nothing more. p. 13

8. d. Gestalt theory emphasizes our tendency to see patterns. p. 15

9. d. Cognitive psychology is the study of mental processes in the broadest sense. p. 16

10. b. Naturalistic observation involves watching a research subject in the natural setting. p. 24

11. d. A case study is a detailed description of one person or a few individuals and may include real life observation, interviews, psychological test scores, and interviews with others. p. 25

12. a. Correlational research is based on a naturally occurring relationship between two variables. p. 26

13. d. Only the experimental method can prove cause and effect. p. 27

14. b. A researcher manipulates the independent variable. p. 28

15. d. A representative sample is carefully chosen to correspond closely to the characteristics of the larger population. p. 30

16. c. Milgram's subjects were told the research was about learning but it was really about obedience. p. 33

17. d. Milgram's study sparked such a public uproar that the APA was forced to reassess its ethical guidelines. p. 33

18. d. Psychiatrists are medical doctors and the only mental health professionals licensed to prescribe medication. p. 35

19. c. Critical thinkers question common knowledge. p. 9

20. b. Wundt's primary interest was selective attention and he used the term voluntarism to describe his view of psychology. p. 11

21. a. The tendency to explain virtually all behaviors as aspects of learning and experience is referred to as an environmental bias. p. 15

22. d. Cognitive psychologists study mental processes including, but not limited to, learning and remembering. p. 16

23. c. In the late 1800s and early 1900s academic careers in psychology remained closed to women. Still, women were attracted to the field and many pursued careers in related nonacademic settings such as child development and education. p. 18

24. d. Understanding human diversity is essential in today's world. Psychologists no longer accept that what is true of white, Western males is true of others as well. p. 20

25. a. Race is a biological term used to refer to a genetically similar subpopulation. Ethnicity is based on cultural characteristics shared by a category of people. p. 22

CHAPTER 2
The Biological Basis of Behavior

CHAPTER OVERVIEW

The chapter opens with the compelling story of 5-year-old Nico, a child who had radical surgery to remove the entire right side of his brain. The journey through the brain taken in this chapter is part of the branch of psychology known as **psychobiology**, which deals with the biological bases of behavior and mental processes. Psychobiology overlaps with a much larger interdisciplinary field of study called **neuroscience**, which specifically focuses on the brain and nervous system.

Biological processes are the basis of our thoughts, feelings, and actions. All of our behaviors are kept in tune with our surroundings and coordinated with one another through the work of two interacting systems: the nervous system and the endocrine system.

The basic building block of the nervous system is the **neuron**, or nerve cell. Neurons have several characteristics that distinguish them from other cells. Neurons receive messages from other neurons through short fibers called **dendrites**. A longer fiber, called an **axon**, carries outgoing messages from the cell. A group of axons bundled together forms a **nerve** or **tract**. Some axons are covered with a fatty **myelin sheath** made up of **glial cells**; this increases neuron efficiency and provides insulation. There are many different types of neurons including: **sensory** or **afferent neurons**, **motor** or **efferent neurons**, **interneurons** or **association neurons**, and **mirror neurons**, which are involved in imitation.

When a neuron is at rest (a state called the **resting potential**), there is a slightly higher concentration of negatively charged **ions** inside its membrane than there is outside. The membrane is said to be **polarized**—that is, the electrical charge inside it is negative relative to its outside. When an incoming message is strong enough, this electrical imbalance abruptly changes (the membrane is depolarized), and an **action potential** (**neural impulse**) is generated. Incoming messages cause **graded potentials**, which, when combined, may exceed the minimum **threshold of excitation** and make the neuron "fire." After firing, the neuron briefly goes through the **absolute refractory period**, when it will not fire again, and then through the **relative refractory period**, when firing will occur only if the incoming message is much stronger than usual. According to the **all-or-none law**, every firing of a particular neuron produces an impulse of equal strength. More rapid firing of neurons is what communicates the strength of a message.

Neurotransmitter molecules, released by **synaptic vesicles**, cross the tiny **synaptic space** (or **cleft**) between an **axon terminal** (or **terminal button**) of a sending neuron and a dendrite of a receiving neuron. Here they latch on to **receptor sites**, much as keys fit into locks, and pass on their excitatory or inhibitory messages. Psychologists need to understand how **synapses** function because neurotransmitters affect an enormous range of physical and emotional responses.

Research demonstrates that experiences in our environments can produce changes in the brain, a principle called **neural plasticity**. Human brains also are capable of **neurogenesis**, the production of new brain cells. The study of neurogenesis may help treat neurological disorders, but also raises ethical questions.

The chapter next turns to the nervous system. The nervous system is organized into two parts: the **central nervous system**, which consists of the brain and spinal cord, and the **peripheral nervous system (PNS)**, made up of nerves that radiate throughout the body, linking the body's parts to the CNS.

Physically, the brain has three more-or-less distinct areas: the central core, the limbic system, and the cerebral hemispheres.

The central core consists of the hindbrain, cerebellum, midbrain, thalamus and hypothalamus, and reticular formation. The **hindbrain** is made up of the **medulla**, a narrow structure nearest the spinal cord that controls breathing, heart rate, and blood pressure, and the **pons**, which produces chemicals that maintain our sleep–wake cycle. The medulla is the point at which many of the nerves from the left part of the body cross to the right side of the brain and vice versa. The **cerebellum** controls the sense of balance and coordinates the body's actions. The **midbrain**, which is above the cerebellum, is important for hearing and sight and is one of the places in which pain is registered. The **thalamus** is a relay station that integrates and shapes incoming sensory signals before transmitting them to the higher levels of the brain. The **hypothalamus** is important to motivation, drives, and emotional behavior. The **reticular formation**, which is woven through all of these structures, alerts the higher parts of the brain to incoming messages.

The cerebrum takes up most of the room inside the skull. The outer covering of the cerebral hemispheres is known as the **cerebral cortex**. They are the most recently evolved portion of the brain, and they regulate the most complex behavior. Each cerebral hemisphere is divided into four lobes, delineated by deep fissures on the surface of the brain. The **occipital lobe** of the cortex, located at the back of the head, receives and processes visual information. The **temporal lobe**, located roughly behind the temples, helps us perform complex visual tasks, such as recognizing faces. The **parietal lobe**, which sits on top of the temporal and occipital lobes, receives sensory information from all over the body and oversees spatial abilities. Messages from sensory receptors are registered in the **primary somatosensory cortex**. The **frontal lobe** receives and coordinates messages from the other lobes and keeps track of past and future body movement. The **prefrontal cortex** is primarily responsible for goal-directed behavior, the ability to control impulses, judgment, and metacognition. The **primary motor cortex** is responsible for voluntary movement. The **association areas**—areas that are free to process all kinds of information—make up most of the cerebral cortex and enable the brain to produce behaviors requiring the coordination of many brain areas.

The **limbic system**, a ring of structures located between the central core and the cerebral hemispheres, is a more recent evolutionary development than the central core. It includes the hippocampus, which is essential to forming new memories, and the amygdala, which, together with the hippocampus, governs emotions related to self-preservation. Other portions of the limbic system heighten the experience of pleasure. In times of stress, the limbic system coordinates the nervous system's response.

The two cerebral hemispheres are linked by the **corpus callosum**, through which they communicate and coordinate their activities. Nevertheless, each hemisphere appears to specialize in certain tasks (although they also have overlapping functions). The right hemisphere excels at visual and spatial tasks, nonverbal imagery, and the perception of emotion, whereas the left hemisphere excels at language and perhaps analytical thinking, too. The right hemisphere controls the left side of the body, and the left hemisphere controls the right side.

Particular to the language function of the left side of the brain, crucial distinctions are made in the text between Wernicke's area and Broca's area and the different roles each area plays. Support for these distinctions comes from patients who have suffered left-hemisphere strokes that produce predictable language problems, called **aphasias**.

An increasingly sophisticated technology exists for investigating the brain. Among the most important tools are microelectrode techniques, macroelectrode techniques (EEG), structural imaging (CT scanning and MRI), and functional imaging (EEG imaging, MEG, and MSI). Two new functional imaging techniques, PET scanning and fMRI, allow us to observe not only the structure, but also the functioning of parts of the brain. Scientists often combine these techniques to study brain activity in unprecedented detail—information that can help in the treatment of medical and psychological disorders.

The **spinal cord** is a complex cable of nerves that connects the brain to most of the rest of the body. It is made up of bundles of long nerve fibers and has two basic functions: to permit some reflex movements and to carry messages to and from the brain. When a break in the cord disrupts the flow of impulses from the brain below that point, paralysis occurs.

The chapter next looks at the peripheral nervous system. The peripheral nervous system (PNS) contains two types of neurons: **afferent neurons,** which carry sensory messages *to* the central nervous system, and **efferent neurons**, which carry messages *from* the CNS. Neurons involved in making voluntary movements of the skeletal muscles belong to a part of the PNS called the **somatic nervous system**, whereas neurons involved in governing the actions of internal organs belong to a part of the PNS called the autonomic nervous system. The **autonomic nervous system** is itself divided into two parts: the **sympathetic division**, which acts primarily to arouse the body when it is faced with threat, and the **parasympathetic division**, which acts to calm the body down, restoring it to normal levels of arousal.

The chapter moves into a discussion of the endocrine system, and the interest psychologists have in hormones and their effects. The endocrine system is the other communication system in the body. It is made up of **endocrine glands** that produce **hormones**, chemical substances released into the bloodstream to either *trigger* developmental changes in the body or to activate certain behavioral responses. The **thyroid gland** secretes thyroxin, a hormone involved in regulating the body's rate of metabolism. Symptoms of an overactive thyroid are agitation and tension, whereas an underactive thyroid produces lethargy. The **parathyroids** control and balance the levels of calcium and phosphate in the blood and tissue fluids. This process in turn affects the excitability of the nervous system. The **pineal gland** regulates activity levels over the course of the day and also regulates the sleep–wake cycle. The **pancreas** controls the level of sugar in the blood by secreting insulin and glucagon. When the pancreas secretes too much insulin, the person can suffer *hypoglycemia*. Too little insulin can result in *diabetes mellitus*. Of all the endocrine glands, the **pituitary gland** regulates the largest number of different activities in the body. It affects blood pressure, thirst, uterine contractions in childbirth, milk production, sexual behavior and interest, and the amount and timing of body growth, among other functions. Because of its influences on other glands, it is often called the "master gland." The **gonads**—the testes in males and the ovaries in females—secrete hormones called androgens (including testosterone) and estrogens. Testosterone has long been linked to aggressive behavior, and recent research suggests that estrogen may also play a role in aggression, as well as cognitive ability. Each of the two **adrenal glands** has two parts: an outer covering, the *adrenal cortex*, and an inner core, the *adrenal medulla*. Both affect our response to stress, although the adrenal cortex affects other body functions, too. One stress-related hormone of the adrenal medulla is epinephrine, which amplifies the effects of the sympathetic nervous system.

The chapter concludes with an examination of genes, evolution, and behavior—how genes are passed from one generation to the next, methods psychologists use to study their effects (and those of natural selection) on behavior, as well as some of the ethical issues that arise as society gains more control over genetics.

The related fields of **behavior genetics** and **evolutionary psychology** explore the influences of heredity on human behavior. Both are helping to settle the nature-versus-nurture debate over the relative contributions of genes and the environment to human similarities and differences. **Genetics** is the study of how traits are passed on from one generation to the next via genes. This process is called heredity. Each **gene**, or basic unit of inheritance, is lined up on tiny threadlike bodies called **chromosomes**, which in turn are made up predominantly of a complex molecule called **deoxyribonucleic acid (DNA)**. The **human genome** is the full complement of genes necessary to build a human body—approximately 20,000 to 25,000 genes. The Human Genome Project has produced a rough map of the genes on the 23 pairs of human chromosomes. Each member of a gene pair can be either **dominant** or **recessive**. In **polygenic inheritance** a number of genes interact to produce a trait. One's unique genetic "blueprint" is called the **genotype**, while the outward expression of a trait is called a **phenotype**.

Psychologists use a variety of methods to study *heritability*—that is, the contribution of genes in determining variations in certain traits. **Strain studies** approach the problem by observing strains of highly inbred, genetically similar animals, whereas **selection studies** try to determine the extent to which an animal's traits can be passed on from one generation to another. In the study of humans, **family studies** tackle heritability by looking for similarities in traits as a function of biological closeness. Also useful in studying human heritability are **twin studies**, which focus on characteristics of **identical twins** and **fraternal twins**, and **adoption studies**.

The theory of evolution by **natural selection** states that organisms best adapted to their environment tend to survive, transmitting their genetic characteristics to succeeding generations, whereas organisms with fewer adaptive characteristics tend to die off. Evolutionary psychology analyzes human behavioral tendencies by examining their adaptive value from an evolutionary perspective. While not without its critics, it has proved useful in helping to explain some of the commonalities in human behavior that occur across cultures.

Manipulating human genes in an effort to change how people develop is a new technology that makes many people uneasy, but their concerns may be exaggerated because genes are not all-powerful. Both heredity and environment play a part in shaping most significant human behaviors and traits.

LEARNING OBJECTIVES EXERCISE

After you have read and studied the chapter, you should be able to answer the following learning objectives.

NEURONS: THE MESSENGERS

- Describe a typical neuron. Distinguish between afferent, efferent, and association neurons.

- Describe how neurons transmit information including the concepts of resting potential, polarization, action potential, graded potential, threshold of excitation, and the all-or-none law.

- Describe the parts of the synapse and the role of neurotransmitters in the synapse.

- Explain "neural plasticity" and "neurogenesis."

THE CENTRAL NERVOUS SYSTEM

- Identify the parts of the brain and their function. Explain what is meant by "hemispheric specialization" and the functional differences between the two cerebral hemispheres.

- Discuss how microelectrode techniques, macroelectrode techniques, structural imaging, and functional imaging provide information about the brain.

- Explain how the spinal cord works.

THE PERIPHERAL NERVOUS SYSTEM

- Identify the peripheral nervous system and contrast the functions of the somatic and autonomic nervous systems.

- Explain the differences between the sympathetic and the parasympathetic nervous systems.

THE ENDOCRINE SYSTEM

- Describe the endocrine glands and the way their hormones affect behavior.

GENES, EVOLUTION, AND BEHAVIOR

- Distinguish between genetics, behavior genetics, and evolutionary psychology.

- Differentiate between genes, chromosomes, DNA, and the human genome. Describe what is meant by dominant and recessive genes, polygenic inheritance, and genotype vs. phenotype.

- Compare and contrast strain studies, selection studies, family studies, twin studies, and adoption studies as sources of information about the effects of heredity.

- Identify the key ethical issues that arise as society gains more control over genetics.

- Describe how evolutionary psychologists view the influence of natural selection on human social behavior.

CHAPTER OUTLINE

KEY TERMS

Adoption studies	Research carried out on children, adopted at birth by parents not related to them, to determine the relative influence of heredity and environment on human behavior. (p. 72)
Adrenal glands	Two endocrine glands located just above the kidneys. (p. 67)
Afferent neurons	Neurons that carry messages from sense organs to the spinal cord or brain. (p. 63)
All-or-none law	Principle that the action potential in a neuron does not vary in strength; either the neuron fires at full strength, or it does not fire at all. (p. 44)
Aphasias	Impairments of the ability to use (expressive aphasia) or understand (receptive aphasia) language that usually results from brain damage. (p. 58)
Association areas	Areas of the cerebral cortex where incoming messages from the separate senses are combined into meaningful impressions and outgoing messages from the motor areas are integrated. (p. 53)
Autonomic nervous system	The part of the peripheral nervous system that carries messages between the central nervous system and the internal organs. (p. 63)
Axon	Single long fiber extending from the cell body; it carries outgoing messages. (p. 42)
Behavior genetics	Study of the relationship between heredity and behavior. (p. 68)
Central nervous system (CNS)	Division of the nervous system that consists of the brain and spinal cord. (p. 50)
Cerebellum	Structure in the hindbrain that controls certain reflexes and coordinates the body's movements. (p. 52)
Cerebral cortex	The outer surface of the two cerebral hemispheres that regulates most complex behavior. (p. 52)
Chromosomes	Pairs of threadlike bodies within the cell nucleus that contain the genes. (p. 69)
Corpus callosum	A thick band of nerve fibers connecting the left and right cerebral hemispheres. (p. 56)
Dendrites	Short fibers that branch out from the cell body and pick up incoming messages. (p. 42)
Deoxyribonucleic acid (DNA)	Complex molecule in a double-helix configuration that is the main ingredient of chromosomes and genes and that forms the code for all genetic information. (p. 70)
Dominant gene	Member of a gene pair that controls the appearance of a certain trait. (p. 70)
Efferent neurons	Neurons that carry messages from the spinal cord or brain to the muscles and glands. (p. 63)
Endocrine glands	Glands of the endocrine system that release hormones into the bloodstream. (p. 65)
Evolutionary psychology	An approach to, and subfield of, psychology that is concerned with the evolutionary origins of behaviors and mental processes, their adaptive value, and the purposes they continue to serve. (p. 68)
Family studies	Studies of heritability in humans based on the assumption that if genes influence a certain trait, close relatives should be more similar on that trait than distant relatives. (p. 72)
Fraternal twins	Twins developed from two separate fertilized ova and therefore different in genetic makeup. (p. 72)
Frontal lobe	Part of the cerebral cortex that is responsible for voluntary movement; it is also important for attention, goal-directed behavior, and appropriate emotional experiences. (p. 53)

Genes	Elements that control the transmission of traits; they are found on the chromosomes. (p. 69)
Genetics	Study of how traits are transmitted from one generation to the next. (p. 69)
Genotype	An organism's entire unique genetic makeup. (p. 70)
Glial cells (or glia)	Cells that insulate and support neurons by holding them together, provide nourishment and remove waste products, prevent harmful substances from passing into the brain, and form the myelin sheath. (p. 42)
Gonads	The reproductive glands—testes in males and ovaries in females. (p. 67)
Graded potential	A shift in the electrical charge in a tiny area of a neuron. (p. 44)
Hindbrain	Area containing the medulla, pons, and cerebellum. (p. 52)
Hormones	Chemical substances released by the endocrine glands; they help regulate bodily activities. (p. 65)
Human genome	The full complement of genes within a human cell. (p. 70)
Hypothalamus	Forebrain region that governs motivation and emotional responses. (p. 52)
Identical twins	Twins developed from a single fertilized ovum and therefore identical in genetic makeup at the time of conception. (p. 72)
Interneurons (or association neurons)	Neurons that carry messages from one neuron to another. (p. 42)
Ions	Electrically charged particles found both inside and outside the neuron. (p. 44)
Limbic system	Ring of structures that plays a role in learning and emotional behavior. (p. 55)
Medulla	Structure in the hindbrain that controls essential life support functions including breathing, heart rate and blood pressure. (p. 52)
Midbrain	Region between the hindbrain and the forebrain; it is important for hearing and sight, and it is one of several places in the brain where pain is registered. (p. 52)
Mirror neurons	Specialized neurons that respond when we observe others perform a behavior or express an emotion. (p. 42)
Motor (or efferent) neurons	Neurons that carry messages from the spinal cord or brain to the muscles and glands. (p. 42)
Myelin sheath	White fatty covering found on some axons. (p. 42)
Natural selection	The mechanism proposed by Darwin in his theory of evolution, which states that organisms best adapted to their environment tend to survive, transmitting their genetic characteristics to succeeding generations, whereas organisms with less adaptive characteristics tend to vanish from the earth. (p. 75)
Nerve (or tract)	Group of axons bundled together. (p. 42)
Neural impulse (or action potential)	The firing of a nerve cell. (p. 44)
Neural plasticity	The ability of the brain to change in response to experience. (p. 49)
Neurogenesis	The growth of new neurons. (p. 50)
Neurons	Individual cells that are the smallest unit of the nervous system. (p. 42)
Neuroscience	The study of the brain and the nervous system. (p. 41)
Neurotransmitters	Chemicals released by the synaptic vesicles that travel across the synaptic space and affect adjacent neurons. (p. 47)
Occipital lobe	Part of the cerebral hemisphere that receives and interprets visual information. (p. 55)
Pancreas	Organ lying between the stomach and small intestine; it secretes insulin and glucagon to regulate blood-sugar levels. (p. 67)
Parasympathetic division	Branch of the autonomic nervous system; it calms and relaxes the body. (p. 65)
Parathyroids	Four tiny glands embedded in the thyroid. (p. 67)
Parietal lobe	Part of the cerebral cortex that receives sensory information from throughout the body. (p. 55)
Peripheral nervous system (PNS)	Division of the nervous system that connects the central nervous system to the rest of the body. (p. 50)

Phenotype	The characteristics of an organism; determined by both genetics and experience. (p. 70)
Pineal gland	A gland located roughly in the center of the brain that appears to regulate activity levels over the course of a day. (p. 66)
Pituitary gland	Gland located on the underside of the brain; it produces the largest number of the body's hormones. (p. 66)
Polarization	Shift in attitudes by members of a group toward more extreme positions than the ones held before group discussion. (p. 44)
Polygenic inheritance	Process by which several genes interact to produce a certain trait; responsible for our most important traits. (p. 70)
Pons	Structure in the midbrain that regulates sleep and wake cycles. (p. 52)
Prefrontal cortex	The forward most region of the frontal cortex involved in impulse control, judgment, and conscious awareness. (p. 55)
Primary motor cortex	The section of the frontal lobe responsible for voluntary movement. (p. 53)
Primary somatosensory cortex	Area of the parietal lobe where messages from the sense receptors are registered. (p. 55)
Psychobiology	The area of psychology that focuses on the biological foundations of behavior and mental processes. (p. 41)
Receptor sites	Locations on a receptor neuron into which a specific neurotransmitter fits like a key into a lock. (p. 47)
Recessive gene	Member of a gene pair that can control the appearance of a certain trait only if it is paired with another recessive gene. (p. 70)
Resting potential	Electrical charge across a neuron membrane resulting from more positive ions concentrated on the outside and more negative ions on the inside. (p. 44)
Reticular formation (RF)	Network of neurons in the hindbrain, the midbrain, and part of the forebrain, whose primary function is to alert and arouse the higher parts of the brain. (p. 52)
Selection studies	Studies that estimate the heritability of a trait by breeding animals with other animals that have the same trait. (p. 72)
Sensory (or afferent) neurons	Neurons that carry messages from sense organs to the spinal cord or brain. (p. 42)
Somatic nervous system	The part of the peripheral nervous system that carries messages from the senses to the central nervous system and between the central nervous system and the skeletal muscles. (p. 63)
Spinal cord	Complex cable of neurons that runs down the spine, connecting the brain to most of the rest of the body. (p. 62)
Strain studies	Studies of the heritability of behavioral traits using animals that have been inbred to produce strains that are genetically similar to one another. (p. 72)
Sympathetic division	Branch of the autonomic nervous system; it prepares the body for quick action in an emergency. (p. 63)
Synapse	Area composed of the axon terminal of one neuron, the synaptic space, and the dendrite or cell body of the next neuron. (p. 44)
Synaptic space (or synaptic cleft)	Tiny gap between the axon terminal of one neuron and the dendrites or cell body of the next neuron. (p. 44)
Synaptic vesicles	Tiny sacs in a terminal button that release chemicals into the synapse. (p. 47)
Temporal lobe	Part of the cerebral hemisphere that helps regulate hearing, balance and equilibrium, and certain emotions and motivations. (p. 55)
Terminal button (or synaptic knob)	Structure at the end of an axon terminal branch. (p. 47)
Thalamus	Forebrain region that relays and translates incoming messages from the sense receptors, except those for smell. (p. 52)
Threshold of excitation	The level an impulse must exceed to cause a neuron to fire. (p. 44)

Thyroid gland   Endocrine gland located below the voice box; it produces the hormone thyroxin. (p. 66)

Twin studies   Studies of identical and fraternal twins to determine the relative influence of heredity and environment on human behavior. (p. 72)

POSTTEST

After studying the text and completing the Study Guide activities, answer these questions to determine if you need to review any areas before the course exam.

MULTIPLE CHOICE

1. The term "plasticity" as it regards the brain, refers to _____.
   a. brittleness or rigidity
   b. levels of complexity
   c. softness or crevices
   d. ability to adapt to new conditions

2. The field of psychobiology explores the ways in which ____.
   a. biological processes affect our behavior
   b. our mental state affects our physical health
   c. behavioral patterns affect biological development
   d. evolution has shaped our instincts, drives, urges, and needs

3. The smallest unit of the nervous system and the cell that underlies the activity of the entire nervous system is the _____.
   a. glial cell
   b. epidermal cell
   c. neuron
   d. T-cell

4. Neurons that receive information from sensory organs and relay that information to the spinal cord and the brain are called _____.
   a. association neurons
   b. efferent neurons
   c. afferent neurons
   d eons

5. When a neuron is polarized, _____.
   a. potassium ions pass freely through the cell membrane
   b. the electrical charge inside is positive relative to the outside
   c. it cannot fire
   d. the electrical charge inside is negative relative to the outside

6. The entire area composed of the axon terminal of one neuron, the synaptic cleft, and the dendrite or cell body of the next neuron is called the _____.
   a. synaptic vesicle
   b. synaptic knob
   c. synaptic space
   d. synapse

7. The "all or none" law refers to _____.
   a. a group of neurons firing together
   b. a neuron fires at full strength or not at all
   c. all the dendrites must be receiving messages telling the neuron to fire or it will not fire at all
   d. all the neurons in a single nerve fire simultaneously

8. People with Parkinson's disease and schizophenia probably have a deficiency of the neurotransmitter _____.
   a. norepinephrine
   b. serotonin
   c. dopamine
   d. acetylcholine

9. Morphine and other opiates are able to bind to the receptor sites for _____.
   a. acetylcholine
   b. hypothalamus
   c. dopamine
   d. endorphins

10. Eating, drinking, sexual behavior, sleeping, and temperature control are regulated by the _____.
    a. thalamus
    b. hypothalamus
    c. cerebral cortex
    d. corpus callosum

11. The outer covering of the brain and the part most people think of when they consider the brain is the _____.
    a. cerebral cortex
    b. pons
    c. medulla
    d. cerebellum

12. What structure connects the two hemispheres of the brain and coordinates their activities?
    a. reticular formation
    b. amygadala
    c. hippocampus
    d. corpus callosum

13. The part of the brain that helps regulate hearing, balance and equilibrium, certain emotions and motivation, and recognizing faces is the _____.
    a. occipital lobe
    b. temporal lobe
    c. parietal lobe
    d. frontal lobe

14. A part of the brain that sends the signal "Alert" to higher centers of the brain in response to incoming messages is _____.
    a. limbic system
    b. reticular formation
    c. amygdala
    d. hippocampus

15. The thyroid gland controls _____.
    a. glucose absorption
    b. emotions
    c. metabolism
    d. sexuality

16. The _____ hemisphere of the cerebral cortex is usually dominant in spatial tasks while the _____ hemisphere usually dominant in language tasks.
    a. frontal, lateral
    b. left, right
    c. right, left
    d. lateral, frontal

17. The limbic system is responsible for _____.
    a. controlling learning and emotional behavior
    b. providing a bridge for numerous brain areas
    c. analyzing problematic situations
    d. fighting pathogens

18. The system that coordinates and integrates behavior by secreting chemicals into the bloodstream is called the _____.
    a. somatic system
    b. autonomic system
    c. limbic system
    d. endocrine system

19. The endocrine glands located just above the kidneys that release hormones important for dealing with stress are the _____.
    a. gonads
    b. adrenal glands
    c. parathyroid glands
    d. pituitary glands

20. The complex molecule that forms the code for all genetic information is the ____.
    a. DNA
    b. messenger RNA
    c. RNA
    d. monoamine oxidase

21. _____ is a test on a fetus to determine if there are any genetic abnormalities.
    a. Amniocentesis
    b. Positron emission tomography
    c. Magnetic resonance
    d. CT-scans

22. Which of the following would provide the best map of physical structures in the brains of living human beings?
    a. magnetic resonance imaging (MRI)
    b. magnetoencephalography (MEG)
    c. positron emission tomography (PET) scan
    d. electroencephalography (EEG) imaging

23. The goal of the Human Genome Project is to:
    a. clone humans
    b. slow the aging process by identifying genes that play a role in development
    c. find cures for people afflicted by Alzheimer's disease and schizophrenia
    d. identify chromosomes and determine which genes influence human characteristics

24. Studies of heritability in humans that assume that if genes influence a certain trait, close relatives should be more similar with that trait than distant relatives are called _____.
    a. family studies
    b. twin studies
    c. strain studies
    d. selection studies

25. Research on human brain tissue has found that human adult brains ____ have stem cells and neurogenesis ____ occur in human adult brains.
    a. do not, does not
    b. do, does not
    c. do not, does
    d. do, does

26. Messages transmitted and received by neurons may be either _____ or ____ telling a neuron to fire or not to fire an action potential.
    a. all; none
    b. excitatory; inhibitory
    c. synaptic; nonsynaptic
    d. dendritic; axonic

27. Which of the following statements is true regarding research findings on the role of experience in neural development?
    a. Rats raised in impoverished conditions showed no difference in the number of synaptic connections later in life when compared to rats raised in enriched environments.
    b. Rats raised in stimulating environments performed worse on problem-solving tasks than rats raised in impoverished conditions.
    c. Rats raised in stimulating environments may form more synapses as a result of performing complex cognitive tasks.
    d. Rats raised in impoverished environments may form more synapses as a result of barren conditions.

28. Damage to the cerebellum is most likely to result in which of the following?
    a. severe problems in movement
    b. loss of language
    c. reduced ability to think abstractly
    d. vision impairment

29. Which of the following is true regarding split-brain operations?
    a. It has been performed on patients with severe epilepsy.
    b. The two hemispheres of the brain are disconnected by severing the corpus callosum.
    c. Normal functioning is possible since sensory information is sent to both hemispheres.
    d. all of the above

30. Distinctions between Broca's and Wernicke's areas came from studying ____.
    a. people with schizophrenia
    b. victims of stroke
    c. Parkinson's patients
    d. none of the above

31. Which of the following is most likely to describe a person with an overactive thyroid?
    a. feeling tired and wanting to sleep
    b. depressed and low excitability
    c. difficulty focusing on tasks and reduced concentration
    d. increased attention span

32. The gland connected to the hypothalamus that influences blood pressure, thirst, sexual behavior, body growth, and other functions is the ____ gland.
    a. pituitary
    b. pancreas
    c. thalamus
    d. pineal

33. Which statement regarding sex hormones is true?
    a. Women perform better on cognitive tasks during the ovulatory phase of their menstrual cycles.
    b. Elderly men with lower testosterone levels perform better on cognitive tasks.
    c. Married men with children have higher testosterone levels than unmarried men.
    d. all of the above

SHORT ESSAY QUESTIONS

1. Discuss how cocaine, curare, caffeine, opiates, and LSD block or disrupt neural communication. Which receptor sites do these drugs specifically affect?

2. What are the reasons for, and the results of, split-brain operations? What is the difference between split-brain surgery and hemispherectomies?

3. Briefly describe the functions of the reticular formation, the limbic system, and the spinal cord. What kind of problems can result from damage or destruction of these areas?

4. Briefly discuss the purposes of and procedures for studying the brain within each of the following general areas: microelectrode techniques; macroelectrode techniques; structural imaging, functional imaging.

5. Compare and contrast strain studies and selection studies. What are they used for and what has been learned from them? Discuss any limitations of these techniques.

6. Identify and briefly explain the four major principles of Darwin's theory of natural selection. What scientific fields have been impacted by his ideas and how large has that impact been?

7. Discuss some social implications of behavior genetics.

8. Identify several approaches to studying heritability of a trait.

9. Explain the concepts of dominant and recessive genes and discuss how a child's eye color may be influenced if the father has blue eyes and the mother has brown eyes.

10. Briefly summarize the research regarding stem cells and the possibility of growing new neurons in the human brain. Define neuronal plasticity and neurogenesis. Which specific disorders or diseases may be helped by this method?

11. What are some of the ethical concerns regarding stem cell research and development?

LABEL DRAWINGS

A. Label the parts of a neuron.

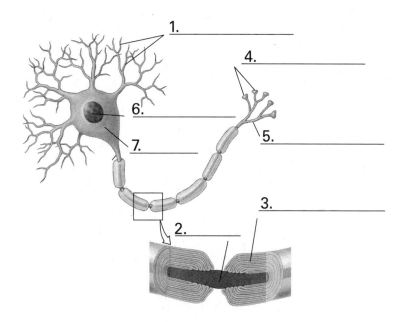

1. _____

4. _____

6. _____

5. _____

7. _____

3. _____

2. _____

B. Label the parts of the neuron at the synapse.

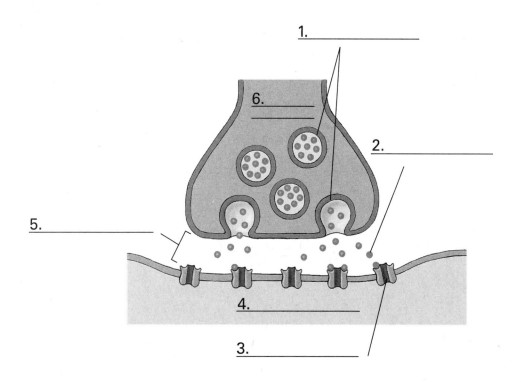

1. _____

6. _____

2. _____

5. _____

4. _____

3. _____

C. Name each lobe of the brain and identify the parts of the brain.

1. _____

2. _____

3. _____

10. _____

9. _____

4. _____

5. _____

6. _____

7. _____

11. _____

8. _____

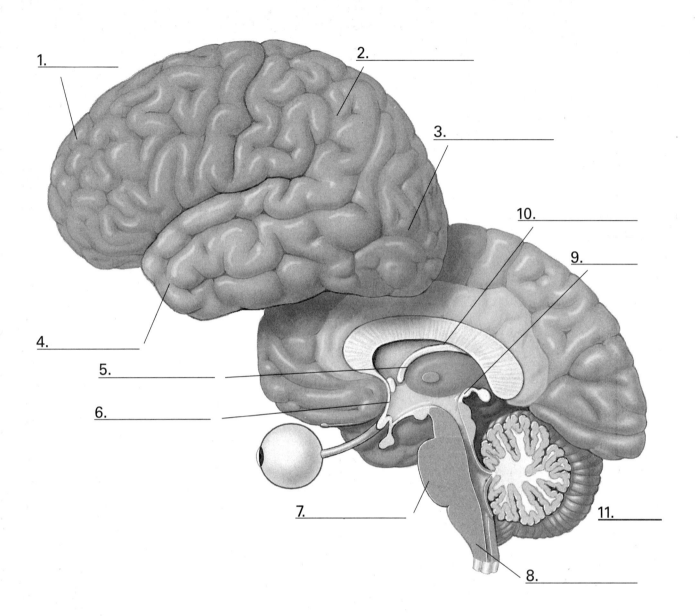

Answers and Explanations to Multiple Choice Posttest

1. d. Plasticity in the human brain is the ability to adapt to new environmental conditions. p. 41

2. a. Psychobiology is the branch of psychology that deals with the biological basis of behavior and mental processes. p. 41

3. c. A neuron is the smallest unit of the nervous system and underlies the activity of the entire nervous system. p. 42

4. c. Afferent (sensory) neurons carry messages from sense organs to the spinal cord or brain. p. 42

5. d. When the electrical charge inside the neuron is negative relative to the outside, it is called polarized or polarization. p. 44

6. d. A synapse is composed of the axon terminal of one neuron, the synaptic space, and the dendrite or cell body of the next neuron. p. 45

7. b. The all-or-none law operates on the principle that the action potential in a neuron either fires at full strength or not at all. p. 45

8. c. The neurotransmitter dopamine is involved in a wide variety of behaviors and emotions and is implicated in schizophrenia and Parkinson's disease. p. 47

9. d. Opiates such as morphine and heroin bind to the receptor sites for endorphins and shed information on addictive behavior. p. 47

10. b. Portions of the hypothalamus govern hunger, thirst, sexual drive, body temperature, rage, terror, and pleasure. p. 52

11. a. Most people think of or refer to the cerebral cortex when talking about "the brain." p. 52

12. d. The corpus callosum is a thick, ribbonlike band of nerve fibers that is the primary connection between the left and right hemispheres. p. 56

13. b. The temporal lobe of the brain regulates hearing, balance, equilibrium, some emotions and motivation, and facial recognition. p. 55

14. b. The reticular formation's main job is to send "alert!" signals to the higher brain in response to incoming messages. p. 52

15. c. The thyroid gland regulates the body's rate of metabolism and how alert and energetic people are. p. 66

16. c. The right hemisphere tends to dominate in spatial and holistic tasks; the left hemisphere tends to dominate in language and sequential activities. p. 57

17. a. The limbic system plays a role in learning and emotional behavior and forming new memories. p. 55

18. d. The endocrine system secretes hormones into the bloodstream that coordinate and integrate behavior. p. 65

19. b. The adrenal glands (adrenal cortex and adrenal medulla) affect the body's reaction to stress by releasing hormones into the bloodstream. p. 67

20. a. Deoxyribonucleic acid (DNA) is a complex, double helix shaped molecule that is the main ingredient of chromosomes and genes and forms the code for all genetic information. p. 70

21. a. Amniocentesis is a prenatal screening procedure that harvests cells taken from the amniotic fluid to determine defects. p. 74

22. a. (MRI) Magnetic resonance imaging observes computerized colored brain images to detect abnormal brain activity and map structures in the brain. p. 60

23. d. The Human Genome Project was launched in 1990 with the goal to map all 23 pairs of human chromosomes and to determine which genes influence which characteristics. p. 71

24. a. Family studies assume that close relatives should have more heritability than distant relatives on certain traits. p. 72

25. d. Major breakthrough research in 1998 has proven that adult brains do have stem cells and that neurogenesis does occur in human adult brains. p. 50

26. b. Excitatory signals tell neurons to "fire," while inhibitory signals tell them to "rest." p. 44

27. c. Studies have shown that rats raised in enriched conditions have larger neurons with more synapses compared to rats raised in impoverished conditions. p. 49

28. a. Also known as the "little brain," the cerebellum is known primarily for control of balance and coordinating action; jerky movements and stumbling may result if the cerebellum is damaged. New evidence shows it may be involved in psychological processes. p. 52

29. d. In severe cases of epilepsy, the corpus callosum may be cut separating the two brain hemispheres. Normal functioning is possible, but certain experiments have revealed the specialized roles of the left and right hemispheres. p. 56

30. b. Strokes often produce language problems called aphasias. Expressive aphasias are seen in damage to Broca's area and receptive aphasias are seen in patients with damage to Wernicke's area. p. 58

31. c. The thyroid gland affects alertness and energy. Among other things, hyperthyroidism results in overexcitability, insomnia, reduced attention span, agitation, as well as reduced concentration and difficulty focusing on a task. p. 66

32. a. Often called the "master gland," the pituitary produces many different hormones and has a wide range of effects on the body functions. p. 66

33. a. Sex hormones such as estrogen and testosterone influence performance on cognitive tasks. Also, testosterone levels vary in males, they are lower in married men and married men with children. p. 67

ANSWERS TO LABEL DRAWINGS

A. Parts of a neuron. Refer to Figure 2-1, p. 43
   1. dendrites
   2. axon
   3. myelin
   4. terminal buttons
   5. axon terminals
   6. cell nucleus
   7. cell body

B. Parts of the neuron at the synapse. Refer to Figure 2-4, p. 46
   1. synaptic vesicles
   2. neurotransmitters
   3. receptor
   4. dendrite or cell body
   5. synaptic space
   6. terminal button

C. Lobes and parts of the brain. Refer to Figure 2-7, p. 53

   1. Frontal lobe
   2. Parietal lobe
   3. Temporal lobe
   4. Occipital lobe
   5. Thalamus
   6. Hypothalamus
   7. Pons
   8. Medulla
   9. Pineal gland
   10. Corpus callosum
   11. Cerebellum

CHAPTER 3

Sensation and Perception

CHAPTER OVERVIEW

The chapter opens with a series of anecdotes illustrating how senses give us a "window on the world" by enabling us to acquire information from our external (and internal) environment, and how the mental process of perception helps us sort, identify, and arrange these bits of raw data into coherent patterns.

Humans have sensory experiences of sight, hearing, smell, taste, touch, pain, and balance, which are known as **sensations**. These experiences begin when the body's sensory receptors are stimulated. In each case, some form of physical energy is converted into neural impulses that are carried to the brain.

The process of sending a sensory message to the brain begins when energy stimulates **receptor cells** in one of the sense organs. Through the process of **transduction**, receptor cells convert the stimulation into coded signals that vary according to the characteristics of the stimulus. Further coding occurs as the signal passes along sensory nerve fibers, so that the message finally reaching the brain is very detailed and precise.

The amount of physical energy that reaches sensory receptors must be of a minimal intensity to produce a detectable sensation. The least amount of energy needed to produce a sensation 50% of the time is called the **absolute threshold**. For hearing, the absolute threshold is roughly the tick of a watch from 6 m (20 feet) away in a very quiet room, and for vision, it is a candle flame seen from 50 km (30 miles) on a clear, dark night. Absolute thresholds vary according to the intensity of the stimulus present at any given time—a process called **adaptation**. Also, we are very sensitive to *changes* in the stimulus intensity. The **difference threshold** or the **just-noticeable difference (jnd)** is the smallest change in stimulation that can be detected 50% of the time. In the 1830s,

Ernst Weber concluded that the difference threshold is a constant *fraction or proportion* of the original stimulus; this is a theory known as **Weber's law**.

When people respond to sensory messages that are below their threshold level of awareness, they are said to be responding subliminally. Such subliminal processing can occur in controlled laboratory settings, but there is no scientific evidence that subliminal messages have any effect in everyday life.

The chapter next focuses on the sense of vision, and why psychologists have studied vision more than any other sense. Different animal species depend more on some senses than others. In bats and dogs, hearing and sense of smell, respectively, are particularly important. In humans, vision is paramount, which is why it has received the most research attention.

Light enters an eye through the **cornea** (a transparent protective coating) and passes through the **pupil** (the opening in the **iris**) as well as through the **lens**, which focuses it onto the eye's light-sensitive inner lining called the **retina**. Directly behind the lens is a depressed spot in the retina called the **fovea**.

The retina contains the receptor cells responsible for vision. These cells are sensitive to only one small part of the spectrum of electromagnetic energy known as *visible light*. Energies in the electromagnetic spectrum are referred to by their **wavelength**.

Neural impulses are generated in the retina by receptor cells known as **rods** and **cones**. The rods and cones connect to nerve cells called **bipolar cells**, which in turn connect to **ganglion cells**. The axons of ganglion cells converge to form the **optic nerve**, which carries to the brain the neural impulses triggered in the retina. The place on the retina where the axons of all the ganglion cells join to form the optic nerve is called the **blind spot**.

After the nerve fibers that make up the optic nerves leave the eyes, they separate, and some of them cross to the other side of the head at the **optic chiasm**. **Light** and **dark adaptation** occur as the sensitivity of rods and cones changes with the availability of light. Dark and light adaptation can cause an **afterimage**.

In the brain itself, certain brain cells—called **feature detectors**—are highly specialized to detect particular elements of the visual field, such as horizontal or vertical lines.

The **trichromatic theory** of color vision is based on the principles of **additive color mixing**, in which each light adds additional wavelengths to the overall mix (this is opposed to **subtractive color mixing**, a process used in paint mixing). Trichromatic theory holds that the eyes contain three different kinds of color receptors, one of which is most responsive to red, another to green, and another to blue. By combining signals from these three types of receptors, the brain can detect a wide range of shades. In contrast, the **opponent-process theory** of color vision maintains that receptors in the eyes are specialized to respond to one member of three basic color pairs: red–green, yellow–blue, and black–white (or light–dark). Research gives some support for both these theories. There are indeed three kinds of color receptors in the retinas, but the messages they initiate are coded by other neurons into opponent-process form. **Hue**, **saturation**, and **brightness** are properties of color vision.

The chapter next turns to a discussion of the sense of hearing. Our ability to hear **sound** is important as it permits us to understand language and communicate with other people.

The physical stimuli for the sense of hearing are **sound waves**, which produce vibration in the eardrums. **Frequency**, the number of cycles per second in a sound wave (expressed in a unit called **hertz (Hz)**), is the primary determinant of **pitch** (how high or low the tones seems to be). The complex patterns of **overtones** which accompany real world sounds determine the **timbre** or texture of sound. **Amplitude**, or loudness, refers to the magnitude of sound wave, and is measured using a **decibel** scale.

When sound waves strike an eardrum and cause it to vibrate, three bones in the middle ear—the hammer, the anvil, and the stirrup—are stimulated to vibrate in sequence. These vibrations are magnified in their passage through the middle ear and into the inner ear beyond it. (The student should note the following relationships between parts of the inner ear: the stirrup is attached to a membrane called the **oval window**; vibrations of the oval window, in turn, are transmitted to the fluid inside a snail-shaped structure called the **cochlea**. The cochlea is divided lengthwise by the **basilar membrane**.) In the inner ear, movement of the basilar membrane stimulates sensory receptors in the **organ of Corti**. This stimulation of the hair cells produces auditory signals that travel to the brain through the **auditory nerve**.

The **place theory** holds that the brain distinguishes low-frequency sounds from high-frequency sounds by noting the place on the basilar membrane at which the greatest stimulation is occurring. For high-frequency sounds, this is the base of the basilar membrane; for low-frequency sounds, it is the membrane's opposite end. According to the **frequency theory** of pitch discrimination, the frequency of vibrations on the basilar membrane as a whole is translated into an equivalent frequency of nerve impulses that travel to the brain. This theory, with its associated **volley principle**, can account for pitch detection up to frequencies of about 4000 Hz. Above that, the place theory seems to provide a better explanation.

The chapter next moves into the broader topic of the "other senses."

Two senses—smell and taste— are designed to detect the presence of various chemical substances in the air and in food.

Substances carried by airborne molecules into the nasal cavities activate highly specialized receptors for smell. From here, messages are carried directly to the **olfactory bulb** in the brain, where they are sent to the brain's temporal lobe, resulting in our awareness of smell. **Pheromones** are chemicals produced by organisms to communicate using their sense of smell.

Flavor is a complex blend of taste and smell. There are five basic ones—sweet, sour, salty, bitter, and umami—and other tastes derive from combinations of these. The five receptors for taste are housed in the **taste buds** on the tongue. When these receptors are activated by the chemical substances in food, their adjacent neurons fire, sending nerve impulses to the brain.

The **vestibular senses** provide information about our orientation or position in space, such as whether we are right side up or upside down. The receptors for these senses are in two vestibular organs in the inner ear—the semicircular canals and the vestibular sacs. The vestibular organs are responsible for a motion sickness. This queasy feeling may be triggered by discrepancies between visual information and vestibular sensations. The **kinesthetic senses** provide information about the speed and direction of our movements. They rely on feedback from specialized receptors, which are attached to muscle fibers and the tendons that connect muscle to bone.

The skin is the largest sense organ, and sensations that arise from the receptors embedded in it produce our sensation of touch, which includes pressure, temperature, and pain. Research has not yet established a simple, direct connection between these three sensations and the various types of skin receptors whose nerve fibers lead to the brain.

People have varying degrees of sensitivity to pain based on their physiological makeup, their current mental and emotional state, their expectations, and their cultural beliefs and values. One commonly accepted explanation of pain is the **gate-control theory**, which holds that a "neurological gate" in the spinal cord controls the transmission of pain messages to the brain. **Biopsychosocial theory** proposes that pain results from the interaction of biological, psychological, and social mechanisms. As pain reducers, placebos and acupuncture work in part through the release of pain-blocking neurotransmitters called endorphins. No doubt many home remedies and secret cures rely on the **placebo effect**.

The chapter concludes with a detailed section on perception, first dealing with how perception differs from sensation. Sensation refers to the raw sensory data that the brain receives from the senses of sight, hearing, smell, taste, balance, touch, and pain. **Perception**, which takes place in the brain, is the process of organizing, interpreting, and giving meaning to those data.

Twentieth-century Gestalt psychologists believed the brain creates a coherent perceptual experience that is more than simply the sum of the available sensory data. The brain imposes order on the data it receives partly by distinguishing patterns such as figure and ground, proximity, similarity, closure, and continuity.

Perceptual constancy is our tendency to perceive objects as unchanging even given many changes in sensory stimulation. Once we have formed a stable perception of something, we see it as essentially the same regardless of differences in viewing angle, distance, lighting, and so forth. These **size**, **shape**, **brightness**, and **color constancies** help us better to understand and relate to the world.

We perceive distance and depth through both **monocular cues** (received even by one eye alone) and **binocular cues** (requiring the interaction of both eyes). Examples of monocular cues are **interposition** (in which one object partly covers another), **linear perspective**, **aerial perspective**, **elevation** (or closeness of something to the horizon), **texture gradient** (from coarser to finer depending on distance), **shadowing**, and **motion parallax** (differences in the relative movement of close and distant objects as we change position). An important binocular cue is **stereoscopic vision**, which is derived from combining our two retinal images to produce a 3-D effect. Two other binocular cues are **retinal disparity** (the difference between the two separate images received by the eyes) and **convergence** of the eyes as viewing distance decreases. Just as we use monocular and binocular cues to sense depth and distance, we use **monaural** (one-ear) and **binaural** (two-ear) cues to locate the source of sounds.

Perception of movement is a complicated process involving both visual messages from the retina and messages from the muscles around the eyes as they shift to follow a moving object. At times our perceptual processes trick us into believing that an object is moving when in fact it is not. There is a difference, then, between real movement and apparent movement. Examples of apparent movement are the **autokinetic illusion** (caused by the absence of visual cues surrounding a stationary object), **stroboscopic motion** (produced by rapidly flashing a series of pictures), and the **phi phenomenon** (produced by a pattern of flashing lights).

Visual illusions occur when we use a variety of sensory cues to create perceptual experiences that do not actually exist. Some are *physical illusions*, such as the bent appearance of a stick in water. Others are *perceptual illusions*, which occur because a stimulus contains misleading cues that lead to inaccurate perceptions.

In addition to past experience and learning, our perceptions are also influenced by our motivation, values, expectations, cognitive style, experience and culture, and personality.

LEARNING OBJECTIVES EXERCISE

After you have read and studied the chapter, you should be able to answer the following learning objectives.

THE NATURE OF SENSATION

*   Explain the difference between absolute and difference thresholds and the effect of adaptation on sensory thresholds. Summarize the evidence for subliminal perception and extrasensory perception.

VISION

*   Describe the role of rods, cones, bipolar cells, ganglion cells, the optic nerve, the optic chiasm, and feature detectors in the brain in causing a visual experience.

*   Explain how dark and light adaptation affect our vision and how they cause afterimages.

*   Distinguish between hue, saturation, brightness, additive and subtractive color mixing. Explain the two major theories of color perception.

HEARING

*   Explain the characteristics of sound waves and their effect on the sensation we call sound.

*   Decribe the path that information about sound travels from the ears to the brain. Explain place theory, frequency theory, and the volley principle.

*   Explain the two major kinds of hearing disorders (deafness and tinnitus).

THE OTHER SENSES

*   Describe how stimuli give rise to smells and tastes.

*   Distinguish between the kinesthetic and vestibular senses.

*   Explain how sensory messages are sent from the skin to the brain. Summarize the sources of differences among people in the degree of pain they experience.

- Distinguish between sensation and perception. Explain the Gestalt principles of perceptual organization. Describe the several perceptual constancies.

- Identify the major cues to distance and depth, distinguishing between monocular and binocular cues.

- Explain how we can localize sound and perceive movement, distinguishing between real movement and apparent movement.

- Explain how visual illusions arise.

- Describe how observer characteristics and culture can influence perception.

I.   Enduring Issues in Sensation and Perception (page 81)

II. The Nature of Sensation (page 81)
    A.   Sensory Thresholds
- Transduction
- Absolute Threshold
- Adaptation
- Difference Threshold or Just-Noticeable Difference (JND)
- Weber's Law

    B.   Subliminal Perception
        i.   Extrasensory Perception

III. Vision (page 85)
    A.   The Visual System
        i.   The Receptor Cells
        ii. Adaptation
        iii. From Eye to Brain
    B.   Color Vision
        i.   Properties of Color
        ii. Theories of Color Vision
        iii. Color Vision in Other Species
    C.   APPLYING PSYCHOLOGY: A ROSE BY ANY OTHER NAME

IV. Hearing (page 93)
    A.   Sound
- Sound Waves
- Frequency
- Hertz (Hz)
- Pitch
- Amplitude
- Decibel
- Overtones
- Timbre

    B.   The Ear
        i.   Neural Connections
    C.   Theories of Hearing
- Place Theory
- Freqency Theory
- Volley Principle
        i.   Hearing Disorders

V.   The Other Senses (page 99)
    A.   Smell
- Olfactory Bulb
- Odor Sensitivity and Gender
- Anosmia

    B.   Taste
- Taste Buds
- Sweet, Salty, Sour, Bitter, Umami

    C.   Kinesthetic and Vestibular Senses
- Motion Sickness

    D.   The Skin Senses
- Numerous Nerve Receptors
- Give Rise to Sensations

    E.   Pain
        i.   Gate-Control Theory
        ii. Biopsychosocial Theory
        iii. Alternative Treatments

VI. Perception (page 106)
    A.   Perceptual Organization
- Proximity
- Similarity
- Closure
- Continuity

    B.   Perceptual Constancies
- Size Constancy
- Shape Constancy
- Color Constancy
- Brightness Constancy

    C.   Perception of Distance and Depth
        i.   Monocular Cues
        ii. Binocular Cues
        iii. Location of Sounds

    D.   Perception of Movement
- Real Movement
- Apparent Movement
- Autokinetic Illusion
- Stroboscopic Motion
- Phi Phenomenon

    E.   Visual Illusions
- Physical Illusion
- Perceptual Illusion
- Depth Cues
- Induced Movement

    F.   Observer Characteristics
        i.   Motivation and Emotion
        ii. Values
        iii. Expectations
        iv. Cognitive Style
        v.   Experience and Culture
        vi. Personality

KEY TERMS

Absolute threshold	The least amount of energy that can be detected as a stimulation 50% of the time. (p. 82)
Adaptation	An adjustment of the senses to the level of stimulation they are receiving. (p. 82)
Additive color mixing	The process of mixing lights of different wavelengths to create new hues. (p. 90)
Aerial perspective	Monocular cue to distance and depth based on the fact that more distant objects are likely to appear hazy and blurred. (p. 112)
Afterimage	Sense experience that occurs after a visual stimulus has been removed. (p. 89)
Amplitude	The magnitude of a wave; in sound, the primary determinant of loudness. (p. 94)
Auditory nerve	The bundle of axons that carries signals from each ear to the brain. (p. 94)
Autokinetic illusion	The perception that a stationary object is actually moving. (p. 114)
Basilar membrane	Vibrating membrane in the cochlea of the inner ear; it contains sense receptors for sound. (p. 94)
Binaural cues	Cues to sound location that involve both ears working together. (p. 113)
Binocular cues	Visual cues requiring the use of both eyes. (p. 111)
Biopsychosocial theory	The theory that the interaction of biological, psychological, and cultural factors influences the intensity and duration of pain. (p. 104)
Bipolar cells	Neurons that have only one axon and one dendrite; in the eye, these neurons connect the receptors on the retina to the ganglion cells. (p. 87)
Blind spot	The place on the retina where the axons of all the ganglion cells leave the eye and where there are no receptors. (p. 89)
Brightness	The nearness of a color to white as opposed to black. (p. 90)
Brightness constancy	The perception of brightness as the same, even though the amount of light reaching the retina changes. (p. 111)
Cochlea	Part of the inner ear containing fluid that vibrates, which in turn causes the basilar membrane to vibrate. (p. 94)
Color constancy	An inclination to perceive familiar objects as retaining their color despite changes in sensory information. (p. 110)
Cones	Receptor cells in the retina responsible for color vision. (p. 86)
Convergence	A visual depth cue that comes from muscles controlling eye movement as the eyes turn inward to view a nearby stimulus. (p. 113)
Cornea	The transparent protective coating over the front part of the eye. (p. 85)
Dark adaptation	Increased sensitivity of rods and cones in darkness. (p. 87)
Decibel	Unit of measurement for the loudness of sounds. (p. 94)
Difference threshold or just-noticeable difference (jnd)	The smallest change in stimulation that can be detected 50% of the time. (p. 82)
Elevation	Monocular cue to distance and depth based on the fact that the higher on the horizontal plane an object is, the farther away it appears. (p. 112)
Feature detectors	Specialized brain cells that only respond to particular elements in the visual field such as movement or lines of specific orientation. (p. 90)
Fovea	The area of the retina that is the center of the visual field. (p. 86)
Frequency	The number of cycles per second in a wave; in sound, the primary determinant of pitch. (p. 94)
Frequency theory	Theory that pitch is determined by the frequency with which hair cells in the cochlea fire. (p. 97)
Ganglion cells	Neurons that connect the bipolar cells in the eyes to the brain. (p. 89)
Gate-control theory	The theory that a "neurological gate" in the spinal cord controls the transmission of pain messages to the brain. (p. 104)

Hertz (Hz)	Cycles per second; unit of measurement for the frequency of sound waves. (p. 94)
Hues	The aspects of color that correspond to names such as red, green, and blue. (p. 90)
Interposition	Monocular distance cue in which one object, by partly blocking a second object, is perceived as being closer. (p. 111)
Iris	The colored part of the eye that regulates the size of the pupil. (p. 85)
Kinesthetic senses	Senses of muscle movement, posture, and strain on muscles and joints. (p. 101)
Lens	The transparent part of the eye behind the pupil that focuses light onto the retina. (p. 86)
Light adaptation	Decreased sensitivity of rods and cones in bright light. (p. 89)
Linear perspective	Monocular cue to distance and depth based on the fact that two parallel lines seem to come together at the horizon. (p. 112)
Monaural cues	Cues to sound location that require just one ear. (p. 113)
Monocular cues	Visual cues requiring the use of one eye. (p. 111)
Motion parallax	Monocular distance cue in which objects closer than the point of visual focus seem to move in the direction opposite to the viewer's moving head, and objects beyond the focus point appear to move in the same direction as the viewer's head. (p. 112)
Olfactory bulb	The smell center in the brain. (p. 99)
Opponent-process theory	Theory of color vision that holds that three sets of color receptors (yellow–blue, red–green, black–white) respond to determine the color you experience. (p. 90)
Optic chiasm	The point near the base of the brain where some fibers in the optic nerve from each eye cross to the other side of the brain. (p. 89)
Optic nerve	The bundle of axons of ganglion cells that carries neural messages from each eye to the brain. (p. 89)
Organ of Corti	Structure on the surface of the basilar membrane that contains the receptor cells for hearing. (p. 94)
Oval window	Membrane across the opening between the middle ear and inner ear that conducts vibrations to the cochlea. (p. 94)
Overtones	Tones that result from sound waves that are multiples of the basic tone; primary determinant of timbre. (p. 94)
Perception	The brain's interpretation of sensory information so as to give it meaning. (p. 107)
Perceptual constancy	A tendency to perceive objects as stable and unchanging despite changes in sensory stimulation. (p. 110)
Pheromones	Chemicals that communicate information to other organisms through smell. (p. 101)
Phi phenomenon	Apparent movement caused by flashing lights in sequence, as on theater marquees. (p. 114)
Pitch	Auditory experience corresponding primarily to frequency of sound vibrations, resulting in a higher or lower tone. (p. 94)
Place theory	Theory that pitch is determined by the location of greatest vibration on the basilar membrane. (p. 97)
Placebo effect	Pain relief that occurs when a person believes a pill or procedure will reduce pain. The actual cause of the relief seems to come from endorphins. (p. 105)
Pupil	A small opening in the iris through which light enters the eye. (p. 85)
Receptor cell	A specialized cell that responds to a particular type of energy. (p. 81)
Retina	The lining of the eye containing receptor cells that are sensitive to light. (p. 86)
Retinal disparity	Binocular distance cue based on the difference between the images cast on the two retinas when both eyes are focused on the same object. (p. 113)
Rods	Receptor cells in the retina responsible for night vision and perception of brightness. (p. 86)
Saturation	The vividness or richness of a hue. (p. 90)

Sensation	The experience of sensory stimulation. (p. 81)
Shadowing	Monocular cue to distance and depth based on the fact that shadows often appear on the parts of objects that are more distant. (p. 112)
Shape constancy	A tendency to see an object as the same shape no matter what angle it is viewed from. (p. 110)
Size constancy	The perception of an object as the same size regardless of the distance from which it is viewed. (p. 110)
Sound	A psychological experience created by the brain in response to changes in air pressure that are received by the auditory system. (p. 94)
Sound waves	Changes in pressure caused when molecules of air or fluid collide with one another and then move apart again. (p. 94)
Stereoscopic vision	Combination of two retinal images to give a three-dimensional perceptual experience. (p. 113)
Stroboscopic motion	Apparent movement that results from flashing a series of still pictures in rapid succession, as in a motion picture. (p. 114)
Subtractive color mixing	The process of mixing pigments, each of which absorbs some wavelengths of light and reflects others. (p. 90)
Taste buds	Structures on the tongue that contain the receptor cells for taste. (p. 101)
Texture gradient	Monocular cue to distance and depth based on the fact that objects seen at greater distances appear to be smoother and less textured. (p. 112)
Timbre	The quality or texture of sound; caused by overtones. (p. 94)
Transduction	The conversion of physical energy into coded neural signals. (p. 82)
Trichromatic (or three-color) theory	The theory of color vision that holds that all color perception derives from three different color receptors in the retina (usually red, green, and blue receptors). (p. 90)
Vestibular senses	The senses of equilibrium and body position in space. (p. 102)
Visual acuity	The ability to distinguish fine details visually. (p. 87)
Volley principle	Refinement of frequency theory; it suggests that receptors in the ear fire in sequence, with one group responding, then a second, then a third, and so on, so that the complete pattern of firing corresponds to the frequency of the sound wave. (p. 97)
Wavelengths	The different energies represented in the electromagnetic spectrum. (p. 86)
Weber's law	The principle that the jnd for any given sense is a constant fraction or proportion of the stimulation being judged. (p. 82)

**Phi
phenomenon**

Apparent movement caused by
flashing lights in sequence, as
on theater marquees.

After studying the text and completing the Study Guide activities, answer these questions to determine if you need to review any areas before the course exam.

MULTIPLE CHOICE

1. Sensation is to _____ as perception is to _____.
   a. stimulation; interpretation
   b. interpretation; stimulation
   c. sensory ability; sensory acuity
   d. sensory acuity; sensory ability

2. The _____ is reached when a person can detect a stimulus 50 percent of the time.
   a. difference threshold
   b. just noticeable difference threshold
   c. absolute threshold
   d. separation threshold

3. Which of the following is NOT true of subliminal perception?
   a. The effects attributed to subliminal perception may be the results of conscious expectations.
   b. Subliminal messages may be able to change attitudes.
   c. People can perceive stimuli they cannot consciously describe.
   d. It works equally as well in all people.

4. _____ are receptor cells in the retina responsible for night vision and perceiving brightness, and _____ are receptor cells in the retina responsible for color vision.
   a. Rods; cones
   b. Rods; reels
   c. Cones; rods
   d. Cornea; iris

5. The ability of the eye to distinguish fine details is called _____.
   a. visual dilation
   b. visual acuity
   c. visual sensitivity
   d. adaptation

6. On the chart below, label the energies in the electromagnetic spectrum in order: FM radio waves, AC circuits, X-rays, radar, TV radio waves, infrared rays, gamma rays, AM radio waves, ultra violet rays.

7. Motion sickness arises in the _____.
   a. kinesthetic organs
   b. cutaneous organs
   c. cerebral cortex
   d. vestibular organs

8. The process of mixing various pigments together to create different colors is called _____.
   a. blending
   b. trichromatic color mixing
   c. subtractive color mixing
   d. additive color mixing

9. The psychological experience created by the brain in response to changes in air pressure that are perceived in the auditory system is known as

   _____.
   a. vibration
   b. harmonics
   c. sound
   d. amplitude

10. On the chart below, label the amount of decibels of the following common sounds: patter of rain; revolver firing at close range; subway train; normal conversation; whisper; average office interior; sonic boom; power lawnmower; food blender; air raid siren; live rock music; heavy truck; leaves rustling; window air conditioner, jet plane; personal stereo; pain threshold; potential ear damage; heavy traffic; vacuum; dishwasher.

11. Hertz is a unit of measurement of

    _____.
    a. the timbre of a sound
    b. how high or low a sound is
    c. the frequency of a sound
    d. the amplitude of a sound

12. A chemical that communicates information to other organisms through the sense of smell is called _____.
    a. a saccule
    b. a pheromone
    c. odorant protein binding
    d. a scent

13. Flavor is _____.
    a. a combination of texture and taste
    b. a combination of taste and smell
    c. a combination of texture and smell
    d. taste

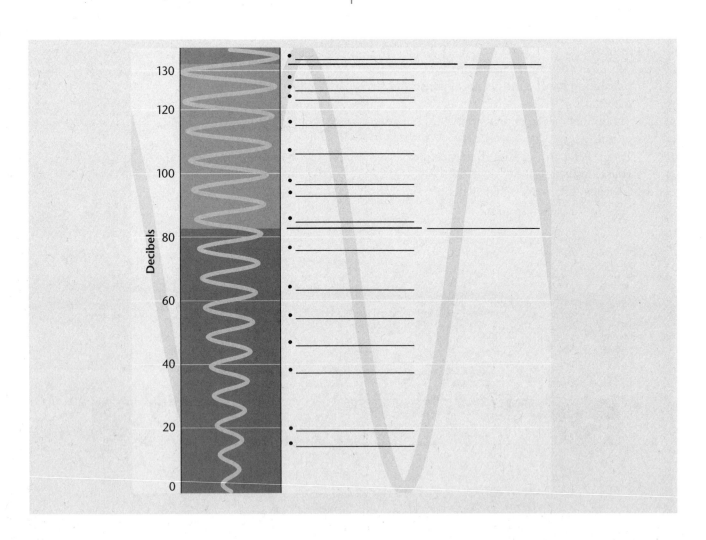

14. The _____ has the most numerous receptors.
    a. eye
    b. ear
    c. nose
    d. skin

15. Optical illusions result from distortion in _____.
    a. transduction
    b. sensation
    c. perception
    d. adaptation

16. You know a house is the same size whether you are standing right next to it or a mile away from it because of _____.
    a. phi phenomenon
    b. the figure-ground distinction
    c. retinal disparity
    d. perceptual constancy

17. Our general method for dealing with the environment is known as _____.
    a. intelligence
    b. perceptual style
    c. personality
    d. cognitive style

18. Visual distance and depth cues that require the use of both eyes are called _____.
    a. monocular cues
    b. diocular cues
    c. binocular cues
    d. dichromatic cues

19. Placebo pills and acupuncture have been effective in reducing pain. The common element in these methods may be their ability to stimulate the ____.
    a. production of adrenal hormones
    b. opening of neurological gates in the spine
    c. arousal of the peripheral nervous system
    d. production of endorphins

20. The phenomenon whereby items that continue a pattern or direction tend to be grouped together as part of a pattern is _____.
    a. proximity
    b. similarity
    c. closure
    d. continuity

21. The phenomenon in which we perceive movement in objects that are actually standing still is known as _____.
    a. apparent movement
    b. real movement
    c. biological movement
    d. induced movement

22. On the chart below, match the Gestalt principles of perceptual organization with the appropriate pattern.
    a. continuity
    b. closure
    c. proximity
    d. similarity

23. Which of the following best describes the process of adaptation in a dimly lit environment?
    a. Rods and cones have equal sensitivity to light in low levels of illumination.
    b. The best vision will occur once the rods have adapted.
    c. Cones will become increasingly sensitive to the dim light.
    d. Once the rods and cones have adapted, seeing in color is possible.

24. The term blind spot refers to _____.
    a. the place on the retina that does not have any receptor cells
    b. the place on the retina that does not have cones
    c. the place on the retina that does not have rods
    d. the complete inability to process vision

25. A person who has tinnitus suffers from _____.
    a. the perception of a constant visual image, as if seeing stars
    b. a chronic sensation of being touched
    c. hearing a persistent sound, like screeching or ringing, from inside the head
    d. an inflammation of the sensory receptors

26. Which of the following statements is true regarding anosmia?
    a. It is most commonly reported in the elderly.
    b. Taste buds detect salty, bitter, sour, or sweet flavors.
    c. It is the complete loss of smell.
    d. all of the above

27. Which of the following is NOT true regarding the experience of pain?
    a. Individuals vary widely in their thresholds for pain.
    b. Genetics may play a role in the perception of pain.
    c. Culture and belief systems play a role in coping with pain.
    d. Pain receptors are easy to locate in the body.

SHORT ESSAY QUESTIONS

1. Define pitch, amplitude, decibels, overtones, and timbre.

2. Differentiate among hue, brightness, and saturation. Explain the difference between additive and subtractive color mixing.

3. Distinguish between rods and cones and list their characteristics and functions with respect to light, color, and how they connect to other cells.

4. Describe hearing disorders and explain the causes of deafness and tinnitus.

5. Describe autokinetic illusion, stroboscopic movement, the phi phenomenon, and the illusion of induced movement.

6. Explain subliminal perception and discuss research findings on the effectiveness of subliminal messages on people's behavior.

7. Explain extrasensory perception, telepathy, and clairvoyance. Define parapsychology and discuss research findings in this field.

8. Describe how we use monaural and binaural cues to locate the source of sounds.

9. Discuss the principles of perceptual organization identified by the Gestaltists.

10. Compare and contrast real and apparent movement and provide three examples of apparent movement.

ANSWERS AND EXPLANATIONS TO MULTIPLE CHOICE POSTTEST

1. a. Sensation is the stimulation of a receptor cell (p. 81) and perception is our interpretation of that stimulation (p. 107).

2. c. Absolute threshold is a sensation detected 50 percent of the time. p. 82

3. d. Subliminal perception has not been shown to affect everyone in the same way. p. 84

4. a. Rods are receptors for night vision and brightness, and cones are receptors for color vision. p. 86

5. b. Visual acuity refers to our ability to see fine details. p. 87

6.   Fig. 3–4, p. 87. From left to right: gamma rays; x rays; ultraviolet rays (visible light); infrared rays; radar; radio waves: FM – TV – AM; AC circuits.

7. d. Motion sickness originates in the vestibular organs. p. 102

8. c. Mixing of pigments is called subtractive color mixing. p. 90

9. c. Sound is our brain's interpretation of the changes in air pressure in our eardrums. p. 94

10.   Fig. 3–15, p. 95 From top to bottom: revolver; 130 decibels: pain threshold; sonic boom; air raid siren; jackhammer; 120 decibels: jet plane; personal stereo; live rock music; 100 decibels: subway train; heavy truck; power lawn mower; food blender; 80 decibels: potential ear damage; heavy traffic/vacuum/dishwasher; normal conversation; 60 decibels: window air conditioner; patter of rain; 40 decibels: average office interior; 20 decibels: leaves rustling; whisper.

11. c. Hertz refers to the frequency of the sound wave. p. 94

12. b. Pheromones are chemicals that communicate information to other organisms through smell. p. 101

13. b. Flavor is a combination of taste and smell. p. 101

14. a. The skin is the largest sense organ and contains the most receptors. p. 102

15. c. Optical illusions are the result of distortions in perception. p. 107

16. d. Perceptual constancy enables us to see distant objects as the same size as when viewed close by. p. 110

17. d. Our cognitive style determines how we deal with our environment. p. 117

18. c. Binocular cues require both eyes. p. 111

19. d. Placebos and acupuncture both work through the release of endorphins. p. 105

20. d. Continuity is perceived as a pattern or direction of items grouped together. p. 109

21. a. Apparent motion is when we perceive movement in objects that are actually standing still. p. 114

22.   Fig. 3–28, p. 109. c. proximity; d. similarity; b. closure; a. continuity

23. b. Rods continue adapting until they reach maximum sensitivity about 30 minutes after entering the environment. This is when the best vision occurs. p. 87

24. a. The place on the retina where the axons of all ganglion cells join to form the optic nerve is called the blind spot and has no receptor cells. p. 89

25. c. Tinnitus is a persistent sound that seems to come from inside the head. p. 98

26. d. Although taste buds may still work, anosmia is a devastating disorder resulting in the loss of smell. It is reported in greater prevalence in people over 65 years old. p. 99

27. d. There is no simple relationship between pain receptors and the experience of pain. In fact, finding pain receptors has proven difficult. p. 103

CHAPTER 4

States of Consciousness

CHAPTER OVERVIEW

The chapter opens with a vivid real-world description of extreme fatigue, setting a frame from which to explore states of consciousness and their effects. **Consciousness** is our awareness of various cognitive processes that operate in our daily lives such as sleeping, dreaming, concentrating, and making decisions. To make sense of our complex environment, we selectively choose which stimuli to absorb and we filter out the rest. Psychologists divide consciousness into two broad areas: **waking consciousness**, which includes thoughts, feelings, and perceptions that arise when we are awake and reasonably alert; and **altered states of consciousness**, during which our mental state differs noticeably from normal waking consciousness.

The chapter first tackles the fascinating subject of sleep. Nobody knows exactly why we need to sleep, although sleep appears to play an important restorative function, both physically and mentally. Getting adequate sleep boosts our immune response and cleanses the body of chemicals like adenosine, which is released when cells use energy. Sleep also appears to play a crucial role in long-term memory formation.

Like many other biological functions, sleep and waking follow a daily biological cycle known as a **circadian rhythm**. The human *biological clock* is governed by a tiny cluster of neurons in the brain known as the **suprachiasmatic nucleus (SCN)** that regulates proteins related to metabolism and alertness. Normally, the rhythms and chemistry of the body's cycles interact smoothly; but when we cross several time zones in one day, hormonal, temperature, and digestive cycles become desynchronized.

Normal sleep consists of several stages. During *Stage 1*, the pulse slows, muscles relax, and the eyes move from side to side. The sleeper is easily awakened from Stage 1 sleep. In *Stages 2 and 3*, the sleeper is hard to awaken and does not respond to noise or light. Heart rate, blood pressure, and temperature continue to drop. During *Stage 4* sleep, heart and breathing rates, blood pressure, and body temperature are at their lowest points of the night. About an hour after first falling asleep, the sleeper begins to ascend through the stages back to Stage 1—a process that takes about 40 minutes. At this stage in the sleep cycle, heart rate and blood pressure increase, the muscles become more relaxed than at any other time in the cycle, and the eyes move rapidly under closed eyelids. This stage of sleep is known as **rapid-eye movement (REM)** or **paradoxical sleep**.

Between one-third and one-half of adults fail to get enough sleep. Among adolescents, not getting enough sleep may result in falling asleep at school. Sleep deprivation negatively affects reaction time, memory, judgment and the ability to pay attention. Driving while sleepy is just as dangerous as driving drunk. Sleep deprivation has been associated with errors and poor performance at work leading to serious mishaps in high-risk professions such as medicine or working at a nuclear power plant. The lack of sleep also contributes to such diseases as heart attacks, asthma, strokes, high blood pressure, and diabetes and is associated with depression and being overweight. Unfortunately, people do not always know when they are not getting enough sleep.

Sleep disorders include sleeptalking, sleepwalking, night terrors, insomnia, apnea, and narcolepsy. Most episodes of sleeptalking and sleepwalking occur during a deep stage of sleep. Unlike **nightmares**, frightening dreams that most often occur during REM sleep and are remembered, **night terrors** are more common among children than adults, prove difficult to be awakened from, and are rarely remembered the next morning. **Insomnia** is characterized by difficulty in falling asleep or remaining asleep throughout the night. **Apnea** is marked by breathing difficulties during the night and feelings of exhaustion during the day. **Narcolepsy** is a hereditary sleep disorder characterized by sudden nodding off during the day and sudden loss of muscle tone following moments of emotional excitement.

The chapter turns next to a discussion of dreams. **Dreams** are visual or auditory experiences that occur primarily during REM periods of sleep. Less vivid experiences that resemble conscious thinking tend to occur during **NREM** sleep.

Several theories have been developed to explain the nature and content of dreams. According to Freud, dreams have two kinds of contents: manifest (the surface content of the dream itself) and latent (the disguised, unconscious meaning of the dream). According to a more recent hypothesis, dreams arise out of the mind's reprocessing of daytime information that is important to the survival of the organism. With this hypothesis, dreaming thus strengthens our memories of important information.

The chapter shifts gears into a wide-ranging discussion of drug-altered consciousness, with a starting point of how today's drug problem compares to drug use in other societies and times. Chemical substances that change moods and perceptions are known as **psychoactive drugs**. Although many of the psychoactive drugs available today have been used for thousands of years, the motivation for using drugs is different today. Traditionally, these drugs were used in religious rituals, as nutrient beverages, or as culturally approved stimulants. Today, most psychoactive drug use is recreational, divorced from religious or family traditions.

Substance abuse is a pattern of drug use that diminishes the person's ability to fulfill responsibilities at home, work, or school and that results in repeated use of a drug in dangerous situations or that leads to legal difficulties related to drug use. Continued abuse over time can lead to **substance dependence**, a pattern of compulsive drug taking that is much more serious than substance abuse. It is often marked by tolerance, the need to take higher doses of a drug to produce its original effects or to prevent withdrawal symptoms. Withdrawal symptoms are the unpleasant physical or psychological effects that follow discontinuance of the psychoactive substance. When studying drug effects, most researchers use the **double-blind procedure** in which some participants receive the active drug while others take a neutral, inactive substance called a **placebo**.

Depressants are chemicals that slow down behavior or cognitive processes. **Alcohol** calms down the nervous system, working like a general anesthetic. It is often experienced subjectively as a stimulant because it inhibits centers in the brain that govern critical judgment and impulsive behavior. This accounts for its involvement in a substantial proportion of violent and accidental deaths. **Barbiturates** are potentially deadly depressants, first used for their sedative and anticonvulsant properties, but today their use is limited to the treatment of such conditions as epilepsy and arthritis. The **opiates** are highly addictive drugs such as opium, morphine, and heroin that dull the senses and induce feelings of euphoria, well-being, and relaxation. Morphine and heroin are derivatives of opium.

Stimulants are drugs that stimulate the sympathetic nervous system and produce feelings of optimism and boundless energy, making the potential for their abuse significant. Caffeine occurs naturally in coffee, tea, and cocoa. Considered a benign drug, in large doses caffeine can cause anxiety, insomnia, and other unpleasant conditions. Nicotine occurs naturally only in tobacco. Although it is a stimulant, it acts like a depressant when taken in large doses. **Amphetamines** are stimulants that initially produce "rushes" of euphoria often followed by sudden "crashes" and, sometimes, depression. **Cocaine** brings on a sense of euphoria by stimulating the sympathetic nervous system, but it can also cause anxiety, depression, and addictive cravings. Its crystalline form— crack—is highly addictive.

Hallucinogens include drugs such as **LSD**, psilocybin, and mescaline that distort visual and auditory perception. **Marijuana** is a mild hallucinogen capable of producing feelings of euphoria, a sense of well-being, and swings in mood from gaiety to relaxation to paranoia. Though similar to hallucinogens in certain respects, marijuana is far less potent, and its effects on consciousness are far less profound. Marijuana can disrupt memory, causing people to forget what they are talking about in midsentence.

A possible genetic predisposition, the person's expectations, the social setting, and cultural beliefs and values make drug abuse more likely.

The chapter concludes with material on meditation and hypnosis. **Meditation** refers to any of several methods of concentration, reflection, or focusing of thoughts intended to suppress the activity of the sympathetic nervous system. Meditation not only lowers the metabolic rate but also reduces heart and respiratory rates. Brain activity during meditation resembles that experienced during relaxed wakefulness; and the accompanying decrease in blood lactate reduces stress.

Hypnosis is a trancelike state in which the hypnotized person responds readily to suggestions. Susceptibility to hypnosis depends on how easily people can become absorbed in concentration. Hypnosis can ease the pain of certain medical conditions and can help people stop smoking and break other habits.

LEARNING OBJECTIVES EXERCISE

After you have read and studied the chapter, you should be able to answer the following learning objectives.

SLEEP

- Summarize current thinking about why we sleep.

- Describe circadian rhythms and their relationship to jet lag.

- Describe the sleep cycle, distinguishing between the various sleep stages. Explain why REM sleep is also called paradoxical sleep. Explain how the sleep cycle changes across the life span.

- Identify the key sleep disorders, distinguishing between nightmares and night terrors and between insomnia, apnea, and narcolepsy.

DREAMS

- Explain what dreams are. Summarize the explanations of dream activity and content as set forth in Freudian theory, information processing theory, and neural activation theory.

DRUG-ALTERED CONSCIOUSNESS

- Define psychoactive drugs and summarize how their use has changed over the centuries.

- Differentiate substance abuse and substance dependence.

- Explain how double-blind procedures and placebos are used in drug research.

- Describe the major depressants, their effects, the effects of an overdose, and the extent to which they are susceptible to dependence.

- Describe the major stimulants, their effects, the effects of an overdose, and the extent to which they are susceptible to dependence.

- Describe the effects of LSD and marijuana.

- Describe the biological, psychological, social, and cultural factors that make it more likely someone will abuse drugs.

- Describe the biological and psychological effects of meditation.

- Explain why it is difficult to define hypnosis, the process of inducing hypnosis, and the role of hypnotic suggestions.

CHAPTER OUTLINE

KEY TERMS

Alcohol	Depressant that is the intoxicating ingredient in whiskey, beer, wine, and other fermented or distilled liquors. (p. 136)
Altered states of consciousness	Mental states that differ noticeably from normal waking consciousness. (p. 123)
Amphetamines	Stimulant drugs that initially produce "rushes" of euphoria often followed by sudden "crashes" and, sometimes, severe depression. (p. 143)
Apnea	Sleep disorder characterized by breathing difficulty during the night and feelings of exhaustion during the day. (p. 130)
Barbiturates	Potentially deadly depressants, first used for their sedative and anticonvulsant properties, now used only to treat such conditions as epilepsy and arthritis. (p. 140)
Circadian rhythm	A regular biological rhythm with a period of approximately 24 hours. (p. 125)
Cocaine	Drug derived from the coca plant that, although producing a sense of euphoria by stimulating the sympathetic nervous system, also leads to anxiety, depression, and addictive cravings. (p. 143)
Consciousness	Our awareness of various cognitive processes, such as sleeping, dreaming, concentrating, and making decisions. (p. 123)
Depressants	Chemicals that slow down behavior or cognitive processes. (p. 136)
Double-blind procedure	Experimental design useful in studies of the effects of drugs, in which neither the subject nor the researcher knows at the time of administration which subjects are receiving an active drug and which are receiving an inactive substance. (p. 136)
Dreams	Vivid visual and auditory experiences that occur primarily during REM periods of sleep. (p. 131)
Hallucinogens	Any of a number of drugs, such as LSD and mescaline, that distort visual and auditory perception. (p. 144)
Hypnosis	Trancelike state in which a person responds readily to suggestions. (p. 150)
Insomnia	Sleep disorder characterized by difficulty in falling asleep or remaining asleep throughout the night. (p. 130)
Lysergic acid diethylamide (LSD)	Hallucinogenic or "psychedelic" drug that produces hallucinations and delusions similar to those occurring in a psychotic state. (p. 144)
Marijuana	A mild hallucinogen that produces a "high" often characterized by feelings of euphoria, a sense of well-being, and swings in mood from gaiety to relaxation; may also cause feelings of anxiety and paranoia. (p. 144)
Meditation	Any of the various methods of concentration, reflection, or focusing of thoughts undertaken to suppress the activity of the sympathetic nervous system. (p. 148)
Narcolepsy	Hereditary sleep disorder characterized by sudden nodding off during the day and sudden loss of muscle tone following moments of emotional excitement. (p. 131)
Night terrors	Frightening, often terrifying dreams that occur during NREM sleep from which a person is difficult to awaken and doesn't remember the content. (p. 130)
Nightmares	Frightening dreams that occur during REM sleep and are remembered. (p. 130)
Non-REM (NREM) sleep	Non-rapid-eye-movement stages of sleep that alternate with REM stages during the sleep cycle. (p. 126)
Opiates	Drugs, such as opium and heroin, derived from the opium poppy, that dull the senses and induce feelings of euphoria, well-being, and relaxation. Synthetic drugs resembling opium derivatives are also classified as opiates. (p. 141)
Placebo	Chemically inactive substance used for comparison with active drugs in experiments on the effects of drugs. (p. 136)
Psychoactive drugs	Chemical substances that change moods and perceptions. (p. 135)

Rapid-eye movement (REM) or paradoxical sleep	Sleep stage characterized by rapid-eye movements and increased dreaming. (p. 126)
Stimulants	Drugs, including amphetamines and cocaine, that stimulate the sympathetic nervous system and produce feelings of optimism and boundless energy. (p. 141)
Substance abuse	A pattern of drug use that diminishes the ability to fulfill responsibilities at home, work, or school that results in repeated use of a drug in dangerous situations or that leads to legal difficulties related to drug use. (p. 135)
Substance dependence	A pattern of compulsive drug taking that results in tolerance, withdrawal symptoms, or other specific symptoms for at least a year. (p. 135)
Suprachiasmatic nucleus (SCN)	A cluster of neurons in the hypothalamus that receives input from the retina regarding light and dark cycles and is involved in regulating the biological clock. (p. 125)
Waking consciousness	Mental state that encompasses the thoughts, feelings, and perceptions that occur when we are awake and reasonably alert. (p. 123)

Vocabulary Flashcards

Cut out each term and use as study cards. The definition is on the back side of each term.

Consciousness	**Rapid-eye movement (REM) or paradoxical sleep**
Waking consciousness	**Non-REM (NREM) sleep**
Altered states of consciousness	**Nightmares**
Circadian rhythm	**Night terrors**
Suprachiasmatic nucleus (SCN)	**Insomnia**

Sleep stage characterized by rapid-eye movements and increased dreaming.	Our awareness of various cognitive processes, such as sleeping, dreaming, concentrating, and making decisions.
Non-rapid-eye-movement stages of sleep that alternate with REM stages during the sleep cycle.	Mental state that encompasses the thoughts, feelings, and perceptions that occur when we are awake and reasonably alert.
Frightening dreams that occur during REM sleep and are remembered.	Mental states that differ noticeably from normal waking consciousness.
Frightening, often terrifying dreams that occur during NREM sleep from which a person is difficult to awaken and doesn't remember the content.	A regular biological rhythm with a period of approximately 24 hours.
Sleep disorder characterized by difficulty in falling asleep or remaining asleep throughout the night.	A cluster of neurons in the hypothalamus that receives input from the retina regarding light and dark cycles and is involved in regulating the biological clock.

Apnea	Substance dependence
Narcolepsy	Double-blind procedure
Dreams	Placebo
Psychoactive drugs	Depressants
Substance abuse	Alcohol

A pattern of compulsive drug taking that results in tolerance, withdrawal symptoms, or other specific symptoms for at least a year.

Sleep disorder characterized by breathing difficulty during the night and feelings of exhaustion during the day.

Experimental design useful in studies of the effects of drugs, in which neither the subject nor the researcher knows at the time of administration which subjects are receiving an active drug and which are receiving an inactive substance.

Hereditary sleep disorder characterized by sudden nodding off during the day and sudden loss of muscle tone following moments of emotional excitement.

Chemically inactive substance used for comparison with active drugs in experiments on the effects of drugs.

Vivid visual and auditory experiences that occur primarily during REM periods of sleep.

Chemicals that slow down behavior or cognitive processes.

Chemical substances that change moods and perceptions.

Depressant that is the intoxicating ingredient in whiskey, beer, wine, and other fermented or distilled liquors.

A pattern of drug use that diminishes the ability to fulfill responsibilities at home, work, or school that results in repeated use of a drug in dangerous situations or that leads to legal difficulties related to drug use.

Barbiturates	Hallucinogens
Opiates	Lysergic acid diethylamide (LSD)
Stimulants	Marijuana
Amphetamines	Meditation
Cocaine	Hypnosis

Any of a number of drugs, such as LSD and mescaline, that distort visual and auditory perception.

Potentially deadly depressants, first used for their sedative and anticonvulsant properties, now used only to treat such conditions as epilepsy and arthritis.

Hallucinogenic or "psychedelic" drug that produces hallucinations and delusions similar to those occurring in a psychotic state.

Drugs, such as opium and heroin, derived from the opium poppy, that dull the senses and induce feelings of euphoria, well-being, and relaxation. Synthetic drugs resembling opium derivatives are also classified as opiates.

A mild hallucinogen that produces a "high" often characterized by feelings of euphoria, a sense of well-being, and swings in mood from gaiety to relaxation; may also cause feelings of anxiety and paranoia.

Drugs, including amphetamines and cocaine, that stimulate the sympathetic nervous system and produce feelings of optimism and boundless energy.

Any of the various methods of concentration, reflection, or focusing of thoughts undertaken to suppress the activity of the sympathetic nervous system.

Stimulant drugs that initially produce "rushes" of euphoria often followed by sudden "crashes" and, sometimes, severe depression.

Trancelike state in which a person responds readily to suggestions.

Drug derived from the coca plant that, although producing a sense of euphoria by stimulating the sympathetic nervous system, also leads to anxiety, depression, and addictive cravings.

After studying the text and completing the Study Guide activities, answer these questions to determine if you need to review any areas before the course exam.

MULTIPLE CHOICE

1. Daydreaming, meditation, intoxication, sleep, and hypnosis are all types of _____.
   a. self-awareness
   b. waking consciousness
   c. self-absorption
   d. altered states of consciousness

2. Our sleeping-waking cycle follows a _____ rhythm.
   a. ultradian
   b. monaural
   c. diurnal
   d. circadian

3. People may be able to adjust their biological clocks to prevent jet lag by taking small amount of the hormone _____.
   a. serotonin
   b. epinephrine
   c. dopamine
   d. melatonin

4. Which of the following is NOT seen in REM sleep?
   a. paralysis of body muscles
   b. periods of REM sleep get shorter as the night continues
   c. rapid eye movement
   d. arousal of brain activity

5. The low voltage brain waves produced during relaxed wakefulness or the twilight stage between waking and sleeping are called _____ waves.
   a. alpha
   b. beta
   c. delta
   d. theta

6. In children and young adults, periods of REM sleep get progressively ____ and periods of Stage 4 sleep get progressively _____ throughout the night.
   a. shorter; shorter
   b. longer; shorter
   c. shorter; longer
   d. longer; shorter

7. Freud believed that sleep and dreams expressed ideas that were free from the _____.
   a. memories of worrisome daily events
   b. instinctive feelings of anger, jealousy, or ambition
   c. conscious controls and moral rules
   d. case study method

8. Which of the following is NOT a suggestion to help overcome insomnia?
   a. establish regular sleeping habits
   b. have a strong alcoholic drink before bed
   c. change bedtime routine
   d. get out of bed and do something until feeling sleepy

9. Most episodes of insomnia are ____ and stem from ____.
   a. temporary; stressful events
   b. chronic; stressful events
   c. temporary; underlying psychological problems
   d. chronic; underlying psychological problems

10. Alice's strange adventures in Wonderland and Dorothy's bizarre journey through the Land of Oz most probably occurred when they were in _____ sleep.
    a. Stage 1
    b. Stage 2
    c. Stage 4
    d. REM

11. Albert is meditating. He is likely to experience each of the following EXCEPT _____.
    a. increased sensory awareness
    b. a sense of timelessness
    c. a sense of well-being
    d. feelings of total relaxation

12. Drugs, such as heroin, that dull the senses and induce feelings of euphoria and relaxation are called _____.
    a. hallucinogens
    b. opiates
    c. barbiturates
    d. placebos

13. Chemical substances that change moods and perceptions are called _____ drugs.
    a. psychoactive
    b. psychedelic
    c. psychoanalytic
    d. psychoactive

14. In the double-blind procedure, some subjects receive a medication while the control group receives an inactive substance called _____.
    a. control treatment
    b. hawthorne reactor
    c. a placebo
    d. dependent variable

15. Which of the following statements about marijuana is NOT true?
    a. Marijuana interferes with attention and short-term memory.
    b. Marijuana use can lead to cardiovascular and respiratory damage.
    c. Marijuana is the most popular drug among college students today.
    d. Marijuana users experience distortions in time perception.

16. The most common contributing factor to automobile accidents after alcohol use is _____.
    a. other drug use
    b. sleep deprivation
    c. cell phone use while driving
    d. talking to others in the car

17. Which of the following drugs can lead to psychosis similar to paranoid schizophrenia?
    a. nicotine
    b. marijuana
    c. amphetamines
    d. heroin

18. The trancelike state in which a subject responds readily to suggestions is _____.
    a. Stage 4 sleep
    b. hypnosis
    c. meditation
    d. coma

19. Which of the following statements best explains why we need sleep?
    a. It helps with physical restoration.
    b. It helps with mental restoration.
    c. It may enhance creativity and problem solving skills.
    d. all of the above

20. The human biological clock is regulated by the _____ in the brain.
    a. optic chiasm
    b. suprachiasmatic nucleus
    c. retina
    d. none of the above

21. An effective way to reduce sleep debt may be to _____.
    a. take a nap during the day
    b. condition yourself to sleep fewer hours each night
    c. take prescription drugs for insomnia
    d. reduce REM sleep

22. Which of the following is NOT true regarding nightmares?
    a. They are commonly experienced during childhood.
    b. They occur during REM sleep.
    c. They are a sign of underlying psychological problems.
    d. Their occurrence is associated with stress in adults.

23. Which of the following does NOT describe the drug Ecstasy?
    a. High doses may damage dopamine and serotonin neurons.
    b. It is a form of methamphetamine.
    c. Use may lead to an increase in intelligence test scores.
    d. Use during pregnancy may lead to birth defects.

SHORT ESSAY QUESTIONS

1. Discuss the research findings in regard to sleep deprivation: its prevalence, symptoms, and the effects of long-term deprivation.

2. List five of the eleven signs of alcoholism.

3. Summarize the trend of "binge drinking" on college campuses and discuss factors that may contribute to binge drinking as well as its effects.

4. Describe the effect of addictive drugs on neurotransmitters and the brain.

5. Discuss how researchers design and carry out experiments and studies of alcohol and drug use and abuse.

6. Outline the path of alcohol in the brain; list the parts of the brain affected by alcohol chronologically and why some people perceive alcohol as a stimulant.

7. Define insomnia, its prevalence and its causes, and the steps a person can take to overcome this sleep disorder.

ANSWERS AND EXPLANATIONS TO MULTIPLE CHOICE POSTTEST

1. d. All are considered to be altered states of consciousness. p. 123

2. d. Circadian cycles represent the body's biological clock adapted to a 24-hour sleep/wake cycle. p. 124

3. d. A small amount of melatonin may prevent jet lag. p. 124

4. b. Periods of REM sleep get longer, not shorter, throughout the night. p. 126

5. a. As measured by the EEG, low voltage alpha waves are produced during twilight sleep. p. 126

6. b. REM sleep gets progressively longer and Stage 4 gets shorter for children and young adults. p. 127

7. c. Freud believed that dreams were free from conscious control and moral rules (ego and superego). p. 132

8. b. Alcohol interferes with getting a good night's sleep. p. 129

9. a. Although some insomnia is part of a larger psychological problem, most insomnia is temporary and grows out of stressful events. p. 130

10. d. Most graphic dreams are reported to occur in REM sleep. p. 131

11. a. Regular meditators report increased sensory awareness, timelessness, well-being, and total relaxation. p. 149

12. b. Heroin is an opiate. p. 141

13. d. Psychoactive drugs are chemical substances that alter moods and perceptions. p. 135

14. c. A placebo is an inactive substance given to the control group. p. 136

15. c. Marijuana, the most popularly used illegal drug in the U.S., is only the fourth most popular drug among students after alcohol, caffeine, and nicotine. p. 144

16. b. Driving while sleepy is just as dangerous as driving while drunk. p. 128

17. c. Chronic users may develop amphetamine psychosis, which resembles paranoid schizophrenia. p. 143

18. b. Hypnosis is a trancelike state in which a person responds readily to suggestions. p. 150

19. d. Evidence suggests sleep may be important in all of these factors. p. 123

20. b. The suprachiasmatic nucleus of the hypothalamus regulates our internal biological clock. p. 124

21. a. Naps from 20–60 minutes can reduce sleep debt and increase alertness and performance. p. 130

22. c. Neither nightmares nor night terrors alone indicate psychological problems. p. 130

23. c. Use of Ecstasy may lead to a decrease in intelligence test scores. p. 143

CHAPTER 5
Learning

CHAPTER OVERVIEW

The chapter opens with several very different anecdotes whose common element is learning, and then aims to address the enduring issue of how humans and other animals acquire new behaviors as a result of their experiences. **Learning** is the process by which experience or practice produces a relatively permanent change in behavior or potential behavior. One basic form of learning involves learning to associate one event with another. **Classical conditioning** is a type of associative learning that Pavlov discovered while studying digestion. Pavlov trained a dog to salivate at the sound of a bell when he rang the bell just before food was given. The dog learned to associate the bell with food and began to salivate at the sound of the bell alone.

Suppose you wanted to classically condition salivation in your own dog. You know that food is an **unconditioned stimulus (US)** that automatically evokes the **unconditioned response (UR)** of salivation. By repeatedly pairing food with a second, initially neutral stimulus (such as a bell), the second stimulus would eventually become a **conditioned stimulus (CS)** eliciting a **conditioned response (CR)** of salivation.

Establishing a classically conditioned response usually is easier if the US and CS are paired with each other repeatedly, rather than a single time or even once in a while (**intermittent pairing**). That is why a single incident—for example, burning your finger on a match while listening to a certain song—is not usually enough to produce a classically conditioned response. It is also important that the spacing of pairings be neither too far apart nor too close together.

In the case of Little Albert, Watson conditioned a child to fear white rats by always pairing a loud, frightening noise with a rat. Perhaps you have acquired a classically conditioned fear or anxiety (to the sound of a dentist's drill, for instance) in much the same way; or perhaps you have also unlearned a conditioned fear by repeatedly pairing the feared object with something pleasant. Mary Cover Jones paired the sight of a feared rat (at gradually decreasing distances) with a child's pleasant experience of eating candy. This procedure was the precursor to **desensitization therapy**.

The concept of **preparedness** accounts for the fact that certain conditioned responses are acquired very easily. The ease with which we develop **conditioned taste aversions** illustrates preparedness. Because animals are biologically prepared to learn them, conditioned taste aversions can occur with only one pairing of the taste of a tainted food and later illness, even when there is a lengthy interval between eating the food and becoming ill. A fear of snakes may also be something that humans are prepared to learn.

The chapter turns its focus to the subject of operant conditioning. **Operant** or **instrumental conditioning** is learning to make or withhold a certain response because of its consequences. **Operant behaviors** are different from the responses involved in classical conditioning because they are voluntarily emitted, whereas those involved in classical conditioning are elicited by stimuli.

There are two essential elements involved in operant conditioning. One is an operant behavior, or a behavior performed by one's own volition while "operating" on the environment. The second essential element is a consequence associated with that operant behavior. When a consequence increases the likelihood of an operant behavior's being emitted, it is called a **reinforcer**. When a consequence decreases the likelihood of an operant behavior, it is called a **punisher**. These relationships are the basis of the **law of effect**, or **principle of** reinforcement: Consistently rewarded behaviors are likely to be repeated, whereas consistently punished behaviors are likely to be suppressed.

To speed up establishing an operantly conditioned response in the laboratory, the number of potential responses may be reduced by restricting the environment, as in a **Skinner box**. For behaviors outside the laboratory, which cannot be controlled so conveniently, the process of **shaping** is often useful. In shaping, reinforcement is given for successive approximations to the desired response. For example, a speech therapist might use shaping to teach a child to pronounce a certain sound correctly.

Several kinds of reinforcers strengthen or increase the likelihood of behavior. **Positive reinforcers** (such as food) add something rewarding to a situation. **Negative reinforcers** (for example, stopping an electric shock) subtracts something unpleasant. When an action is followed closely by a reinforcer, we tend to repeat the action, even if it did not actually produce the reinforcement. Such behaviors are called *superstitious*.

Punishment is any unpleasant consequence that decreases the likelihood that the preceding behavior will recur. Whereas negative reinforcement strengthens behavior, punishment weakens it. Although punishment can be effective, it also can stir up negative feelings and serve to model aggressive behavior. Also, rather than teaching a more desirable response; it only suppresses an undesirable one. After punishment has occurred a few times, further repetitions sometimes are unnecessary because the threat of punishment is enough. With this process, called **avoidance training**, people learn to avoid the possibility of a punishing consequence.

When people or other animals are unable to escape from a punishing situation, they may acquire a "giving-up" response, called **learned helplessness**. Learned helplessness can generalize to new situations, causing resignation in the face of unpleasant outcomes, even when the outcomes can be avoided. For example, a college student who gives up trying to do well in school after a few poor grades on tests is exhibiting learned helplessness.

When operant conditioning is used to control biological functions, such as blood pressure or heart rate, it is referred to as **biofeedback**. When it is used to control brain waves it is called **neurofeedback**. Biofeedback and neurofeedback have been successfully applied to a variety of medical problems, including migraine headaches, hypertension, and asthma. Biofeedback has also been used by athletes and musicians to improve performance and control anxiety.

The chapter ties the previous material together by looking at factors that are shared by both classical and operant conditioning. Despite the differences between classical and operant conditioning, these two forms of learning have many things in common. (1) Both cases involve learned associations; (2) in both cases, responses come under control of stimuli in the environment; (3) in both cases, the responses will gradually disappear if they are not periodically renewed; and (4) in both cases, new behaviors can build upon previously established ones.

In both classical and operant conditioning, an "if–then" relationship, or **contingency**, exists either between two stimuli or between a stimulus and a response. In both these kinds of learning, perceived contingencies are very important.

In classical conditioning, the contingency is between the CS and the US. The CS comes to be viewed as a signal that the US is about to happen. For that reason, the CS must not only occur in close proximity to the US, but must also precede the US and provide predictive information about it. If the CS occurs *after* the US, it will come to serve as a signal that the US is over, not that the US is imminent. **Blocking** is a process whereby prior conditioning prevents conditioning to a second stimulus even when the two stimuli are presented simultaneously.

In operant conditioning, contingencies exist between responses and consequences. Contingencies between responses and rewards are called **schedules of reinforcement**. *Partial reinforcement*, in which rewards are given only for some correct responses, generates behavior that persists longer than that learned by *continuous reinforcement*. A **fixed-interval schedule**, by which reinforcement is given for the first correct response after a fixed time period, tends to result in a flurry of responding right before a reward is due. A **variable-interval schedule**, which reinforces the first correct response after an unpredictable period of time, tends to result in a slow, but steady pattern of responding. In a **fixed-ratio schedule**, behavior is rewarded after a fixed number of correct responses, so the result is usually a high rate of responding. Finally, a **variable-ratio schedule** provides reinforcement after a varying number of correct responses. It encourages a high rate of response that is especially persistent.

Learned responses sometimes weaken and may even disappear, a phenomenon called **extinction**. The learning is not necessarily completely forgotten, however. Sometimes a **spontaneous recovery** occurs, in which the learned response suddenly reappears on its own, with no retraining.

Extinction is produced in classical conditioning by failure to continue pairing the CS and the US. The CS no longer serves as a signal that the US is about to happen, and so the conditioned response dies out. An important contributing factor is often new, learned associations that interfere with the old one. In situations in which you are reminded of the old association, spontaneous recovery may occur.

Extinction occurs in operant conditioning when reinforcement is withheld until the learned response is no longer emitted. The ease with which an operantly conditioned behavior is extinguished varies according to several factors: the strength of the original learning, the variety of settings in which learning took place, and the schedule of reinforcement used during conditioning.

When conditioned responses are influenced by surrounding cues in the environment, **stimulus control** occurs. The tendency to respond to cues that are similar, but not identical, to those that prevailed during the original learning is known as **stimulus generalization**. An example of stimulus generalization in classical conditioning is a student's feeling anxious about studying math in college because he or she had a bad experience learning math in grade school. **Stimulus discrimination** enables learners to perceive differences among cues so as not to respond to all of them.

In operant conditioning, the learned response is under the control of whatever cues come to be associated with delivery of reward or punishment. Learners often generalize about these cues, responding to others that are broadly similar to the ones that prevailed during the original learning. An example is slapping any face card in a game of slapjack. Learners may also generalize their responses by performing behaviors that are similar to the ones that were originally reinforced. This result is called **response generalization**. Discrimination in operant conditioning is taught by reinforcing only a certain response and only in the presence of a certain stimulus.

In both classical and operant conditioning, original learning serves as a building block for new learning. In classical conditioning, an earlier CS can be used as an US for further training. For example, Pavlov used the bell to condition his dogs to salivate at the sight of a black square. This effect, which is called **higher order conditioning**, is difficult to achieve because of extinction. Unless the original unconditioned stimulus is presented occasionally, the initial conditioned response will die out.

In operant conditioning, initially neutral stimuli can become reinforcers by being associated with other reinforcers. A **primary reinforcer** is one that, like food and water, is rewarding in and of itself. A **secondary reinforcer** is one whose value is learned through its association with primary reinforcers or with other secondary reinforcers. Money is such a good secondary reinforcer because it can be exchanged for so many different primary and secondary rewards.

Despite their differences, classical and operant conditioning share many similarities: Both involve associations between stimuli and responses; both are subject to extinction and spontaneous recovery as well as generalization and discrimination; in both, new learning can be based on original learning. Operant conditioning can even be used, in **biofeedback** and **neurofeedback** training, to learn to control physiological responses that are usually learned through classical conditioning. Many psychologists now wonder whether classical and operant conditioning aren't just two ways of bringing about the same kind of learning.

The chapter concludes with a detailed look at cognitive learning. **Cognitive learning** refers to the mental processes that go on inside us when we learn. Some kinds of learning, such as memorizing the layout of a chessboard, seem to be purely cognitive, because the learner does not appear to be "behaving" while the learning takes place. Cognitive learning, however, can always affect future behavior, such as reproducing the layout of a memorized chessboard after it is cleared away. It is from such observable behavior that cognitive learning is inferred.

Latent learning is any learning that has not yet been demonstrated in behavior. Your knowledge of psychology is latent if you have not yet displayed it in what you say, write, and do. One kind of latent learning is knowledge of spatial layouts and relationships, which is usually stored in the form of a **cognitive map**. Rewards or punishments aren't essential for latent learning to take place. You did not need rewards and punishments to learn the layout of your campus, for example. You acquired this cognitive map simply by storing your visual perceptions.

A **learning set** is a concept or procedure that provides a key to solving a problem even when its demands are slightly different from those of problems you have solved in the past. As a student, you probably have a learning set for writing a term paper that allows you successfully to develop papers on many different topics. A learning set can sometimes encourage **insight** or the sudden perception of a solution even to a problem that at first seems totally new. In this case, you are perceiving similarities between old and new problems that weren't initially apparent.

Social learning theorists argue that we learn much by observing other people who model a behavior or by simply hearing about something. This process is called **observational** (or **vicarious**) **learning**. It would be harder to learn to drive a car without ever having been in one because you would lack a model of "driving behavior." It is hard for deaf children to learn spoken language because they have no auditory model of correct speech.

The extent to which we imitate behaviors learned through observation depends on our motivation to do so. One important motivation is any reward or punishment that we have seen the behavior bring. When a consequence isn't experienced firsthand, but only occurs to other people, it is called **vicarious reinforcement** or **vicarious punishment**.

Research has shown that many animals, including chimpanzees, dolphins, whales, rats, octopi, and even bumblebees are capable of various forms of cognitive learning.

LEARNING OBJECTIVES EXERCISE

After you have read and studied the chapter, you should be able to answer the following learning objectives.

CLASSICAL CONDITIONING

- Define learning.

- Describe the elements of classical conditioning, distinguishing between unconditioned stimulus, unconditioned response, conditioned stimulus and conditioned response. Describe the process of establishing a classically conditioned response, including the effect of intermittent pairing.

- Provide examples of classical conditioning in humans, including desensitization therapy. Explain the statement that "classical conditioning is selective" and illustrate with examples of conditioned taste aversions.

OPERANT CONDITIONING

- Explain how operant conditioning differs from classical conditioning.

- Explain the law of effect (the principle of reinforcement) and the role of reinforcers, punishers, and shaping in establishing an operantly conditioned response. Differentiate between positive reinforcers, negative reinforcers, and punishment. Explain the circumstances under which punishment can be effective and the drawbacks to using punishment.

- Explain what is meant by learned helplessness.

- Describe how biofeedback and neurofeedback can be used to change behavior.

FACTORS SHARED BY CLASSICAL AND OPERANT CONDITIONING

- Describe the importance of contingencies in both operant and classical conditioning.

- Differentiate between the four schedules of reinforcement in operant conditioning and their effect on learned behavior.

- Describe the processes of extinction, spontaneous recovery, generalization, and discrimination in classical and operant conditioning.

- Explain what is meant by higher order conditioning and differentiate between primary and secondary reinforcers.

- Define cognitive learning and how it can be inferred from evidence of latent learning and cognitive maps.

- Explain what is meant by insight and its relation to learning sets.

- Explain the process of observational (vicarious) learning and the conditions under which it is most likely to be reflected in behavior.

- Give examples of cognitive learning in nonhumans.

CHAPTER OUTLINE

KEY TERMS

Avoidance training	Learning a desirable behavior to prevent the occurrence of something unpleasant, such as punishment. (p. 166)
Biofeedback	A technique that uses monitoring devices to provide precise information about internal physiological processes, such as heart rate or blood pressure, to teach people to gain voluntary control over these functions. (p. 167)
Blocking	A process whereby prior conditioning prevents conditioning to a second stimulus even when the two stimuli are presented simultaneously. (p. 169)
Classical (or Pavlovian) conditioning	The type of learning in which a response naturally elicited by one stimulus comes to be elicited by a different, formerly neutral, stimulus. (p. 156)
Cognitive learning	Learning that depends on mental processes that are not directly observable. (p. 177)
Cognitive map	A learned mental image of a spatial environment that may be called on to solve problems when stimuli in the environment change. (p. 177)
Conditioned response (CR)	After conditioning, the response an organism produces when a conditioned stimulus is presented. (p. 156)
Conditioned stimulus (CS)	An originally neutral stimulus that is paired with an unconditioned stimulus and eventually produces the desired response in an organism when presented alone. (p. 156)
Conditioned taste aversion	Conditioned avoidance of certain foods even if there is only one pairing of conditioned and unconditioned stimuli. (p. 159)
Contingency	A reliable "if–then" relationship between two events, such as a CS and a US. (p. 169)
Desensitization therapy	A conditioning technique designed to gradually reduce anxiety about a particular object or situation. (p. 158)
Extinction	A decrease in the strength or frequency, or stopping, of a learned response because of failure to continue pairing the US and CS (classical conditioning) or withholding of reinforcement (operant conditioning). (p. 170)
Fixed-interval schedule	A reinforcement schedule in which the correct response is reinforced after a fixed length of time since the last reinforcement. (p. 170)
Fixed-ratio schedule	A reinforcement schedule in which the correct response is reinforced after a fixed number of correct responses. (p. 170)
Higher order conditioning	Conditioning based on previous learning; the conditioned stimulus serves as an unconditioned stimulus for further training. (p. 175)
Insight	Awareness of previously unconscious feelings and memories and how they influence present feelings and behavior. (p. 178)
Intermittent pairing	Pairing the conditioned stimulus and the unconditioned stimulus on only a portion of the learning trials. (p. 158)
Latent learning	Learning that is not immediately reflected in a behavior change. (p. 177)
Law of effect (principle of reinforcement)	Thorndike's theory that behavior consistently rewarded will be "stamped in" as learned behavior, and behavior that brings about discomfort will be "stamped out." (p. 161)
Learned helplessness	Failure to take steps to avoid or escape from an unpleasant or aversive stimulus that occurs as a result of previous exposure to unavoidable painful stimuli. (p. 166)
Learning	The process by which experience or practice results in a relatively permanent change in behavior or potential behavior. (p. 156)
Learning set	The ability to become increasingly more effective in solving problems as more problems are solved. (p. 179)

Negative reinforcers	Events whose reduction or termination increases the likelihood that ongoing behavior will recur. (p. 163)
Neurofeedback	A biofeedback technique that monitors brain waves with the use of an EEG to teach people to gain voluntary control over their brain wave activity. (p. 167)
Observational (or vicarious) learning	Learning by observing other people's behavior. (p. 179)
Operant (or instrumental) conditioning	The type of learning in which behaviors are emitted (in the presence of specific stimuli) to earn rewards or avoid punishments. (p. 161)
Operant behaviors	Behaviors designed to operate on the environment in a way that will gain something desired or avoid something unpleasant. (p. 161)
Positive reinforcers	Events whose presence increases the likelihood that ongoing behavior will recur. (p. 163)
Preparedness	A biological readiness to learn certain associations because of their survival advantages. (p. 159)
Primary reinforcers	Reinforcers that are rewarding in themselves, such as food, water, or sex. (p. 175)
Punishers	Stimuli that follows a behavior and decreases the likelihood that the behavior will be repeated. (p. 161)
Punishment	Any event whose presence decreases the likelihood that ongoing behavior will recur. (p. 164)
Reinforcers	A stimuli that follows a behavior and increases the likelihood that the behavior will be repeated. (p. 161)
Response generalization	Giving a response that is somewhat different from the response originally learned to that stimulus. (p. 174)
Schedule of reinforcement	In operant conditioning, the rule for determining when and how often reinforcers will be delivered. (p. 170)
Secondary reinforcers	Reinforcers whose value is acquired through association with other primary or secondary reinforcers. (p. 175)
Shaping	Reinforcing successive approximations to a desired behavior. (p. 163)
Skinner box	A box often used in operant conditioning of animals; it limits the available responses and thus increases the likelihood that the desired response will occur. (p. 163)
Social learning theorists	Psychologists whose view of learning emphasizes the ability to learn by observing a model or receiving instructions, without firsthand experience by the learner. (p. 179)
Spontaneous recovery	The reappearance of an extinguished response after the passage of time, without training. (p. 173)
Stimulus control	Control of conditioned responses by cues or stimuli in the environment. (p. 174)
Stimulus discrimination	Learning to respond to only one stimulus and to inhibit the response to all other stimuli. (p. 174)
Stimulus generalization	The transfer of a learned response to different but similar stimuli. (p. 174)
Unconditioned response (UR)	A response that takes place in an organism whenever an unconditioned stimulus occurs. (p. 156)
Unconditioned stimulus (US)	A stimulus that invariably causes an organism to respond in a specific way. (p. 156)
Variable-interval schedule	A reinforcement schedule in which the correct response is reinforced after varying lengths of time following the last reinforcement. (p. 170)
Variable-ratio schedule	A reinforcement schedule in which a varying number of correct responses must occur before reinforcement is presented. (p. 170)
Vicarious reinforcement (or punishment)	Reinforcement or punishment experienced by models that affects the willingness of others to perform the behaviors they learned by observing those models. (p. 180)

After studying the text and completing the Study Guide activities, answer these questions to determine if you need to review any areas before the course exam.

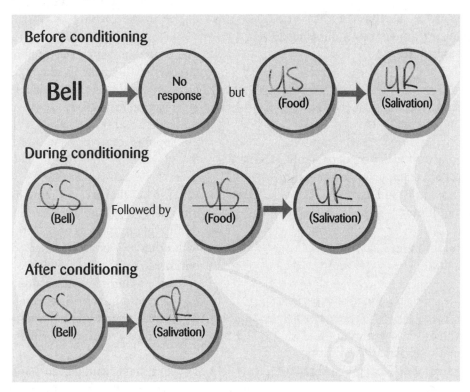

Before conditioning

Bell → No response

but

US (Food) → UR (Salivation)

During conditioning

CS (Bell) — Followed by — US (Food) → UR (Salivation)

After conditioning

CS (Bell) → CR (Salivation)

MULTIPLE CHOICE

1. In the chart above, provide the correct elements in the three stages of Pavlov's classical conditioning experiment.
   a. conditioned response (CR)
   b. unconditioned stimulus (US)
   c. conditioned stimulus (CS)
   d. unconditioned response (UR)

2. In Watson's experiment with Little Albert, the conditioned response (CR) was _____.
   a. fear of the experimenter (Watson)
   b. fear of the laboratory
   c. fear of the rat
   d. fear of the loud noise

3. The idea that a behavior will increase or decrease based on the consequences that follow the behavior is crucial to _____.
   a. operant conditioning
   b. vicarious learning
   c. classical conditioning
   d. insight learning

4. In classical conditioning the learner is _____, and in operant conditioning the learner is _____.
   a. passive; passive
   b. passive; active
   c. active; passive
   d. active; active

5. Any stimulus that follows a behavior and increases the likelihood that the behavior will be repeated is called a _____.
   a. cue
   b. situational stimulus
   ç. reinforcer
   d. higher-order conditioner

6. Any stimulus that follows a behavior and decreases the likelihood that the behavior will be repeated is called a _____.
   a. cue
   b. situational stimulus
   c. reinforcer
   d. punisher

7. Changing behavior through the reinforcement of partial responses is called _____.
   a. modeling
   b. shaping
   c. negative reinforcement
   d. classical conditioning

8. _____ therapy for treating anxiety involves the pairing of relaxation training with systematic exposure to the fearful stimulus.
   a. Operant conditioning
   b. Shaping
   c. Aversive conditioning
   d. Desensitization

9. The process of learning is defined as experience resulting in _____.
   a. amplification of sensory stimuli
   b. delayed genetic behavioral contributions
   c. relatively permanent behavior change
   d. acquisition of motivation

10. A dolphin learns to swim toward a blue platform but not toward a platform of a different color. This shows the concept of _____.
    a. discrimination
    b. modeling
    c. higher-order conditioning
    d. stimulus generalization

11. Reacting to a stimulus that is similar to one that you have already learned to react to is called _____.
    a. response generalization
    b. modeling
    c. higher-order conditioning
    d. stimulus generalization

12. Failure to take steps to avoid or escape from an unpleasant or aversive stimulus that occurs as a result of previous exposure to unavoidable painful stimuli is called _____.
    a. learned helplessness
    b. avoidance learning
    c. aversive conditioning
    d. vicarious learning

13. The process in which a learned response, which has been extinguished suddenly, reappears on its own with no retraining, is called _____.
    a. reaction formation
    b. generalization
    c. spontaneous recovery
    d. shaping

14. A reinforcer that is reinforcing in and of itself is called a _____, and a reinforcer that takes on reinforcing properties only through association with other reinforcers is called a (n) _____ reinforcer.
    a. direct reinforcer/indirect reinforcer
    b. delayed reinforcer/immediate reinforcer
    c. primary reinforcer/secondary reinforcer
    d. secondary reinforcer/primary reinforcer

15. The idea that learning occurs and is stored up, even when behaviors are not reinforced is called _____.
    a. insight
    b. latent learning
    c. placebo learning
    d. innate learning

16. The type of learning that involves elements suddenly coming together so that the solution to a problem is clear is called _____.
    a. latent learning
    b. insight
    c. cognitive mapping
    d. vicarious learning

17. The mental picture of an area, such as a floor plan of a building, is called _____.
    a. a perceptual illusion
    b. a mental set
    c. subliminal perception
    d. a cognitive map

CHAPTER 6 Memory

CHAPTER OVERVIEW

The chapter, which opens by featuring the extraordinary case of Jill Price's "overdeveloped memory," explores the biological bases of memory, the ways that memory differs among people and across cultures, and the ways that memory changes in the first few years of life. It also examines how memories can be changed by events outside the person as well as environmental cues that trigger them.

Many psychologists view **memory** as a series of steps in which we encode, store, and retrieve information, much as a computer does. This is called the **information-processing model** of memory. The first step in the model is inputting data through our senses into temporary holding bins, called **sensory registers**. These registers give us a brief moment to decide whether something deserves our attention.

Information entering a sensory register disappears very quickly if it isn't processed further. Information in the visual register lasts for only about a quarter of a second before it is replaced by new information. If sounds faded from our auditory register as rapidly as this, spoken language would be more difficult to understand. Luckily, information in the auditory register can linger for several seconds.

The next step in the memory process is **attention**—selectively looking at, listening to, smelling, tasting, or feeling what we deem to be important. The nervous system filters out peripheral information, allowing us to zero in on what is essential at a particular time. Unattended information receives at least some processing, however, so that we can quickly shift attention to it if it suddenly strikes us as significant.

The chapter next delves into the topic of short-term memory. **Short-term memory (STM)**, also called *working memory*, holds whatever information we are actively attending to at any given time. Its two primary tasks are to store new information briefly and to "work" on information that we currently have in mind. We can process more information in STM by grouping it into larger meaningful units, a process called **chunking**.

Information can be stored in STM according to the way it sounds, the way it looks, or its meaning. Verbal information is encoded by sound, even if it is written rather than heard. The capacity for visual encoding in STM is greater than for encoding by sound.

Through **rote rehearsal**, or maintenance rehearsal, we retain information in STM for a minute or two by repeating it over and over again. However, rote memorization does not promote long-term memory.

The chapter moves from short-term memory into a parallel exploration of long-term memory. **Long-term memory (LTM)** stores everything we learn. It can store a vast amount of information for many years. Most of the information in LTM seems to be encoded according to its meaning.

Short- and long-term memory work together to explain the **serial position effect**, in which people tend to recall the first and last items in a list better than items in the middle. The *recency effect* explains that items at the end are still held in STM, whereas the *primacy effect* describes the extra LTM rehearsal given to items early in the list.

The way in which we encode material for storage in LTM affects the ease with which we can retrieve it later on. Rote rehearsal is particularly useful for holding conceptually meaningless material, such as phone numbers, in LTM. Through the deeper and more meaningful mechanism of **elaborative rehearsal**, we extract the meaning of information and link it to as much material as possible that is already in LTM. Memory techniques such as **mnemonics** rely on elaborative processing.

A **schema** is a mental representation of an object or event that is stored in memory. Schemata provide a framework into which incoming information is fitted. They may prompt the formation of stereotypes and the drawing of inferences.

Episodic memories are personal memories for events experienced in a specific time and place. **Semantic memories** are facts and concepts not linked to a particular time. **Procedural memories** are motor skills and habits. **Emotional memories** are learned emotional responses to various stimuli.

Explicit memory refers to memories we are aware of, including episodic and semantic memories. **Implicit memory** refers to memories for information that either was not intentionally committed to LTM or is retrieved unintentionally from LTM, including procedural and emotional memories. This distinction is illustrated by research on *priming*, in which people are more likely to complete fragments of stimuli with items seen earlier than with other, equally plausible items. **Tip-of-the-tongue phenomenon (TOT)** involves knowing a word, but not being able to immediately recall it.

The chapter continues into a look at the biology of memory. Memories consist of changes in the chemistry and structure of neurons. The process by which these changes occur is called **long-term potentiation (LTP)**.

Different parts of the brain are specialized for the storage of memories. Short-term memories seem to be located primarily in the prefrontal cortex and temporal lobe. Long-term memories seem to involve both subcortical and cortical structures. Semantic and episodic memories seem to be located primarily in the frontal and temporal lobes of the cortex, and procedural memories appear to be located primarily in the cerebellum and motor cortex. The hippocampus seems especially important in the formation of semantic, episodic, and procedural memories. Emotional memories are dependent on the amygdala.

During deep sleep, the same hippocampal neurons and patterns of neuron activity that accompany initial learning are reactivated. As a result, new memories are further strengthened.

Examining the flip side of memory, the topic of forgetting is featured next in the chapter. Both biological and experiential factors can contribute to our inability to recall information.

According to the **decay theory**, memories deteriorate because of the passage of time. Severe memory loss can be traced to brain damage caused by accidents, surgery, poor diet, or disease. Head injuries can cause **retrograde amnesia**, the inability of people to remember what happened shortly before their accident. The hippocampus may have a role in long-term memory formation. Below-normal levels of the neurotransmitter acetylcholine may be implicated in memory loss seen in Alzheimer's disease.

Certain environmental factors contribute to our inability to remember. To the extent that information is apparently lost from LTM, researchers attribute the cause to inadequate learning or to interference from competing information. Interference may come from two directions: In **retroactive interference**, new information interferes with old information already in LTM; **proactive interference** refers to the process by which old information already in LTM interferes with new information.

When environmental cues present during learning are absent during recall, context-dependent forgetting may occur. The ability to recall information is also affected by one's physiological state when the material was learned; this process is known as *state-dependent memory*.

Sometimes we "reconstruct" memories for social or personal self-defense. Research on long-term memory and on forgetting offers ideas for a number of steps that can be taken to improve recall.

The chapter concludes by taking a snapshot look at several wide-ranging "special topics" in memory, beginning with the relationship between culture and memory.

Cultural values and customs profoundly affect what people remember and how easily they recall it. So do the emotions we attach to a memory, with some emotion-laden events being remembered for life. Also affecting how well we remember are the strategies we use to store and retrieve information.

Many Western schools stress being able to recall long lists of words, facts, and figures that are divorced from everyday life. In contrast, societies in which cultural information is passed on through a rich oral tradition may instead emphasize memory for events that directly affect people's lives.

Autobiographical memory refers to recollection of events from one's life. Not all of these events are recalled with equal clarity, of course, and some are not recalled at all. Autobiographical memories are typically strongest for events that had a major impact on our lives or that aroused strong emotion.

People generally cannot remember events that occurred before age 2, a phenomenon called **childhood amnesia**. Childhood amnesia may result from the incomplete development of brain structures before age 2, from the infants' lack of a clear sense of self, or from the lack of language skills used to consolidate early experience. Research also suggests it may be related to an adult's inability to recall memories that were, in fact, stored during the first 2 years.

People with exceptional memories have carefully developed memory techniques. **Mnemonists** are individuals who are highly skilled at using those techniques. A phenomenon called **eidetic imagery** enables some people to see features of an image in minute detail.

Years after a dramatic or significant event occurs, people often report having vivid memories of that event as well as the incidents surrounding it. These memories are known as **flashbulb memories**. Recent research has challenged the assumptions that flashbulb memories are accurate and stable.

Jurors tend to put their faith in witnesses who saw an event with their own eyes. However, some evidence suggests that eyewitnesses sometimes are unable to tell the difference between what they witnessed and what they merely heard about or imagined.

There are many cases of people who experience a traumatic event, lose all memory of it, but then later recall it. Such recovered memories are highly controversial, since research shows that people can be induced to "remember" events that never happened. So far there is no clear way to distinguish real recovered memories from false ones.

LEARNING OBJECTIVES EXERCISE

After you have read and studied the chapter, you should be able to answer the following learning objectives.

THE SENSORY REGISTERS

- Describe the role of the sensory registers and the length of time information remains there. Distinguish between the *icon* and the *echo*.

- Compare Broadbent and Treisman's theories of attention. Explain what is meant by the "cocktail-party phenomenon" and "inattentional blindness."

SHORT-TERM MEMORY

- Define short-term memory (STM), explain why it is called "working memory" and describe the way information is encoded in STM.

- Describe the capacity of STM including the role of chunking and interference, maintenance of information in STM, and the effect of stress on STM.

LONG-TERM MEMORY

- Define long-term memory (LTM) including the capacity of LTM and the way information is encoded in LTM. Explain the serial position effect.

- Differentiate rote rehearsal from elaborative rehearsal and explain the role of mnemonics and schemata as forms of elaborative rehearsal.

- Distinguish between episodic memories, semantic memories, procedural memories, emotional memories, explicit memories, and implicit memories. Explain how priming and the tip-of-the-tongue phenomenon shed light on memory.

THE BIOLOGY OF MEMORY

- Define long-term potentiation. Identify the areas of the brain that play a role in the formation and storage of long-term memories. Describe the role of sleep in the formation of new memories.

FORGETTING

- Describe the biological factors that influence forgetting, including the phenomenon of retrograde amnesia.

- Differentiate between retroactive and proactive interference.

- Explain what is meant by "statedependent memory" and the "reconstructive" nature of remembering.

SPECIAL TOPICS IN MEMORY

- Describe the influence of culture on memory.

- Define autobiographical memory and describe the several theories that attempt to explain childhood amnesia.

- Describe examples of extraordinary memory (including eidetic imagery and flashbulb memories).

- Discuss the accuracy of eyewitness testimony and recovered memories.

CHAPTER OUTLINE

KEY TERMS

Attention	The selection of some incoming information for further processing. (p. 188)
Childhood amnesia	The difficulty adults have remembering experiences from their first two years of life. (p. 209)
Chunking	The grouping of information into meaningful units for easier handling by short-term memory. (p. 191)
Decay theory	A theory that argues that the passage of time causes forgetting. (p. 204)
Eidetic imagery	The ability to reproduce unusually sharp and detailed images of something one has seen. (p. 209)
Elaborative rehearsal	The linking of new information in short-term memory to familiar material stored in long-term memory. (p. 195)
Emotional memories	Learned emotional responses to various stimuli. (p. 198)
Episodic memories	The portion of long-term memory that stores personally experienced events. (p. 196)
Explicit memory	Memory for information that we can readily express in words and are aware of having; these memories can be intentionally retrieved from memory. (p. 198)
Flashbulb memory	A vivid memory of a certain event and the incidents surrounding it even after a long time has passed. (p. 210)
Implicit memory	Memory for information that we cannot readily express in words and may not be aware of having; these memories cannot be intentionally retrieved from memory. (p. 198)
Information-processing model	A computer-like model used to describe the way humans encode, store, and retrieve information. (p. 187)
Long-term memory (LTM)	A long-lasting change in the structure or function of a synapse that increases the efficiency of neural transmission and is thought to be related to how information is stored by neurons. (p. 193)
Long-term potentiation (LTP)	A method of studying developmental changes by evaluating the same people at different points in their lives. (p. 201)
Memory	The ability to remember the things that we have experienced, imagined, and learned. (p. 187)
Mnemonics	Techniques that make material easier to remember. (p. 195)
Mnemonists	People with highly developed memory skills. (p. 210)
Proactive interference	The process by which information already in memory interferes with new information. (p. 205)
Procedural memories	The portion of long-term memory that stores information relating to skills, habits, and other perceptual-motor tasks. (p. 197)
Retroactive interference	The process by which new information interferes with information already in memory. (p. 205)
Retrograde amnesia	The inability to recall events preceding an accident or injury, but without loss of earlier memory. (p. 204)
Rote rehearsal	Retaining information in memory simply by repeating it over and over. (p. 192)
Schema (skee-mah; plural: schemata)	A set of beliefs or expectations about something that is based on past experience. (p. 196)
Semantic memories	The portion of long-term memory that stores general facts and information. (p. 197)
Sensory registers	Entry points for raw information from the senses. (p. 188)
Serial position effect	The finding that when asked to recall a list of unrelated items, performance is better for the items at the beginning and end of the list. (p. 194)

| Short-term memory (STM) | Working memory; briefly stores and processes selected information from the sensory registers. (p. 190) |
| Tip-of-the-tongue phenomenon (or TOT) | Knowing a word, but not being able to immediately recall it. (p. 199) |

After studying the text and completing the Study Guide activities, answer these questions to determine if you need to review any areas before the course exam.

MULTIPLE CHOICE

1. Label the elements of the information processing model of memory illustrated in Figure 6-1 on page 189. Select from the following terms: a) decay; b) repetition; c) attention; d)sensory register; e) retrieval; f) interference; g) rehearsal; h) long-term memory; i) coding; j) short term memory; k) external stimulus.

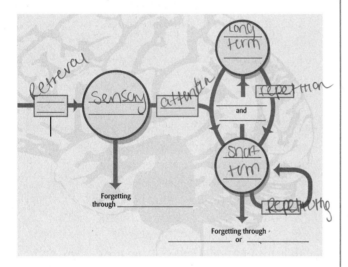

(handwritten labels: retrieval; Sensory; attention; Long term; repetition; Short term; and; repetition)

Forgetting through _____

Forgetting through _____ or _____

2. Our visual impression of our friend walking past us would initially be found in the _____.
   a. sensory registers
   b. short-term memory
   c. long-term memory
   d. hippocampus

3. What we are thinking of at any given moment, or what we commonly know as "consciousness," is _____.
   a. long-term memory
   b. short-term memory
   c. secondary memory
   d. sensory registers

4. Information is grouped for storage in short-term memory through the process of _____.
   a. categorizing
   b. chunking
   c. rote rehearsal
   d. nonsense syllables

5. The linking of new information in short-term memory to familiar material stored in long-term memory is called _____.
   a. elaborative rehearsal
   b. rote rehearsal
   c. semantic rehearsal
   d. chunking

6. The inability to recall events immediately preceding an accident or injury, but without loss of earlier memory is called _____ amnesia.
   a. psychogenic
   b. retroactive
   c. retrograde
   d. fugue

7. The portion of long-term memory that stores general facts and information is called _____.
   a. eidetic
   b. episodic
   c. semantic
   d. procedural

8. While memorizing a list of words, students were exposed to the scent of chocolate. If the students recall more words when there is the scent of chocolate present, then the effect of chocolate is most likely due to _____ memory.
   a. explicit
   b. implicit
   c. procedural
   d. eidetic

9. Proactive interference of long-term memory means that _____.
   a. old material has eliminated memories of new material
   b. old material interferes with remembering new material
   c. new material represses short-term memories
   d. new material interferes with remembering old material

10. When memories are not lost but are transformed into something somewhat different, it is called _____.
   a. retroactive interference
   b. eidetic memory
   c. proactive interference
   d. reconstructive memory

11. The phenomenon whereby most people cannot recall events that occurred in their life before the age of 2, is called _____.
   a. infantile autism
   b. psychogenic amnesia
   c. fugue amnesia
   d. childhood amnesia

12. Our recollection of events that occurred in our life and when those events took place is called _____ memory.
   a. autobiographical
   b. reconstructive
   c. semantic
   d. procedural

13. Memories that concern highly significant events and are vividly remembered, such as the World Trade Center and Pentagon events of September 11th, 2001, are called _____.
   a. eyewitness images
   b. flashbulb memories
   c. now print images
   d. photographic memories

14. The most important determinant of interference is _____.
   a. similarity of material
   b. complexity of material
   c. decay
   d. rehearsal time

15. Remembering a telephone number because it contains the numbers of the year in which you were born is an example of the use of _____.
   a. a mnemonic device
   b. association
   c. eidetic imagery
   d. chunking

16. The hippocampus is important for _____.
   a. transferring information from short-term to long-term memory
   b. the retrieval of memories from long-term memory
   c. maintaining a constant level of attention
   d. the formation of short-term memory

17. The neurotransmitter that appears to be instrumental in the memory process is _____.
   a. serotonin
   b. dopamine
   c. norepinephrine
   d. acetylcholine

18. In more than 1,000 cases in which innocent people were wrongly convicted of a crime, the single most pervasive element leading to the wrongful conviction was _____.
   a. faulty forensic work by police labs
   b. phony evidence "planted" by the police
   c. faulty eyewitness testimony
   d. misinterpretations of the law by judges and juries

19. Each of the following is a recommended strategy for improving your memory abilities EXCEPT _____.
   a. developing your motivation
   b. practicing memory skills
   c. staying focused and minimizing distractions
   d. learning to rely on your memory alone

20. Which of the following statements is true regarding the role of attention in information processing?
    a. Attention involves selectively recognizing sensations.
    b. Attention is believed to work as a large filter, letting most stimuli through.
    c. Attention is not an automatic process but requires constant monitoring of the environment.
    d. none of the above

21. Which of the following statements is not true regarding mnemonics?
    a. Mnemonics may be useful to help tie new material to information already stored in STM.
    b. Mnemonic techniques may include rhymes and jingles.
    c. Relating personal information to mnemonics may facilitate recall.
    d. All of the above are true.

22. Which of the following statements best reflects the role of long-term potentiation in memory processes?
    a. LTP accounts for why we forget—synaptic connections are lost in the brain.
    b. As new memories are formed, old connections are weakened.
    c. Memory formation involves forming new synaptic connections in the brain or strengthening existing ones.
    d. LTP plays an influential role in STM, but a lesser role in LTM.

23. Which of the following statements is true regarding the storage of memories in the brain?
    a. All memories are stored in one place in the brain.
    b. Short-term memories tend to be stored in the cerebellum.
    c. Damage to the hippocampus greatly impairs short-term memories.
    d. Damage to the amygdala impairs recall of new emotional memories.

24. The theory that memories deteriorate because of the passage of time is known as _____.
    a. interference theory
    b. anterograde amnesia theory
    c. decay theory
    d. childhood amnesia theory

SHORT ESSAY QUESTIONS

1. Explain Broadbent's filter theory and Treisman's modified filter theory. Which theory best accounts for how people select what they attend to from the massive amount of information entering the sensory register?

2. Define proactive and retroactive interference. Describe reconstructive memory and give two examples of how we utilize it in real-life situations.

3. Discuss the research on the reliability of eyewitness testimony and how this relates to recovered memories. What do scientists currently believe about the accuracy and reliability of recovered memories?

4. Recall your memories of the incidents surrounding September 11th as they relate to the definition of a flashbulb memory. Discuss the events surrounding your learning of the event, the emotions and thoughts you experienced then, and how this event has affected your present life.

5. Make a commitment to yourself to use at least three steps for improving your memory. List them here and describe how you will make them new habits.

ANSWERS AND EXPLANATIONS TO MULTIPLE CHOICE POSTTEST

1.

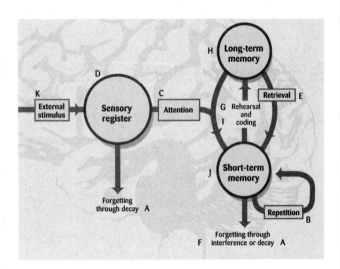

2. a. Visual sensations flow from your senses into the sensory registers. p. 187

3. b. What we are thinking of at any given moment refers to short-term memory. p. 190

4. b. Chunking is grouping information in meaningful units in short-term memory. p. 191

5. a. Elaborative rehearsal relates new information to something we already know. p. 195

6. c. Retrograde amnesia is the inability to recall events preceding an accident or injury, but without loss of earlier memory. p. 204

7. c. Semantic memory stores general facts and information. p. 197

8. b. Implicit memory provides retrieval cues we may not be aware of having made. p. 198

9. b. Old material interfering with remembering new material is called proactive interference. p. 205

10. d. Reconstructive memory changes the original memory. p. 206

11. d. Childhood amnesia refers to the difficulty adults have remembering experiences before age 2. p. 209

12. a. Autobiographical memory is collection of memories for events that took place in our lives. p. 208

13. b. Flashbulb memories are vivid memories of certain events and incidents surrounding them even long after the event occurred. p. 210

14. a. Similarity of material can lead to greater amounts of interference. p. 205

15. a. Mnemonic devices are techniques that make material easier to remember. p. 195

16. a. The hippocampus is important in converting short-term memory into long-term memory. p. 201

17. d. Acetylcholine is the neurotransmitter that is instrumental in memory. p. 205

18. c. Faulty eyewitness testimony was the single most persuasive element leading to false conviction in over 1,000 cases studied. p. 211

19. d. Rely on more than memory alone by using other tools. p. 197

20. a. Attention involves selectively looking, listening, smelling, tasting, and feeling. p. 188

21. a. Mnemonics may be useful to help tie new material to information already stored in LTM. p. 195

22. c. As we learn, new connections are formed in the brain and old connections are strengthened. As the number of connections among neurons increases, firing of electrical charges increases. p. 200

23. d. Damage to the amygdala impairs recall of new emotional memories. p. 203

24. c. According to decay theory, memories deteriorate because of the passage of time. p. 204

7 Cognition and Mental Abilities

CHAPTER OVERVIEW

The chapter opens with Oliver Sacks' case description of Joseph, an 11-year-old deaf boy who longed to communicate but could not. As illustrated by Sacks, language and thought are intertwined, and the chapter focuses on three "characteristically human" cognitive processes: thinking, problem solving, and decision making. The term **cognition** involves the processes whereby we acquire and use knowledge.

The three most important building blocks of thought are language, images, and concepts. As we think, we use words, sensory "snapshots," and categories that classify things.

Language is a flexible system of symbols that allows us to communicate ideas to others. When we express thoughts as statements, we must conform to our language's rules. Every language has rules indicating which sounds (or **phonemes**) are part of that particular language, how those sounds can be combined into meaningful units (or **morphemes**), and how those meaningful units can be ordered into phrases and sentences (rules of **grammar**). To communicate an idea, we start with a thought and then choose sounds, words, and phrases that will express the idea clearly. To understand the speech of others, the task is reversed.

Images are mental representations of sensory experiences. Visual images in particular can be powerful aids in thinking about the relationships between things. Picturing things in our mind's eye can sometimes help us solve problems.

Concepts are categories for classifying objects, people, and experiences based on their common elements. Without the ability to form concepts, we would need a different name for every new thing we encounter. We draw on concepts to anticipate what new experiences will be like. Many concepts are "fuzzy," lacking clear-cut boundaries. Therefore we often use **prototypes**, mental models of the most typical examples of a concept, to classify new objects.

The chapter continues into a discussion of language, thought, and culture. According to Benjamin Whorf's **linguistic relativity hypothesis**, thought is greatly influenced by language. But critics of Whorf's **linguistic determinism** contend that thought and experience can shape and change a language as much as a language can shape and change thought.

Some evidence indicates that the use of "man" and "he" to refer to all people affects the way that English speakers think. Referring to doctors, college professors, bankers, and executives by the generic "he" may contribute to the gender stereotyping of these respected occupations as appropriate for men but not for women. In contrast, referring to secretaries and housekeepers as "she" may reinforce the stereotype that those occupations are appropriate for women, not men.

The chapter next moves into the realm of nonhuman language and thought. Nonhuman animals communicate primarily through **signs**: general or global statements about the animal's current state. Using the distinguishing features of language, which include semantics, displacement, and productivity as criteria, no other species has its own language, although chimpanzees have been taught to use American Sign Language. Research indicates that some animals have humanlike cognitive capacities, such as the ability to form concepts and to reason. Apes have demonstrated sophisticated problem-solving skills. However, only chimpanzees, bonobos, and orangutans consistently show signs of self-awareness.

The chapter switches focus to the subject of problem solving. Interpreting a problem, formulating a strategy, and evaluating progress toward a solution are three general aspects of the problem-solving process. Each in its own way is critical to success at the task.

Problem representation—defining or interpreting the problem—is the first step in problem solving. We must decide whether to view the problem verbally, mathematically, or visually; and to get clues about how to solve it we must categorize it. Some problems require **convergent thinking**, or searching for a single correct solution, while others call for **divergent thinking**, or generating many possible solutions. Representing a problem in an unproductive way can block progress completely.

Selecting a solution strategy and evaluating progress toward the goal are also important steps in the problem-solving process. A solution strategy can range from trial and error, to information retrieval based on similar problems, to a set of step-by-step procedures guaranteed to work (an **algorithm**), to rule-of-thumb approaches known as **heuristics**. An algorithm is often preferable over trial and error because it guarantees a solution and does not waste time. But because we lack algorithms for so many things, heuristics are vital to human problem solving. Some useful heuristics are **hill climbing**, creating **subgoals**, **means-end analysis**, and **working backward**.

A **mental set** is a tendency to perceive and approach a problem in a certain way. Although sets can enable us to draw on past experience to help solve problems, a strong set can also prevent us from using essential new approaches. One set that can seriously hamper problem solving is **functional fixedness**—the tendency to perceive only traditional uses for an object. One way to minimize mental sets is the technique of **brainstorming** in which an individual or group collects numerous ideas and evaluates them only after all possible ideas have been collected.

The chapter continues from problem solving to the related topic of decision making. Decision making is a special kind of problem solving in which all possible solutions or choices are known. The task is not to come up with new solutions, but rather to identify the best one available based on whatever criteria are being used.

The logical way to make a decision is to rate each available choice in terms of weighted criteria and then to total the ratings for each choice. This approach is called a **compensatory model** because heavily weighted attractive features can compensate for lightly weighted unattractive ones.

Heuristics can save a great deal of time and effort, but they do not always result in the best choices.

Errors in judgment may occur based on the **representativeness** heuristic, which involves making decisions based on information that matches our model of the "typical" member of a category. Other examples are overreliance on the **availability** heuristic (making choices based on whatever information we can most easily retrieve from memory, even though it may not be accurate) and the **confirmation bias** (the tendency to seek evidence in support of our existing beliefs and to ignore evidence that contradicts them).

Framing, or perspective in which a problem is presented, can also affect the outcome of a decision. And regardless of whether a decision proves to be good or bad, we often use **hindsight bias**, which refers to our tendency to view outcomes as inevitable or predictable after we know the outcome to "correct" our memories so that the decision seems to be a good one. **Counterfactual thinking** involves revisiting our decisions by considering "what if "alternatives.

Next, the chapter briefly jumps into a discussion of multitasking. Contrary to what many people believe, multitasking often results in reduced speed, decreased accuracy, and increased stress. Numerous studies have shown that driving is particularly affected by multitasking. Talking on a cell phone or texting while driving may be as bad as driving legally drunk.

Shifting gears, the chapter next takes on intelligence and mental abilities. Psychologists who study **intelligence** ask what intelligence entails and how it can be measured. To accomplish this, they use a variety of questions to assess general knowledge, vocabulary, arithmetic reasoning, and spatial manipulation.

Intelligence theories fall into two categories: those that argue in favor of a "general intelligence" that affects all aspects of cognitive functioning, and those that say intelligence is composed of many separate abilities, in which a person will not necessarily score high in all. Spearman's theory of intelligence is an example of the first category. Thurstone's theory is an example of the second category, as are Sternberg's **triarchic theory of intelligence** and Gardner's **theory of multiple intelligences**. Goleman's theory of **emotional intelligence** emphasizes skill in social relationships and awareness of others' and one's own emotions.

The Binet–Simon Scale, developed in France by Alfred Binet and Theodore Simon, was adapted by Stanford University's L. M. Terman to create a test that yields an **intelligence quotient (IQ)**, the Stanford–Binet Intelligence Scale. The **Wechsler Adult**

Intelligence Scale and the **Wechsler Intelligence Scale for Children** were the first intelligence tests to yield both a verbal and performance IQ score as well as an overall IQ score. In contrast to these individual intelligence tests, **group tests** of intelligence are administered by one examiner to many people at a time. Alternatives to traditional IQ tests include **performance tests** of mental abilities that exclude the use of language and **culture-fair tests** that reduce cultural bias in a variety of ways.

Reliability refers to the ability of a test to produce consistent and stable scores. **Split-half reliability** is a method of determining test reliability by dividing the test into two parts and checking the agreement of scores on both parts. Psychologists express reliability in terms of **correlation coefficients**, which measure the relationship between two sets of scores. **Validity** is the ability of a test to measure what it has been designed to measure. **Content validity** exists if a test contains an adequate sample of questions relating to the skills or knowledge it is supposed to measure. **Criterion-related validity** refers to the relationship between test scores and whatever the test is designed to measure. In the case of intelligence, the most common independent measure is academic achievement. Although the reliability of IQ tests is seldom questioned, their validity is questioned. Critics charge that these tests assess a very limited set of mental skills and that some tests may be unfairly biased against minority groups. Also, poor school performance may be the result of, rather than caused by, low test scores. Finally, although IQ tests tend to predict occupational success and performance on the job after college, they are not ideally suited to that important task. New tests are being developed to address these concerns.

The chapter continues forward with an indepth treatment of heredity, environment, and intelligence, starting with a discussion of IQ scores. Although there has been extended debate about the extent to which heredity and environment contribute to IQ, studies comparing the IQ scores of identical and fraternal twins raised in the same and different families indicate that approximately 50% of differences in intelligence are due to genetics and the other half due to differences in environment, including education.

With such a sizable percentage of the differences in IQ scores being attributable to the environment and education, many psychologists are strongly in favor of compensatory education programs for young children from disadvantaged homes. Two such programs are the Milwaukee Project and Head Start. Although they may not boost IQ scores greatly in the long run, such programs do seem to have significant educational benefits.

Conceptually, observations from the study of plants may be able to help us understand the relationship between heredity and the environment. Plants grown in rich soil under ideal environmental conditions generally do better than plants grown in poor soil under less than ideal conditions, thus showing the importance of environment. But differences between plants grown under the same environmental conditions demonstrate the importance of heredity. Similarly, individual differences in human intelligence reflect both the genetic and environmental factors. However, psychologists cannot yet account for the fact that IQ scores on the whole are increasing (the Flynn Effect).

While males and females do not differ in general intelligence, females do tend to have slightly stronger verbal skills while males tend to have slightly stronger visual-spatial skills. Research indicates that these differences emerge in early infancy. As for cultural differences, research does not support the notion that people from certain cultures have a natural tendency to excel at academic skills.

The IQs of nearly 70% of the population fall between 85 and 115; and all but 5% have IQs between 70 and 130. **Mental retardation** and **giftedness** are the two extremes of intelligence. About 25% of cases of mental retardation can be traced to biological causes, including Down syndrome, but causes of the remaining 75% are not fully understood; nor are the causes of giftedness. Gifted people do not necessarily excel in all mental abilities.

The chapter concludes with a look at creativity and its relation to intelligence. **Creativity** is the ability to produce novel and socially valued ideas or objects.

The threshold theory holds that a minimum level of intelligence is needed for creativity, but above that threshold level, higher intelligence doesn't necessarily make for greater creativity. Apparently factors other than intelligence contribute to creativity.

Creativity tests are scored on the originality of answers and, frequently, on the number of responses (demonstrating divergent thinking). Some psychologists question how valid these tests are, however.

LEARNING OBJECTIVES EXERCISE

After you have read and studied the chapter, you should be able to answer the following learning objectives.

BUILDING BLOCKS OF THOUGHT

- Describe the three basic building blocks of thought and give an example of each. Explain how phonemes, morphemes, and grammar (syntax and semantics) work together to form a language.

LANGUAGE, THOUGHT, AND CULTURE

- Summarize the evidence for the idea that people in different cultures perceive and think about the world in different ways. Explain what is meant by "linguistic determinism" and summarize the evidence for and against it.

NONHUMAN LANGUAGE AND THOUGHT

- Summarize research evidence that supports the statement that "nonhuman animals have some humanlike cognitive capacities." Explain the following statement: "All animals communicate, but only humans use language to communicate."

PROBLEM SOLVING

- Explain why problem representation is an important first step in solving problems. In your explanation include divergent and convergent thinking, verbal, mathematical and visual representation, and problem categorization.

- Distinguish between trial and error, information retrieval, algorithms, and heuristics as ways of solving problems. Give an example of hill-climbing, subgoals, means-end analysis, and working backward. Explain how "mental sets" can help or hinder problem solving.

DECISION MAKING

- Explain how decision making differs from problem solving. Describe the process of compensatory decision making and the use of decision-making heuristics. Explain how framing can affect decisions, and how hindsight bias and counterfactual thinking affect that way we view our decisions after the fact.

INTELLIGENCE AND MENTAL ABILITIES

- Compare and contrast the theories of intelligence put forth by Spearman, Thurstone, Sternberg, Gardner, and Goleman.

- Describe the similarities and differences between the Stanford-Binet Intelligence Scale and the Wechsler Intelligence Scales, and explain how they differ from group tests, performance tests, and culture-fair tests of intelligence. Explain what is meant by test "reliability" and "validity" and how psychologists determine whether an intelligence test is reliable or valid.

- Summarize the criticisms of intelligence tests and the relationship between IQ test scores and job success.

HEREDITY, ENVIRONMENT, AND INTELLIGENCE

- Summarize the evidence that both heredity and environment (including intervention programs) affect intelligence.

- What is the "Flynn Effect"? What are some of the explanations that have been offered for it?

- Summarize the evidence regarding gender differences and cultural differences in mental abilities.

- Explain what is required for a diagnosis of mental retardation and summarize what is known about its causes. Describe what is meant by "inclusion" and whether it has been shown to be beneficial.

- Explain what is meant by saying a person is "gifted." Explain the pros and cons of special programs for gifted children.

CREATIVITY

- Describe the relationship between creativity and intelligence, and the ways in which creativity has been measured.

I. Enduring Issues in Cognition and Mental Abilities (page 217)

II. Building Blocks of Thought (page 217)
   A. Language
      • Phonemes
      • Morphemes
      • Grammar
   B. Images
      • Can Represent Abstract Ideas
   C. Concepts
      • Prototype (or Model)

III. Language, Thought, and Culture (page 220)
   • Linguistic Relativity Hypothesis
   • Linguistic Determinism
   A. Is Language Male Dominated?
      • Research on Unconscious Nature of Gender Stereotyping

IV. Nonhuman Language and Thought (page 222)
   A. The Question of Language
      • Signs
      • Francine Patterson and "Koko"
   B. Animal Cognition
      • Question of Self-Awareness

V. Problem Solving (page 224)
   A. Interpreting Problems
      • Problem Representation
      • Divergent Thinking
      • Convergent Thinking
   B. Implementing Strategies and Evaluating Progress
      i. Trial and Error
      ii. Information Retrieval
      iii. Algorithms
      iv. Heuristics
   C. Obstacles to Solving Problems
      • Functional Fixedness
      • Brainstorming
   D. APPLYING PSYCHOLOGY: BECOMING A MORE SKILLFUL PROBLEM SOLVER

VI. Decision Making (page 230)
   A. Compensatory Decision Making
      • Compensatory Model

B. Decision-Making Heuristics
   • Representativeness
   • Availability
   • Confirmation Bias
C. Framing
   • Subtle Changes in Presentation Can Dramatically Affect Decisions
D. Explaining Our Decisions
   i. Hindsight
   ii. "If Only"

VII. Multitasking (page 233)
   • Negative Effects and Dangers

VIII. Intelligence and Mental Abilities (page 234)
   A. Theories of Intelligence
      i. Early Theorists
      ii. Contemporary Theorists
   B. Intelligence Tests
      i. The Stanford–Binet Intelligence Scale
      ii. The Wechsler Intelligence Scales
      iii. Group Tests
      iv. Performance and Culture-Fair Tests
      v. Biological Measures of Intelligence
   C. What Makes a Good Test?
      i. Reliability
      ii. Validity
      iii. Criticisms of IQ Tests

IX. Heredity, Environment, and Intelligence (page 243)
   A. Heredity
   B. Environment
      i. Intervention Programs: How Much Can We Boost IQ?
   C. The IQ Debate: A Useful Model
      i. The Flynn Effect
   D. Mental Abilities and Human Diversity: Gender and Culture
      i. Gender
      ii. Culture
   E. Extremes of Intelligence
      i. Mental Retardation
      ii. Giftedness

X. Creativity (page 250)
   A. Intelligence and Creativity
      • Threshold Theory
   B. Creativity Tests
      • Open-Ended Tests Better

Algorithm	A step-by-step method of problem solving that guarantees a correct solution. (p. 226)
Availability	A heuristic by which a judgment or decision is based on information that is most easily retrieved from memory. (p. 231)
Brainstorming	A problem-solving strategy in which an individual or a group produces numerous ideas and evaluates them only after all ideas have been collected. (p. 229)
Cognition	The processes whereby we acquire and use knowledge. (p. 217)
Compensatory model	A rational decision-making model in which choices are systematically evaluated on various criteria. (p. 231)
Concepts	Mental categories for classifying objects, people, or experiences. (p. 219)
Confirmation bias	The tendency to look for evidence in support of a belief and to ignore evidence that would disprove a belief. (p. 232)
Content validity	Refers to a test's having an adequate sample of questions measuring the skills or knowledge it is supposed to measure. (p. 240)
Convergent thinking	Thinking that is directed toward one correct solution to a problem. (p. 225)
Correlation coefficients	Statistical measures of the degree of association between two variables. (p. 240)
Counterfactual thinking	Thinking about alternative realities and things that never happened. (p. 233)
Creativity	The ability to produce novel and socially valued ideas or objects. (p. 250)
Criterion-related validity	Validity of a test as measured by a comparison of the test score and independent measures of what the test is designed to measure. (p. 241)
Culture-fair tests	Intelligence tests designed to eliminate cultural bias by minimizing skills and values that vary from one culture to another. (p. 239)
Divergent thinking	Thinking that meets the criteria of originality, inventiveness, and flexibility. (p. 225)
Emotional intelligence	According to Goleman, a form of intelligence that refers to how effectively people perceive and understand their own emotions and the emotions of others, and can regulate and manage their emotional behavior. (p. 236)
Framing	The perspective from which we interpret information before making a decision. (p. 232)
Functional fixedness	The tendency to perceive only a limited number of uses for an object, thus interfering with the process of problem solving. (p. 228)
Giftedness	Refers to superior IQ combined with demonstrated or potential ability in such areas as academic aptitude, creativity, and leadership. (p. 249)
Grammar	The language rules that determine how sounds and words can be combined and used to communicate meaning within a language. (p. 218)
Group tests	Written intelligence tests administered by one examiner to many people at one time. (p. 239)
Heuristics	Rules of thumb that help in simplifying and solving problems, although they do not guarantee a correct solution. (p. 227)
Hill climbing	A heuristic, problem-solving strategy in which each step moves you progressively closer to the final goal. (p. 227)
Hindsight bias	The tendency to see outcomes as inevitable and predictable after we know the outcome. (p. 232)
Image	A mental representation of a sensory experience. (p. 219)
Intelligence	A general term referring to the ability or abilities involved in learning and adaptive behavior. (p. 235)

Intelligence quotient (IQ)	A numerical value given to intelligence that is determined from the scores on an intelligence test on the basis of a score of 100 for average intelligence. (p. 237)
Language	A flexible system of communication that uses sounds, rules, gestures, or symbols to convey information. (p. 218)
Linguistic determinism	The belief that thought and experience are determined by language. (p. 221)
Linguistic relativity hypothesis	Whorf's idea that patterns of thinking are determined by the specific language one speaks. (p. 221)
Means-end analysis	A heuristic strategy that aims to reduce the discrepancy between the current situation and the desired goal at a number of intermediate points. (p. 227)
Mental retardation	Condition of significantly subaverage intelligence combined with deficiencies in adaptive behavior. (p. 248)
Mental set	The tendency to perceive and to approach problems in certain ways. (p. 228)
Morphemes	The smallest meaningful units of speech, such as simple words, prefixes, and suffixes. (p. 218)
Performance tests	Intelligence tests that minimize the use of language. (p. 239)
Phonemes	The basic sounds that make up any language. (p. 218)
Problem representation	The first step in solving a problem; it involves interpreting or defining the problem. (p. 225)
Prototype (or model)	According to Rosch, a mental model containing the most typical features of a concept. (p. 219)
Reliability	Ability of a test to produce consistent and stable scores. (p. 239)
Representativeness	A heuristic by which a new situation is judged on the basis of its resemblance to a stereotypical model. (p. 231)
Signs	Stereotyped communications about an animal's current state. (p. 222)
Split-half reliability	A method of determining test reliability by dividing the test into two parts and checking the agreement of scores on both parts. (p. 239)
Subgoals	Intermediate, more manageable goals used in one heuristic strategy to make it easier to reach the final goal. (p. 227)
Theory of multiple intelligences	Howard Gardner's theory that there is not one intelligence, but rather many intelligences, each of which is relatively independent of the others. (p. 236)
Triarchic theory of intelligence	Sternberg's theory that intelligence involves mental skills (analytical intelligence), insight and creative adaptability (creative intelligence), and environmental responsiveness (practical intelligence). (p. 236)
Validity	Ability of a test to measure what it has been designed to measure. (p. 240)
Wechsler Adult Intelligence Scale—Third Edition (WAIS-III)	An individual intelligence test developed especially for adults; measures both verbal and performance abilities. (p. 237)
Wechsler Intelligence Scale for Children—Third Edition (WISC-III)	An individual intelligence test developed especially for school-aged children; measures verbal and performance abilities and also yields an overall IQ score. (p. 238)
Working backward	A heuristic strategy in which one works backward from the desired goal to the given conditions. (p. 228)

Vocabulary Flashcards

Cut out each term and use as study cards. The definition is on the back side of each term.

Cognition	**Image**
Language	**Concepts**
Phonemes	**Prototype (or model)**
Morphemes	**Linguistic relativity hypothesis**
Grammar	**Linguistic determinism**

A mental representation of a sensory experience.

The processes whereby we acquire and use knowledge.

Mental categories for classifying objects, people, or experiences.

A flexible system of communication that uses sounds, rules, gestures, or symbols to convey information.

According to Rosch, a mental model containing the most typical features of a concept.

The basic sounds that make up any language.

Whorf's idea that patterns of thinking are determined by the specific language one speaks.

The smallest meaningful units of speech, such as simple words, prefixes, and suffixes.

The belief that thought and experience are determined by language.

The language rules that determine how sounds and words can be combined and used to communicate meaning within a language.

Signs	**Heuristics**
Problem representation	**Hill climbing**
Divergent thinking	**Subgoals**
Convergent thinking	**Means-end analysis**
Algorithm	**Working backward**

Rules of thumb that help in simplifying and solving problems, although they do not guarantee a correct solution.

Stereotyped communications about an animal's current state.

A heuristic, problem-solving strategy in which each step moves you progressively closer to the final goal.

The first step in solving a problem; it involves interpreting or defining the problem.

Intermediate, more manageable goals used in one heuristic strategy to make it easier to reach the final goal.

Thinking that meets the criteria of originality, inventiveness, and flexibility.

A heuristic strategy that aims to reduce the discrepancy between the current situation and the desired goal at a number of intermediate points.

Thinking that is directed toward one correct solution to a problem.

A heuristic strategy in which one works backward from the desired goal to the given conditions.

A step-by-step method of problem solving that guarantees a correct solution.

Mental set	**Availability**
Functional fixedness	**Confirmation bias**
Brainstorming	**Framing**
Compensatory model	**Hindsight bias**
Representa-tiveness	**Counterfactual thinking**

A heuristic by which a judgment or decision is based on information that is most easily retrieved from memory.

The tendency to perceive and to approach problems in certain ways.

The tendency to look for evidence in support of a belief and to ignore evidence that would disprove a belief.

The tendency to perceive only a limited number of uses for an object, thus interfering with the process of problem solving.

The perspective from which we interpret information before making a decision.

A problem-solving strategy in which an individual or a group produces numerous ideas and evaluates them only after all ideas have been collected.

The tendency to see outcomes as inevitable and predictable after we know the outcome.

A rational decision-making model in which choices are systematically evaluated on various criteria.

Thinking about alternative realities and things that never happened.

A heuristic by which a new situation is judged on the basis of its resemblance to a stereotypical model.

Intelligence	**Wechsler Adult Intelligence Scale—3rd Ed. (WAIS-III)**
Triarchic theory of intelligence	**Wechsler Intelligence Scale for Children— 3rd Ed. (WISC-III)**
Theory of multiple intelligences	**Group tests**
Emotional intelligence	**Performance tests**
Intelligence quotient (IQ)	**Culture-fair tests**

An individual intelligence test developed especially for adults; measures both verbal and performance abilities.	A general term referring to the ability or abilities involved in learning and adaptive behavior.
An individual intelligence test developed especially for school-aged children; measures verbal and performance abilities and also yields an overall IQ score.	Sternberg's theory that intelligence involves mental skills (analytical intelligence), insight and creative adaptability (creative intelligence), and environmental responsiveness (practical intelligence).
Written intelligence tests administered by one examiner to many people at one time.	Howard Gardner's theory that there is not one intelligence, but rather many intelligences, each of which is relatively independent of the others.
Intelligence tests that minimize the use of language.	According to Goleman, a form of intelligence that refers to how effectively people perceive and understand their own emotions and the emotions of others, and can regulate and manage their emotional behavior.
Intelligence tests designed to eliminate cultural bias by minimizing skills and values that vary from one culture to another.	A numerical value given to intelligence that is determined from the scores on an intelligence test on the basis of a score of 100 for average intelligence.

Reliability	**Criterion-related validity**
Split-half reliability	**Mental retardation**
Correlation coefficients	**Giftedness**
Validity	**Creativity**
Content validity	

Validity of a test as measured by a comparison of the test score and independent measures of what the test is designed to measure.	Ability of a test to produce consistent and stable scores.
Condition of significantly subaverage intelligence combined with deficiencies in adaptive behavior.	A method of determining test reliability by dividing the test into two parts and checking the agreement of scores on both parts.
Refers to superior IQ combined with demonstrated or potential ability in such areas as academic aptitude, creativity, and leadership.	Statistical measures of the degree of association between two variables.
The ability to produce novel and socially valued ideas or objects.	Ability of a test to measure what it has been designed to measure.
	Refers to a test's having an adequate sample of questions measuring the skills or knowledge it is supposed to measure.

POSTTEST

After studying the text and completing the Study Guide activities, answer these questions to determine if you need to review any areas before the course exam.

MULTIPLE CHOICE

1. The three most important building blocks of thoughts are ____, _____, and ____.
   a. semantics, phonemes, and morphemes
   b. cognition, feelings, and language
   c. language, images, and concepts
   d. stream of consciousness, sensory register, and perception

2. Label the terms in correct order in the direction of movement in speech production and comprehension in the figure shown below.
   a. Phenomes
   b. Meaning
   c. Morphemes
   d. Sentences

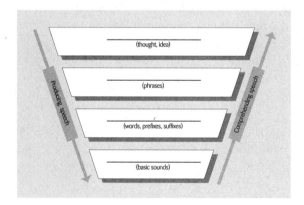

3. _____ consists of the language rules that determine how sounds and words can be combined and used to communicate meaning within a language.
   a. Semantics
   b. Syntax
   c. Morphemes
   d. Grammar

4. Most concepts that people use in thinking _____.
   a. accurately account for critical differences among various images
   b. depend on the magnitude of sensory memory
   c. allow them to generalize but not to think abstractly
   d. are fuzzy and overlap with one another

5. A mental model containing the most typical features of a concept is called a (n) ___.
   a. algorithm
   b. prototype
   c. stereotype
   d. description

6. The problem-solving methods that guarantee solutions if appropriate and properly followed are called _____.
   a. heuristics
   b. trial and error
   c. hill-climbing
   d. algorithm

7. The technique of ____ encourages people to generate a list of ideas without evaluation of those ideas.
   a. convergent thinking
   b. brainstorming
   c. circular thinking
   d. functional thinking

8. People sometimes make decisions based on information that is most easily retrieved from memory, even though this information may not be accurate. This process of decision making is called _____.
   a. compensatory model
   b. means-end analysis
   c. the availability heuristic
   d. functional analysis

9. The tendency to look for evidence in support of a belief and to ignore evidence that would disprove a belief is called _____.
   a. the confirmation bias
   b. means-end analysis
   c. the representativeness heuristic
   d. functional analysis

10. Spearman believed that specific mental abilities are _____ each other, and Thurstone believed that they are ___ each other.
    a. dependent on; dependent on
    b. dependent on; relatively independent of
    c. relatively independent of; dependent on
    d. relatively independent of; relatively independent of

11. Which of the following is NOT one of the three basic kinds of intelligence that comprises Sternberg's triarchic theory of intelligence?
    a. practical intelligence
    b. analytical intelligence
    c. naturalistic intelligence
    d. creative intelligence

12. Which of the following is NOT one of the types of intelligence described in Gardner's theory of multiple intelligences?
    a. practical intelligence
    b. interpersonal intelligence
    c. linguistic intelligence
    d. spatial intelligence

13. The Binet-Simon scale was originally developed to _____.
    a. identify gifted children
    b. identify children who might have difficulty in school
    c. measure the intelligence of normal children
    d. measure scholastic achievement

14. Wechsler hypothesized that adult intelligence:
    a. consists of the ability to solve problems
    b. consists solely of the ability to handle the environment
    c. consists more of the ability to solve problems than of the ability to handle the environment
    d. consists more of the ability to handle life situations than of skill in solving verbal and abstract problems.

15. Performance tests and culture-fair tests are similar in that they _____.
    a. focus on linguistic abilities
    b. are exclusively group tests
    c. minimize or eliminate the use of words
    d. focus only on mathematical and abstraction skills

16. The ability of a test to produce consistent and stable scores is its _____ while the ability of a test to measure what it sets out to measure is its _____.
    A. validity; reliability
    B. standard deviation; validity
    C. reliability; validity
    D. reliability; standard deviation

17. The largest program designed to improve educationally disadvantaged children's chances of school achievement is _____.
    a. the Milwaukee Project
    b. the Perry Preschool Program
    c. the Hobbs and Robinson Program
    d. the Head Start Program

18. Plomin's review of the literature on IQ led him to conclude that a person's IQ is about ___ percent the result of genetic factors and about ___ percent the result of environmental factors.
    a. 80; 20
    b. 70; 30
    c. 50; 50
    d. 30; 70

19. In the majority of cases, the cause of both mental retardation and giftedness is _____.
    a. clearly identified genetic abnormalities
    b. unknown
    c. poor prenatal nutrition
    d. financial status of the parents

20. Creative people are ___ than less creative people with equivalent IQ scores.
    a. more intelligent in their actual job performance
    b. perceived as being more intelligent
    c. less intelligent in their actual job performance
    d. perceived as being less intelligent

21. The type of thinking required to solve problems requiring a creative or flexible, or inventive solution is ____, and the type of thinking needed to solve problems requiring one or a few logically thought-out solutions is _____.
   a. functional thinking; circular thinking
   b. convergent thinking; divergent thinking
   c. divergent thinking; functional thinking
   d. divergent thinking; convergent thinking

22. Each of the following is a characteristic of emotional intelligence EXCEPT _____.
   a. knowing your emotions
   b. using your emotions to motivate yourself
   c. expressing your emotions
   d. managing relationships

23. Which of the following statements accurately reflects the Flynn Effect?
   a. Over the last several decades intelligence test scores have risen.
   b. Young children are less cognitively advanced today compared to 30 years ago.
   c. Compared to today's test scores, the gap in intelligence test scores between blacks and whites was narrower 30 years ago.
   d. Televisions, computers, and video games have caused increases in intelligence test scores.

24. Which of the following is true regarding mental retardation?
   a. Mental retardation is not based entirely on IQ.
   b. Savants can display exceptional skills in specialized areas.
   c. Mental retardation encompasses a vast array of mental deficits with a wide variety of causes, treatments, and outcomes.
   d. all of the above

25. Which of the following statements accurately reflects the criticism over IQ tests?
   a. Content of the tests is too broad and attempts to assess too many skills.
   b. Test scores are a very complex way of summing up a simple set of abilities.
   c. IQ tests only measure a person's ability at a certain point in time, but cannot explain reasons for a good or poor performance.
   d. Questions on IQ tests should reflect intelligence as a single entity that should be measured the same for each culture.

SHORT ESSAY QUESTIONS

1. Define language, phonemes, morphemes, semantics, syntax, and grammar and briefly discuss the role of each of them in the development of communications and language.

2. Identify and describe four tactics for improving your problem-solving abilities and discuss the advantages of each method.

3. Compare and contrast compensatory and noncompensatory models and discuss the roles of representativeness, availability, and the confirmation bias in decision making. Identify the strengths and weaknesses of each technique.

4. Explain "emotional intelligence." Identify the five traits of emotional intelligence.

5. Name at least three group IQ tests and three individual IQ tests. Explain the advantages and disadvantages of each.

6. Summarize current beliefs and research regarding the role of heredity and environment in intelligence. Include research on the effectiveness of intervention programs aimed at improving the academic performance of disadvantaged children.

7. Define creativity and discuss its relationship to intelligence. Identify four types of creativity tests and how they measure creativity.

Answers and Explanations to Multiple Choice Posttest

1. c. Thoughts are believed to be made up of language, images, and concepts. p. 217

2. Top to bottom: b. meaning; d. sentences; c. morphemes; a. phonemes Fig. 7–1; p. 219

3. d. The language rules that determine how to combine and use sounds and words to communicate are called grammar. p. 218

4. d. Most people use fuzzy, poorly defined, and overlapping concepts. p. 219

5. b. A prototype is a mental model containing representative features of a concept. p. 219

6. d. Algorithms are step-by-step problem-solving methods that guarantee a correct solution. p. 226

7. b. Brainstorming involves generating numerous ideas before evaluating them. p. 229

8. c. The availability heuristic relies on the information most easily retrieved from long-term memory. p. 232

9. a. Confirmation bias causes us to find evidence to support our beliefs. p. 236

10. b. Spearman believed that intelligence is generalized to specific mental abilities, while Thurstone believed they are relatively independent of each other. p. 236

11. c. Naturalistic intelligence is part of the theory of multiple intelligences advanced by Howard Gardner. p. 236

12. a. Practical intelligence is not a type of multiple intelligence. p 236

13. b. The Binet-Simon scale was developed in 1905 to identify children that might have difficulty in school. p. 237

14. d. Wechsler believed that adult intelligence is more concerned with the ability to handle life situations than excel at verbal or mathematical problems. p. 237

15. c. Both performance tests and culture-fair tests were designed to eliminate or minimize words and language. p. 238

16. c. Reliability measures a test's ability to produce stable, consistent scores; and validity effectively measures what a test has been designed to measure. p. 239

17. d. The Head Start Program is the largest program created to enrich disadvantaged children's educational opportunities. p. 245

18. c. Plomin found that heredity and environment almost equally contributed to human differences in intelligence. p. 245

19. b. As with mental retardation, the causes of giftedness are largely unknown. p. 249

20. b. Creative people are perceived as being more intelligent than their less creative but equivalent IQ score counterparts. p. 251

21. d. Divergent thinking reflects original, inventive, and flexible thinking; convergent thinking is directed towards finding one correct solution. p. 225

22. c. Expressing your emotions is NOT one of the five traits of emotional intelligence. p. 236

23. a. According to James Flynn, intelligence test scores have risen about 3 points per decade and increases in IQ may be as high as 6 points per decade. p. 246

24. d. All of the statements are true regarding mental retardation. pp. 248–249

25. c. Tests measure our ability at a certain point in time. Test scores do not tell us why someone performs poorly or well. p. 241

CHAPTER 8
Motivation and Emotion

CHAPTER OVERVIEW

The chapter opens with a detective story teaser that shows how motivation and emotion are so closely intertwined that drawing distinctions between them is difficult. A **motive** is a specific need or desire that arouses the organism and directs its behavior toward a goal, while **emotion** refers to the experience of feelings such as fear, joy, surprise, and anger. The heart of the chapter concerns the ways in which motives and emotions affect behavior and are affected by the external environment.

The idea that motivation is based on **instincts** was popular in the early 20th century but since has fallen out of favor. It has also been held that bodily needs create a state of tension or arousal called a **drive** (such as hunger or thirst), whereby human motivation is viewed as an effort toward **drive reduction** and **homeostasis**, or balance in the body. According to drive-reduction theory, drives can generally be divided into two categories: **primary drives**, which are unlearned, and **secondary drives**, which are acquired through learning.

Another perspective, reflected in **arousal theory**, suggests behavior stems from a desire to maintain an optimum level of arousal. However, psychologists agree that there is no "best level" of arousal necessary to perform all tasks—it is largely a question of degree. The **Yerkes–Dodson law** puts it this way: the more complex the task, the lower the level of arousal that can be tolerated before performance deteriorates.

Motivational inducements or incentives can originate from within (**intrinsic motivation**) or from outside (**extrinsic motivation**) the person. The effects of intrinsic motivation are greater and longer-lasting.

Abraham Maslow suggested human motives can be arranged in a **hierarchy of needs**, with primitive ones based on physical needs positioned at the bottom and higher ones such as self-esteem positioned toward the top. Maslow believed that the higher motives don't emerge until the more basic ones have been met, but recent research challenges his view.

The chapter turns to the subject of hunger and thirst. Hunger is regulated by several centers within the brain. These centers are stimulated by receptors that monitor blood levels of **glucose**, fats, and carbohydrates as well as the hormones **leptin** and **ghrelin**. Hunger is also stimulated by **incentives** such as cooking aromas and by emotional, cultural, and social factors.

Eating disorders, particularly **anorexia nervosa** and **bulimia nervosa**, are more prevalent among females than among males. They are characterized by extreme preoccupation with body image and weight. **Muscle dysmorphia** is a disorder generally seen among young men involving an obsession with muscle size leading to inordinate worry about diet and exercise. Another food-related problem, obesity, affects millions of Americans. Obesity has complex causes and negative consequences particularly for obese children, who are likely to have health problems as adults. **Set point theory** holds that our bodies are genetically predisposed to maintaining a certain weight by changing our metabolic rate and activity level in response to caloric intake. The chapter's *Applying Psychology* section offers a series of recommendations for weight control.

Next, the chapter focuses on the interaction between sex and motivation. Sex is a primary drive that gives rise to reproductive behavior essential for the survival of the species.

Although hormones such as **testosterone** are involved in human sexual responses, they don't play as dominant a role as they do in some other species. In humans, the brain exerts a powerful influence on the sex drive as well. The human **sexual response cycle**, which differs somewhat for males and females, has four stages—excitement, plateau, orgasm, and resolution.

Experience and learning affect preferences for sexually arousing stimuli. What is sexually attractive is also influenced by culture. Research suggests a more conservative pattern of sexual behavior in the United States than is portrayed in popular media.

Regarding **sexual orientation**, there are arguments for and against a biological explanation. People with a heterosexual orientation are sexually attracted to members of the opposite sex; those with a homosexual orientation are sexually attracted to members of their own sex. It is likely that both biological and environmental factors play a role in explaining homosexuality.

The chapter next examines other important motives, beginning with stimulus motives. Stimulus motives are less obviously associated with the survival of the organism or the species, although they often help humans adapt to their environments. **Stimulus motives**, such as the urge to explore and manipulate things, are associated with obtaining information about the world.

A gap in understanding may stimulate curiosity, motivating us to explore and, often, to change our environment.

Another important stimulus motive in humans and other primates is to seek various forms of tactile stimulation. The importance of contact has been demonstrated in nonhuman animal studies as well as in premature human infants.

Any behavior intended to inflict physical or psychological harm on others is an act of **aggression**. Some psychologists see aggression as an innate drive in humans that must be channeled to constructive ends, but others see it more as a learned response that is greatly influenced by modeling, norms, and values. Aggression differs markedly across cultures, supporting the latter view. Males generally are more inclined than females to strike out at others and commit acts of violence. This gender difference probably stems from an interaction of nature and nurture.

People who display a desire to excel, to overcome obstacles, and to accomplish difficult things well and quickly score high in **achievement motive**. Although hard work and a strong desire to master challenges both contribute to achievement, excessive competitiveness toward others can actually interfere with achievement.

The **affiliation motive**, or need to be with other people, is especially pronounced when we feel threatened or anxious. Affiliation with others in this situation can counteract fear and bolster spirits.

The chapter next shifts its focus toward the subject of emotions, and then concludes with a section on how emotions are communicated. Robert Plutchik's circular classification system for emotions encompasses eight basic emotions. But not all cultures categorize emotions this way. Some lack a word for emotion; others describe feelings as physical sensations. Cross-cultural research by Paul Ekman argues for the universality of at least six emotions—happiness, surprise, sadness, fear, disgust, and anger. Many psychologists add *love* to this list.

According to the **James–Lange theory**, environmental stimuli can cause physiological changes; and emotions then arise from our awareness of those changes. In contrast, the **Cannon–Bard theory** holds that emotions and bodily responses occur simultaneously. A third perspective, the **cognitive theory** of emotion, contends that our perceptions and judgments of situations are essential to our emotional experiences. Without these cognitions we would have no idea how to label our feelings. Not everyone agrees with this view, however, because emotions sometimes seem to arise too quickly to depend on mental evaluations. Counter to the cognitive view, C. E. Izard argues that certain inborn facial expressions and body postures are automatically triggered in emotion-arousing situations and are then "read" by the brain as particular feelings.

People express emotions verbally through words, tone of voice, exclamations, and other sounds. Facial expressions are the most obvious nonverbal indicators of emotion.

The amygdala and insula play an important role in our ability to correctly interpret facial expressions. Abnormalities in these brain circuits may be a factor in depression and unprovoked aggression.

Other indicators involve body language—our posture, the way we move, our preferred personal distance from others when talking to them, our degree of eye contact. Explicit acts, such as slamming a door, express emotions, too. People vary in their skill at reading these nonverbal cues.

Research confirms some gender differences in expressing and perceiving emotions. For instance, when confronted with a person in distress, women are more likely than men to express emotion, even though the levels of physiological arousal are the same for the two sexes. Also, being betrayed or criticized elicits more anger in men, versus more disappointment and hurt in women. Women are generally better than men at reading other people's emotions: decoding facial expressions, body cues, and tones of voice. This skill may be sharpened by their role as caretakers of infants and their traditional subordinate status to men.

Regardless of a person's cultural background, the facial expressions associated with certain basic emotions appear to be universal. This finding contradicts the culture-learning view, which suggests facial expressions of emotion are learned within a particular culture. This is not to say that there are no cultural differences in emotional expression, however. Overlaying the universal expression of certain emotions are culturally varying **display rules** that govern when it is appropriate to show emotion—to whom, by whom, and under what circumstances. Other forms of nonverbal communication of emotion vary more from culture to culture than facial expressions do.

LEARNING OBJECTIVES EXERCISE

After you have read and studied the chapter, you should be able to answer the following learning objectives.

PERSPECTIVES ON MOTIVATION

- Compare and contrast instincts, drive-reduction theory, and arousal theory (including the Yerkes-Dodson law) as explanations of human behavior. Distinguish between primary and secondary drives, intrinsic and extrinsic motivation, and summarize Maslow's hierarchy of motives.

HUNGER AND THIRST

- Identify the areas of the brain that are involved in hunger and describe the role of glucose, leptin, and ghrelin in determining a biological need for food. Distinguish between the biological need for food and the experience of hunger (including the role of incentives).

- List the symptoms that are used to diagnose anorexia nervosa, bulimia nervosa, muscle dysmorphia, and obesity. Describe the people who are most likely to develop these disorders and the most likely causes of them.

SEX

- Describe how sexual motivation is both similar to and different from other primary drives. Identify the factors (biological and nonbiological) that affect sexual motivation.

- Describe the sexual response cycle and how it differs for men and women. Briefly explain what is meant by the statement that "research indicates that the sex lives of most Americans differ significantly from media portrayals."

- Summarize the research evidence for and against a biological basis for sexual orientation.

OTHER IMPORTANT MOTIVES

- Briefly describe the major stimulus motives: exploration, curiosity, manipulation, and contact.

- Describe the role of learning as a determinant of aggression including evidence for gender and cultural differences in aggressive behavior.

- Identify the components of achievement behavior and the characteristics of people who are high in achievement motivation. Explain the factors that affect the affiliation motive and the likelihood that a person will express their need for affiliation.

EMOTIONS

- Discuss the evidence for a set of basic emotions that are experienced by all humans.

- Compare and contrast the James-Lange theory, Cannon-Bard theory, and cognitive theories of emotion.

COMMUNICATING EMOTION

- Explain the importance of facial expressions in communicating emotion and identify the areas of the brain that are responsible for interpreting facial expressions. Describe the role of body language, gestures, and personal space in communicating emotions.

- Summarize the research evidence regarding gender and cultural differences in emotion, the role of "display rules," and whether it is advantageous to express anger as opposed to "holding it in."

KEY TERMS

Achievement motive	The need to excel, to overcome obstacles. (p. 276)
Affiliation motive	The need to be with others. (p. 277)
Aggression	Behavior aimed at doing harm to others; also, the motive to behave aggressively. (p. 274)
Anorexia nervosa	A serious eating disorder that is associated with an intense fear of weight gain and a distorted body image. (p. 265)
Arousal theory	Theory of motivation that proposes that organisms seek an optimal level of arousal. (p. 260)
Bulimia nervosa	An eating disorder characterized by binges of eating followed by self-induced vomiting. (p. 266)
Cannon–Bard theory	States that the experience of emotion occurs simultaneously with biological changes. (p. 281)
Cognitive theory	States that emotional experience depends on one's perception or judgment of a situation. (p. 281)
Display rules	Culture-specific rules that govern how, when, and why expressions of emotion are appropriate. (p. 286)
Drive	State of tension or arousal that motivates behavior. (p. 260)
Drive-reduction theory	States that motivated behavior is aimed at reducing a state of bodily tension or arousal and returning the organism to homeostasis. (p. 260)
Emotion	Feeling, such as fear, joy, or surprise, that underlies behavior. (p. 259)
Extrinsic motivation	A desire to perform a behavior to obtain an external reward or avoid punishment. (p. 261)
Ghrelin	A hormone produced in the stomach and small intestines that increases appetite. (p. 264)
Glucose	A simple sugar used by the body for energy. (p. 264)
Hierarchy of needs	A theory of motivation advanced by Maslow holding that higher order motives involving social and personal growth only emerge after lower level motives related to survival have been satisfied. (p. 262)
Homeostasis	State of balance and stability in which the organism functions effectively. (p. 260)
Incentive	External stimulus that prompts goal-directed behavior. (p. 265)
Instincts	Inborn, inflexible, goal-directed behaviors that is characteristic of an entire species. (p. 259)
Intrinsic motivation	A desire to perform a behavior that stems from the enjoyment derived from the behavior itself. (p. 261)
James–Lange theory	States that stimuli cause physiological changes in our bodies, and emotions result from those physiological changes. (p. 280)
Leptin	A hormone released by fat cells that reduces appetite. (p. 264)
Motive	Specific need or desire, such as hunger, thirst, or achievement, that prompts goal-directed behavior. (p. 259)
Muscle dysmorphia	A disorder generally seen in young men involving an obsessive concern with muscle size. (p. 266)
Primary drives	Unlearned drive, such as hunger, that are based on a physiological state. (p. 260)
Secondary drives	Learned drives, such as ambition, that are not based on a physiological state. (p. 260)
Set point theory	A theory that our bodies are genetically predisposed to maintaining a certain weight by changing our metabolic rate and activity level in response to caloric intake. (p. 268)

Sexual orientation	Refers to the direction of one's sexual interest toward members of the same sex, the other sex, or both sexes. (p. 272)
Sexual response cycle	The typical sequence of events, including excitement, plateau, orgasm, and resolution, characterizing sexual response in males and females. (p. 270)
Stimulus motives	Unlearned motives, such as curiosity or contact, that prompt us to explore or change the world around us. (p. 273)
Testosterone	The primary male sex hormone. (p. 269)
Yerkes–Dodson law	States that there is an optimal level of arousal for the best performance of any task; the more complex the task, the lower the level of arousal that can be tolerated before performance deteriorates. (p. 260)

POSTTEST

After studying the text and completing the Study Guide activities, answer these questions to determine if you need to review any areas before the course exam.

MULTIPLE CHOICE

1. A (n) _____ is a need that pushes a person to work toward a specific goal.
   a. stimulus
   b. behavior
   c. incentive
   d. motive

2. A (n) _____ is an inborn, goal-directed behavior that is seen in an entire species.
   a. instinct
   b. drive
   c. motive
   d. stimulus

3. External stimuli that lead to goal-directed behavior are called _____.
   a. drives
   b. incentives
   c. needs
   d. reciprocals

4. All of the following are examples of primary drives EXCEPT _____.
   a. hunger
   b. money
   c. thirst
   d. affiliation

5. A desire to perform a behavior that originates within the individual is known as _____, while a desire to perform a behavior to obtain an external reward or avoid punishment is known as _____.
   a. primary motivation; secondary motivation
   b. intrinsic motivation; extrinsic motivation
   c. secondary motivation; primary motivation
   d. extrinsic motivation; intrinsic motivation

6. Increased _____ is the most effective way to increase the body's metabolism when trying to lose weight.
   a. protein consumption
   b. exercise
   c. reduction of calories
   d. sleep

7. A serious eating disorder that is associated with an intense fear of weight gain and a distorted body image is called _____.
   a. anorexia nervosa
   b. Karposi's anemia
   c. bulimia
   d. Huntington's chorea

8. An eating disorder characterized by binges of eating followed by self-induced vomiting or purging is called _____.
   a. anorexia nervosa
   b. Karposi's anemia
   c. bulimia
   d. Huntington's chorea

9. In Harlow's classic experiments, when the infant monkeys were frightened, they ran to a "surrogate mother" that offered _____.
   a. food and warmth
   b. food only
   c. warmth only
   d. warmth and closeness

10. Scents that can be sexually stimulating are called _____.
    a. androgens
    b. corticorsteroids
    c. globulins
    d. pheromones

11. The correct chronological order of the phases of the sexual response cycle is _____.
    a. resolution, excitement, plateau, orgasm
    b. excitement, resolution, orgasm, plateau
    c. plateau, excitement, orgasm, resolution
    d. excitement, plateau, orgasm, resolution

12. _____ are largely unlearned motives that push us to investigate, explore, and often change, the world around us.
    a. Primary drives
    b. Stimulus motives
    c. Secondary motives
    d. Achievement drives

13. Research indicates that ____ factors contribute to gender differences in aggressive behavior.
    a. neither biological nor social
    b. biological, but not social
    c. social, but not biological
    d. both social and biological

14. Which one of the following is NOT of the three separate, but interrelated aspects of achievement-oriented behavior identified by Helmrich and Spence?
    a. work-orientation
    b. curiosity
    c. mastery
    d. competitiveness

15. Label the correct sequential order of Maslow's hierarchy of motives from the most primitive to the most complex and human, using the following needs:
    a. belongingness
    b. esteem
    c. safety
    d. self- actualization
    e. physiological

16. The _____ theory of emotion states that the experience of emotion occurs simultaneously with biological changes.
    a. Cannon-Bard
    b. James-Lange
    c. Schacter-Singer
    d. cognitive

17. The belief that certain facial expressions represent similar emotions across all cultures is known as the _____ position.
    a. universalist
    b. fundamentalist
    c. culture-learning
    d. unidimensional

18. Which of the following is most likely to describe a high sensation seeker as opposed to a low sensation seeker?
    a. classified as an aggressive individual
    b. prefers team sports
    c. has varied sexual activities
    d. chooses high-paying careers

19. Which of the following statements is NOT true regarding biological factors that influence eating?
    a. Regions of the cerebellum and brainstem regulate eating.
    b. Regions of the hypothalamus, cortex, and spinal cord regulate eating.
    c. Changes in glucose, fats, and other substances in the blood signal the need for food.
    d. Presence of the hormone leptin influences eating.

20. Which of the following factors contributes to overeating and obesity in Americans?
    a. sedentary lifestyle
    b. genetics
    c. food availability
    d. All of the above

21. Which of the following statements is true regarding the affiliation motive?
    a. It is aroused when people feel safe or secure.
    b. It is closely tied to fear and anxiety.
    c. It stems from environmental factors alone.
    d. all of the above

SHORT ESSAY QUESTIONS

1. Discuss Harlow's experiments with infant monkeys and "surrogate mothers." Discuss the need for contact and whether or not it is universal and applies to other organisms besides humans. How do Harlow's findings generalize to human infant development of attachment?

2. Discuss the most effective methods for losing weight and maintaining the weight loss. Provide the Five Steps for Losing Weight outlined in the text.

3. Compare and contrast verbal and nonverbal communication in expressing emotion. Give at least three examples of nonverbal communication and how each assists in sending an emotional message. Explain why some people may not be willing or able to report their emotions verbally.

4. Identify and discuss the different types of sexual coercion. Describe what factors contribute to sexual coercion (i.e., motivation of the perpetrator) and the impact it has on the victims.

5. Discuss the characteristics of the stimulus motives of activity, exploration, curiosity, manipulation, and contact. Provide an example of each and discuss how they may contribute to changes in behavior and society.

Answers and Explanations to Multiple Choice Posttest

1. d. Motives are needs that push people to work toward specific goals. p. 259

2. a. Instincts are inborn, goal-directed behavior seen in an entire species. p. 259

3. b. Incentives are external stimuli that lead to goal-directed behavior. p. 265

4. b. Primary drives are basic needs we are born with, such as hunger, thirst, sexual drive, and comfort. p. 260

5. b. Intrinsic motivation originates with the individual, and extrinsic motivation originates from the desire to obtain an external reward. p. 261

6. b. Exercise is the best way to prevent metabolism from dropping when dieting. p. 268

7. a. Anorexia nervosa is a serious eating disorder associated with intense fear of weight gain and a distorted body image. p. 265

8. c. Bulimia is an eating disorder characterized by eating and purging binges. p. 266

9. d. The surrogate mothers chosen by the infant monkeys offered warmth and closeness. p. 274

10. d. Pheromones are sexually stimulating scents produced by the body. p. 269

11. d. The correct chronological order of the sexual response cycle is: excitement, plateau, orgasm, and resolution. p. 270

12. b. Stimulus motives are unlearned motives that push us to investigate and explore. p. 273

13. d. Both sociological and biological factors contribute to gender differences in aggressive behavior. p. 276

14. b. Curiosity is NOT one of the achievement-oriented behavioral aspects. pp. 276–277

15. Maslow's hierarchy of motives from primitive to complex is: e. physiological; c. safety; a. belongingness; b. esteem, and d. self-actualization. p. 262, Fig. 8–2

16. b. The James-Lange theory of emotions states emotion and biological changes occur simultaneously. p. 280

17. a. The universalist position holds that certain facial expressions represent similar emotions across all cultures. p. 285; Fig. 8–9 on p. 280

18. c. High sensation seekers are more likely to have more sexual partners and engage in more varied sexual activities. p. 261

19. a. All of the other statements are true. p. 264

20. d. All of the factors contribute to overeating and obesity. p. 267

21. b. Fear and anxiety are closely tied to the affiliation motive. p. 277

CHAPTER 9

Life-Span Development

CHAPTER OVERVIEW

The chapter begins with a look at the life arc of Barack Obama as a fascinating example of both continuity and change, setting the stage for an examination of **developmental psychology**, the study of changes that occur in people from birth through old age. **Cross-sectional studies** involve studying different age groups of people at the same time, whereas **longitudinal studies** involve the same group of individuals at different times in their lives. Longitudinal studies are more time consuming, but do account for **cohort** differences in the typical experiences of members of different generations. **Biographical**, or **retrospective**, **studies** involve reconstructing a person's past through interviews.

The chapter focuses next on **prenatal development**, and how an organism or another substance can cause devastating effects at one point in the process, but not at others. The period of development from conception to birth is called prenatal development. During this time, **teratogens**—disease-producing organisms or potentially harmful substances, such as drugs—can pass through the placenta and cause irreparable harm to the **embryo** or **fetus**. This harm is greatest if the drug or other substance is introduced at the same time that some major developmental process is occurring. If the same substance is introduced outside this **critical period**, little or even no harm may result. Pregnant women who consume alcohol may give birth to a child with **fetal alcohol spectrum disorder (FASD)**.

The chapter continues from prenatal development into an exploration of the world of the newborn. Although **neonates** (newborn babies) appear helpless, they are much more competent and aware than they seem. Newborns see and hear, are capable of reflexive

behavior, and are distinctly unique in their underlying temperaments.

Certain reflexes are critical to survival. For instance, the *rooting reflex* causes newborns, when touched on the cheek, to turn their head in that direction and locate a nipple with their mouths. Nursing is further facilitated by the *sucking reflex*, which causes newborns to suck on anything placed in their mouth, and the *swallowing reflex*, which enables them to swallow liquids without choking.

Babies are born with individual differences in personality, or **temperament** differences. Often a baby's temperament remains quite stable over time due to a combination of genetic and environmental influences, but stability in temperament is not inevitable. Your own temperament may be both similar to and different from the temperament you displayed as a newborn.

All of a baby's senses are functioning at birth: sight, hearing, taste, smell, and touch. Newborns seem particularly adept at discriminating speech sounds, suggesting their hearing is quite keen. Their least developed sense is probably vision, which takes 6 to 8 months to become as good as the average college student's.

The chapter progresses with a lengthy and detailed discussion of infancy and childhood. During the first dozen years of life, a helpless infant becomes a competent older child. This transformation encompasses many important kinds of changes, including physical, motor, cognitive, and social developments.

During the first 3 years of life, there are rapid increases in the number of connections between neurons in the brain, the speed of conduction between neurons, and the density of synaptic connections. Beginning in the third year of life, both the number and density of synaptic connections decreases markedly as unused neurons are removed.

Growth of the body is most rapid during the first year, with the average baby growing approximately 10 inches and gaining about 15 pounds. It then slows down considerably until early adolescence. When growth does occur, it happens suddenly—almost overnight—rather than through small, steady changes.

Babies tend to reach the major milestones in early motor development at similar ages. The average ages are called *developmental norms*. Those who are somewhat ahead of their peers are not necessarily destined for athletic greatness. Motor development that is slower or faster than the norm tells us little or nothing about a child's future characteristics. **Maturation**, the biological process that leads to developmental changes, also is shaped by experiences with the environment.

According to Jean Piaget, children undergo qualitative cognitive changes as they grow older. During the **sensory-motor stage** (birth to age 2), children acquire **object permanence**, the understanding that things continue to exist even when they are out of sight. In the **preoperational stage** (ages 2 to 7), they become increasingly adept at using **mental representations**; and language assumes an important role in describing, remembering, and reasoning about the world. They are **egocentric** in that they have difficulty appreciating others' viewpoints. Children in the **concrete-operational stage** (ages 7 to 11) are able to pay attention to more than one factor at a time, grasp **principles of conservation**, and can understand someone else's point of view. Finally, in the **formal-operational stage** (adolescence through adulthood), teenagers acquire the ability to think abstractly and test ideas mentally using logic. Not all psychologists agree with Piaget's theory, however.

Lawrence Kohlberg's stage theory of cognition focused exclusively on moral thinking. He proposed that children at different levels of moral reasoning base their moral choices on different factors: first, a concern about physical consequences, next, a concern about what other people think, and finally a concern about abstract principles. One problem with this view is that it doesn't consider how cultural values (associated with being female, African American, Japanese, and so on) may affect moral development.

Language begins with cooing and progresses to **babbling**, the repetition of speechlike sounds. The first word is usually uttered at 12 months. During the next 6 to 8 months, children build a vocabulary of one-word sentences called **holophrases**. Chomsky proposed that children are born with a **language acquisition device**, an innate mechanism that enables them to build a vocabulary, master the rules of grammar, and form intelligible sentences. According to Steven Pinker, human beings have a language instinct. Shaped by natural selection, this language instinct is hardwired into our brains, predisposing infants and young children to focus on the relevant aspects of speech and attach meaning to words. Young children learn a second language more quickly and speak it more fluently than adults.

Parents can help their children become both securely attached and independent. Developing a sense of independence is just one of the tasks that children face in their social development. During the toddler period, a growing awareness of being a separate person makes developing some **autonomy** from parents a very important issue. Parents can encourage independence in their children by allowing them to make choices and do things on their own within a framework of reasonable and consistently enforced limits. Another major task during this period is forming a secure **attachment**, or emotional bond, with other people. Young animals of many species form a strong bond to the first moving object they see, a process known as **imprinting**. In contrast, human newborns only gradually form emotional bonds with their caregivers. Some of the other important tasks during infancy and early childhood include overcoming **stranger anxiety**, trusting other people (infancy), learning to take initiative in tackling new tasks (the preschool years), and mastering some of the many skills that will be needed in adulthood (middle and later childhood). Parenting style affects children's behavior and self-image. The most successful parenting style is authoritative, in which parents provide firm guidance but are willing to listen to the child's opinions. However, parents do not act the same way toward every child in the family because children are different from each other and elicit different parental responses. The **nonshared environment** refers to the unique aspects of the environment that are experienced differently by siblings even though they are reared in the same family.

Socialization, the process by which children learn their cultures' behaviors and attitudes, is an important task of childhood. As children get older, they develop a deeper understanding of the meaning of friendship and come under the influence of a **peer group**.

By age 3, a child has developed a **gender identity**, a girl's knowledge that she is a girl and a boy's knowledge the he is a boy. But children of this age have little idea of what it means to be a particular gender. By 4 or 5, most children develop **gender constancy**, the realization that gender depends on what kind of genitals one has and cannot be changed. Children develop **sex-typed behavior**, or behavior appropriate to their gender, through a process of **gender-role awareness** and the formation of **gender stereotypes** reflected in their culture.

Watching television and playing video games can be worthwhile when the programs or games have an educational context and provide positive role models. However, TV and video games also reduce the time children could spend on other positive activities. When TV and video games contain aggressive content and negative role models, they can encourage aggressive behavior.

The chapter continues through the life span by exploring adolescence. The **growth spurt** is a rapid increase in height and weight that begins, on average, at about age 10 1/2 in girls and 12 1/2 in boys, and reaches its peak at age 12 in girls and 14 in boys. These physical changes of adolescence are just part of the transformation that occurs during this period. The child turns into an adult, not only physically, but also cognitively, socially, and emotionally.

Signs of **puberty**—the onset of sexual maturation—begins around 11 1/2 in boys. In girls, **menarche**, the first menstrual period, occurs at 12 1/2 for the average American girl. But individuals vary widely in when they go through puberty. Very early maturing girls like the admiration they get from other girls, but dislike the embarrassing sexual attention given to them by boys. Boys who mature early do better in sports and in social activities and receive greater respect from their peers.

In terms of cognitive development, teenagers often reach the level of *formal operational thought*, in which they can reason abstractly and speculate about alternatives. These newfound abilities may make them overconfident that their own ideas are right, turning adolescence into a time of cognitive egocentrism.

Identity formation is the process in which a person develops a stable sense of self. Identity formation usually follows an intense period of self-exploration called an **identity crisis**. In Erik Erikson's theory, *identity versus role confusion* is the major challenge of this period. Most adolescents rely on a peer group for social and emotional support, often rigidly conforming to the values of their friends. From small unisex **cliques** in early adolescence, friendship groups change to mixed-sex groups in which short-lived romantic interests are common. Later, stable dating patterns emerge. Parent–child relationships may become temporarily rocky during adolescence as teenagers become aware of their parents' faults and question parental rules.

Developmental problems often emerge for the first time during adolescence. A sizable number of adolescents think about committing suicide; a much smaller number attempt it; however, suicide is the third leading cause of death among adolescents. Statistics reflect a common decline in self-esteem during adolescence, especially among girls.

Emerging out of adolescence, the chapter turns its attention to adulthood. Reaching developmental milestones in adulthood is much less predictable than in earlier years; it is much more a function of the individual's decisions, circumstances, and even luck. Still, certain experiences and changes eventually take place and nearly every adult tries to fulfill certain needs.

Almost every adult forms a long-term loving partnership with at least one other adult at some point in life. According to Erik Erikson, the task of finding intimacy versus being isolated and lonely is especially important during young adulthood. Erikson believed that people are not ready for love until they have formed a firm sense of identity.

The vast majority of adults is moderately or highly satisfied with their jobs and would continue to work even if they didn't need to do so for financial reasons. Balancing the demands of job and family is often difficult, however, especially for women, because they tend to have most of the responsibility for housework and child care. Yet despite this stress of a "double shift," a job outside the home is a positive, self-esteem–boosting factor in most women's lives.

An adult's thinking is more flexible and practical than that of an adolescent. Whereas adolescents search for the one "correct" solution to a problem, adults realize that there may be several "right" solutions—or none at all. Adults also place less faith in authority than adolescents do.

Certain broad patterns of personality change occur in adulthood. As people grow older, they tend to become less self-centered and more comfortable in interpersonal relationships. They also develop better coping skills and new ways of adapting. By middle age, many adults feel an increasing commitment to, and responsibility for, others. This suggests that many adults are successfully meeting what Erik Erikson saw as the major challenge of middle adulthood: *generativity* (the ability to continue being productive and creative, especially in ways that guide and encourage future generations) *versus stagnation* (a sense of boredom or lack of fulfillment, sometimes called a **midlife crisis**). Most adults, however, do not experience dramatic upheaval in their middle years, so this period may be better thought of as one of **midlife transition**.

Middle adulthood brings a decline in the functioning of the reproductive organs. In women, this is marked by **menopause**, the cessation of menstruation, accompanied by a sharp drop in estrogen levels. Although hormone-replacement therapy can alleviate some negative symptoms (such as thinning bones and "hot flashes"), it is associated with cancer and heart risks; thus, women should seek medical advice and supervision. Men experience a slower decline in testosterone levels.

The chapter concludes with a section on late adulthood and the many changes it brings, including coping with the end of life. Over the past century, life expectancy in America has increased mainly because of improved health care and nutrition. There is, however, a sizable gender gap, with women living an average of 5.2 years longer than men. There is also a sizable racial gap, with White Americans living an average of 5 years longer than Blacks.

The physical changes of late adulthood affect outward appearance and the functioning of every organ. We don't yet know why these changes happen. Perhaps our genes program cells to eventually deteriorate and die, or perhaps genetic instructions simply degrade over time. Another possible explanation is that body parts wear out after repeated use, with environmental toxins contributing to the wearing-out process. Whatever the reason, physical aging is inevitable, although it can be slowed by a healthy lifestyle.

Most older adults have an independent lifestyle and engage in activities that interest them. Although their sexual responses may be slowed, most continue to enjoy sex beyond the seventies. Still, gradual social changes occur in late adulthood. Older adults start to interact with fewer people and perform fewer social roles. They may also become less influenced by social rules and expectations. Realizing that there is a limit to the capacity for social involvement, they learn to live with some restrictions.

The aging mind works a little more slowly and certain kinds of memories are more difficult to store and retrieve, but these changes are generally not extensive enough to interfere with most everyday tasks. Healthy older adults who engage in intellectually stimulating activities usually maintain a high level of mental functioning, unless they develop a condition such as **Alzheimer's disease**, a progressive neurological condition characterized by losses of memory and cognition and changes in personality.

Most elderly people fear death less than younger people fear it. They do fear the pain, indignity, depersonalization, and loneliness associated with a terminal illness. They also worry about becoming a financial burden to their families. The death of a spouse may be the most severe challenge that the elderly face. Kübler-Ross described a sequence of five stages that people go through when they are dying: *denial, anger, bargaining, depression,* and *acceptance.*

LEARNING OBJECTIVES EXERCISE

After you have read and studied the chapter, you should be able to answer the following learning objectives.

METHODS IN DEVELOPMENTAL PSYCHOLOGY

- Describe cross-sectional, longitudinal, and retrospective research methods including the advantages and disadvantages of each.

PRENATAL DEVELOPMENT

- Explain how toxic agents, diseases, and maternal stress can affect an unborn child. Include the concept of *critical period* in your explanation.

THE NEWBORN

- Summarize the reflexes and perceptual abilities of newborns. Describe the four basic temperaments that are visible at birth, the extent to which those inborn temperaments remain stable over time, and the reasons for both stability and change.

INFANCY AND CHILDHOOD

- Describe how the human brain changes during infancy and early childhood. Summarize the course of physical and motor development in childhood.

- Describe Piaget's stages of cognitive development and Kohlberg's stages of moral development and summarize the criticisms of each. Describe the course of language development in childhood. Compare and contrast the views of Skinner, Chomsky, and Pinker regarding language development.

- Distinguish *imprinting* from *attachment*. Describe the nature of parent–child relationships in the first 12 years of life with specific reference to Erikson's stages of development. Describe how peer relationships develop during childhood and the importance of *non-shared environments*.

- Distinguish *gender identity*, *gender constancy*, *gender-role awareness*, and *gender stereotypes*. Describe *sex-typed behavior* including the extent to which biology and experience shape sex-typed behavior.

- Summarize the research on the effects of television and video games on children.

ADOLESCENCE

- Describe the physical and cognitive changes that occur during adolescence.

- Summarize the research on whether adolescence is, indeed, a period of "storm and stress" for most teenagers. In your discussion include *identity achievement, identity foreclosure, moratorium, identity diffusion,* relationships with both peers and parents, self-esteem, depression, and violence.

ADULTHOOD

- Explain Erikson's concept of *intimacy versus isolation* in young adulthood, the kinds of partnerships that adults form, parenthood, and the difficulties of ending intimate relationships.

- Describe gender differences in the world of work and the demands of dual-career families.

- Describe the changes and challenges of midlife including Erikson's notion of *generativity versus stagnation* and the concept of *midlife crisis* as opposed to *midlife transition.*

LATE ADULTHOOD

- Describe the factors that affect life expectancy, the physical changes that occur in late adulthood, and the possible reasons for those physical changes. Include in your description an answer to the question "What kind of lifestyle and sex life can be expected after age 65?"

- Describe Kübler-Ross's stages of dying and the criticisms of her model. Discuss the burden of widowhood and whether it falls more heavily on men or women.

CHAPTER OUTLINE

I. Enduring Issues in Life-Span Development (page 291)
- Individual Characteristics vs. Shared Human Traits
- Stability vs. Change
- Heredity vs. Environment

II. Methods in Developmental Psychology (page 292)
- Cross-sectional
- Longitudinal
- Biographical or Retrospective

III. Prenatal Development (page 293)
- Embryo
- Critical Period
- Fetus
- Teratogens

IV. The Newborn (page 295)
- A. Reflexes
  - Rooting, Sucking, Grasping, Stepping Reflexes
- B. Temperament
  - Hereditary Factors
  - Prenatal Factors
- C. Perceptual Abilities
  - i. Vision
  - ii. Depth Perception
  - iii. Other Senses

V. Infancy and Childhood (page 298)
- A. Neurological Development
  - Synaptic Density
- B. Physical Development
  - Body Proportions at Various Ages
- C. Motor Development
  - Maturation
- D. Cognitive Development
  - i. Sensory-Motor Stage (Birth to 2 Years)
  - ii. Preoperational Stage (2 to 7 Years)
  - iii. Concrete-Operational Stage (7 to 11 Years)
  - iv. Formal-Operational Stage (Adolescence Through Adulthood)
  - v. Criticisms of Piaget's Theory
- E. Moral Development
  - Preconventional Level
  - Conventional Level
  - Postconventional Level
- F. Language Development
  - i. Theories of Language Development
  - ii. Bilingualism
- G. Social Development
  - i. Parent–Child Relationships in Infancy: Development of Attachment
  - ii. Parent–Child Relationships In Childhood
  - iii. Relationships with Other Children
  - iv. Non-shared Environments
- H. Sex-Role Development
  - Gender Identity and Constancy
  - Gender-role Awareness
  - Sex-typed Behavior
- I. Television, Video Games, and Children
  - Educational Video Games

VI. Adolescence (page 314)
- A. Physical Changes
  - i. Sexual Development
  - ii. Early and Late Developers
  - iii. Adolescent Sexual Activity
  - iv. Teenage Pregnancy and Childbearing
- B. Cognitive Changes
  - Formal-operational Thought
- C. Personality and Social Development
  - i. How "Stormy and Stressful" is Adolescence?
  - ii. Forming an Identity
  - iii. Relationships with Peers
  - iv. Relationships with Parents
- D. Some Problems of Adolescence
  - i. Declines in Self-Esteem
  - ii. Depression and Suicide
  - iii. Youth Violence

VII. Adulthood (page 319)
- A. Love, Partnerships, and Parenting
  - i. Forming Partnerships
  - ii. Parenthood
  - iii. Ending a Relationship

KEY TERMS

Alzheimer's disease	A neurological disorder, most commonly found in late adulthood, characterized by progressive losses in memory and cognition and by changes in personality. (p. 327)
Attachment	Emotional bond that develops in the first year of life that makes human babies cling to their caregivers for safety and comfort. (p. 307)
Autonomy	Sense of independence; a desire not to be controlled by others. (p. 309)
Babbling	A baby's vocalizations, consisting of repetition of consonant–vowel combinations. (p. 305)
Biographical (or retrospective) study	A method of studying developmental changes by reconstructing a person's past through interviews and inferring the effects of past events on current behaviors. (p. 293)
Cliques	Groups of adolescents with similar interests and strong mutual attachment. (p. 317)
Cohort	A group of people born during the same period in historical time. (p. 293)
Concrete-operational stage	In Piaget's theory, the stage of cognitive development between 7 and 11 years of age in which the individual can attend to more than one thing at a time and understand someone else's point of view, though thinking is limited to concrete matters. (p. 302)
Critical period	A time when certain internal and external influences have a major effect on development; at other periods, the same influences will have little or no effect. (p. 294)
Cross-sectional study	A method of studying developmental changes by comparing people of different ages at about the same time. (p. 293)
Developmental psychology	The study of the changes that occur in people from birth through old age. (p. 292)
Egocentric	Unable to see things from another's point of view. (p. 302)
Embryo	A developing human between 2 weeks and 3 months after conception. (p. 293)
Fetal alcohol spectrum disorder (FASD)	A disorder that occurs in children of women who drink alcohol during pregnancy; this disorder is characterized by facial deformities, heart defects, stunted growth, brain damage and cognitive impairments. (p. 294)
Fetus	A developing human between 3 months after conception and birth. (p. 294)
Formal-operational stage	In Piaget's theory, the stage of cognitive development beginning about 11 years of age in which the individual becomes capable of abstract thought. (p. 303)
Gender constancy	The realization that gender does not change with age. (p. 311)
Gender identity	A little girl's knowledge that she is a girl, and a little boy's knowledge that he is a boy. (p. 311)
Gender stereotypes	General beliefs about characteristics that men and women are presumed to have. (p. 312)
Gender-role awareness	Knowledge of what behavior is appropriate for each gender. (p. 312)
Growth spurt	A rapid increase in height and weight that occurs during adolescence. (p. 314)
Holophrases	One-word sentences commonly used by children under 2 years of age. (p. 305)
Identity crisis	A period of intense self-examination and decision making; part of the process of identity formation. (p. 316)
Identity formation	Erickson's term for the development of a stable sense of self necessary to make the transition from dependence on others to dependence on oneself. (p. 316)
Imprinting	The tendency in certain species to follow the first moving thing (usually its mother) it sees after it is born or hatched. (p. 307)

Language acquisition device	A hypothetical neural mechanism for acquiring language that is presumed to be "wired into" all humans. (p. 306)
Longitudinal studies	The portion of memory that is more or less permanent, corresponding to everything we "know." (p. 293)
Maturation	An automatic biological unfolding of development in an organism as a function of the passage of time. (p. 300)
Menarche	First menstrual period. (p. 314)
Menopause	The time in a woman's life when menstruation ceases. (p. 324)
Mental representations	Mental images or symbols (such as words) used to think about or remember an object, a person, or an event. (p. 302)
Midlife crisis	A time when adults discover they no longer feel fulfilled in their jobs or personal lives and attempt to make a decisive shift in career or lifestyle. (p. 323)
Midlife transition	According to Levinson, a process whereby adults assess the past and formulate new goals for the future. (p. 323)
Neonates	Newborn babies. (p. 295)
Non-shared environment	The unique aspects of the environment that are experienced differently by siblings, even though they are reared in the same family. (p. 311)
Object permanence	The concept that things continue to exist even when they are out of sight. (p. 302)
Peer group	A network of same-aged friends and acquaintances who give one another emotional and social support. (p. 310)
Prenatal development	Development from conception to birth. (p. 293)
Preoperational stage	In Piaget's theory, the stage of cognitive development between 2 and 7 years of age in which the individual becomes able to use mental representations and language to describe, remember, and reason about the world, though only in an egocentric fashion. (p. 302)
Principles of conservation	The concept that the quantity of a substance is not altered by reversible changes in its appearance. (p. 303)
Puberty	The onset of sexual maturation, with accompanying physical development. (p. 314)
Sensory-motor stage	In Piaget's theory, the stage of cognitive development between birth and 2 years of age in which the individual develops object permanence and acquires the ability to form mental representations. (p. 302)
Sex-typed behavior	Socially prescribed ways of behaving that differ for boys and girls. (p. 312)
Socialization	Process by which children learn the behaviors and attitudes appropriate to their family and culture. (p. 309)
Stranger anxiety	Fear of unfamiliar people which usually emerges around 7 months, reaching its peak at 12 months and declining during the second year. (p. 308)
Temperament	Characteristic patterns of emotional reactions and emotional self-regulation. (p. 295)
Teratogens	Toxic substances such as alcohol or nicotine that cross the placenta and may result in birth defects. (p. 294)

POSTTEST

After studying the text and completing the Study Guide activities, answer these questions to determine if you need to review any areas before the course exam.

MULTIPLE CHOICE

1. Times when certain internal and external influences have a major impact on development, whereas at other times those same influences would have little impact, are called _____.
   a. developmental surges
   b. growth stages
   c. critical periods
   d. latency period

2. The term used by psychologists to describe the physical/emotional characteristics of the newborn child and young infant is _____.
   a. cognitive capacity
   b. temperament
   c. maturity
   d. development

3. People born during the same period of historical time are called _____.
   a. a cohort
   b. a cross-sectional group
   c. clique
   d. a peerage

4. Children have developed a capacity for self-recognition by the end of the ___ stage.
   a. concrete operations
   b. preoperational
   c. sensory motor
   d. formal operations

5. A characteristic that first shows up in the formal operations stage is ___.
   a. irreversibility
   b. abstract thinking
   c. egocentrism
   d. logical thinking

6. The _____ process teaches children what behaviors and attitudes are appropriate in their family, friendships, and culture.
   a. attachment
   b. socialization
   c. imprinting
   d. anthropomorphism

7. Authoritative parents are to ____ children as permissive parents are to ____ children.
   a. Distrustful; assertive
   b. Self-reliant; dependent
   c. passive; assertive
   d. distrustful; dependent

8. The onset of sexual maturation in adolescence is known as ____.
   a. the growth spurt
   b. maturation
   c. atrophy
   d. puberty

9. According to Erikson, developing a stable sense of self and making the transition from dependence on others to dependence on oneself is called _____.
   a. self-actualization
   b. identity formation
   c. the personal fable
   d. identity diffusion

10. The low point of parent-child relationships usually occurs in _____.
    a. late childhood
    b. early adolescence
    c. mid-adolescence
    d. late adolescence

11. When adolescents are asked what they MOST dislike about themselves, they are most likely to say they dislike their _____.
    a. personality
    b. social status
    c. physical appearance
    d. lack of control over their life

12. Suicide is the ____ leading cause of death among adolescents.
    a. second
    b. third
    c. fourth
    d. fifth

13. Couples who lived together before getting married are ___ satisfied with their marriages and ___ likely to get divorced.
    a. less; less
    b. less; more
    c. more; less
    d. more; more

14. The major turning point in most adults' lives is _____.
    a. getting their first job
    b. buying their first house
    c. dealing with aging parents
    d. having and raising children

15. A time when some adults discover they no longer feel fulfilled in their jobs or personal lives and attempt to make a decisive shift in career or lifestyle is called _____.
    a. empty nest
    b. midlife transition
    c. midlife crisis syndrome
    d. life review

16. The majority of older adults are _____.
    a. impotent and incapable of sexual response
    b. uninterested in sex
    c. sexually active
    d. none of the above

17. Older people who were often labeled as "senile" in the past, were most likely suffering from _____.
    a. normal aging
    b. Parkinson's disease
    c. Huntington's disease
    d. Alzheimer's disease

18. Kübler-Ross describes the sequence of stages of dying as _____.
    a. anger, denial, depression, bargaining, acceptance
    b. denial, anger, bargaining, depression, acceptance
    c. denial, bargaining, depression, anger, acceptance
    d. anger, bargaining, depression, denial, acceptance

19. Studies of teenage killers have found that most of the killers had _____ experience with guns.
    a. virtually no
    b. little
    c. moderate
    d. extensive

SHORT ESSAY QUESTIONS

1. Define developmental psychology and discuss some limitations of the methods used to study development.

2. Describe prenatal, infancy, and child development.

3. What are the four stages of Piaget's theory of cognitive development?

4. Trace language development from infancy through age 5 or 6.

5. Explain the importance of secure attachments between a caregiver and child.

6. Explain how sex-role identity is formed.

7. Summarize the important physical and cognitive changes that the adolescent undergoes during puberty.

8. Discuss the four problems of adolescence: self-esteem, depression, suicide, and eating disorders.

9. Distinguish between the longitudinal and cross-sectional methods as they relate to the study of adulthood. List the disadvantages of the methods and how the disadvantages can be overcome.

10. Identify the central concerns and crises that characterize the young, middle, and late adulthood stages. Explain moral development.

11. Identify Elisabeth Kübler-Ross's five sequential stages through which people pass as they react to their own impending death.

Answers and Explanations to Multiple Choice Posttest

1. c. The critical period is when certain internal and external influences have a major impact on development and little impact at other times. p. 293

2. b. Temperament refers to the physical and emotional characteristics of the newborn and infant. p. 295

3. a. Cohort refers to a group of people born during the same historical period of time. p. 293

4. c. By the end of the sensory motor stage, Piaget said most toddlers have a capacity for self-recognition and can identify "myself" in the mirror. p. 302

5. b. Abstract thinking first shows up in the formal operations stage, usually in adolescence. p. 303

6. b. The socialization process teaches children socially appropriate behaviors and attitudes. p. 309

7. b. Authoritative parents are to self-reliant children as permissive parents are to dependent children. p. 310

8. d. Puberty is the onset of sexual maturation in adolescence. p. 314

9. b. Erikson termed identity formation as the time when young people make the transition from dependence on others to self-dependency. p. 316

10. b. The low point in parent-child relationships is usually in early adolescence when physical changes are occurring. p. 317

11. c. Adolescents tend to dislike their physical appearance more than anything else about themselves, leading to low self-esteem and possible eating disorders. p. 317

12. b. Suicide is the third leading cause of death among teens, after accidents and homicides. p. 318

13. b. Couples who cohabitated before marriage are less satisfied and more likely to divorce. They may have been more tentative about the relationship to begin with. p. 320

14. d. Having and raising children is the major turning point in most adults' lives due to increased duty, obligation, time, and energy involved. p. 320

15. c. The midlife crisis is a time when some adults discover a lack of fulfillment and attempt to make a radical shift in their career or lifestyle. p. 323

16. c. The majority of older adults are sexually active. p. 327

17. d. Alzheimer's disease used to be considered rare; however, now it is considered what was labeled 'senile' in the past. p. 327

18. b. Kübler-Ross's five stages of accepting one's approaching death as: denial, anger, bargaining, depression, and acceptance. p. 328

19. d. Killer kids were found to have extensive experience with guns and easy access to them. p. 318

CHAPTER 10 Personality

CHAPTER OVERVIEW

The chapter opens with the account of troubled physician Jaylene Smith, framing the chapter with the kind of intriguing questions about personality that psychologists like to ask and answer. **Personality** refers to an individual's unique pattern of thoughts, feelings, and behaviors that persists over time and across situations. Key to this definition is the concept of distinctive differences among individuals and the concept of personality's stability and endurance.

The chapter next moves to the topic of psychodynamic theories. *Psychodynamic theories* of personality consider behavior to be the transformation and expression of psychic energy within the individual. Often these psychological dynamics are **unconscious** processes.

According to Freud, personality is made of three structures. The **id**, the only personality structure present at birth, operates in the unconsciousness according to the **pleasure principle**. The **ego**, operating at the conscious level according to the **reality principle**, controls all conscious thinking and reasoning. The **superego** acts as the moral guardian or conscience helping the person function in society by comparing the ego's actions with the **ego ideal** of perfection. Freud used the term *sexual instinct* to refer to the desire for virtually any form of pleasure. As infants mature, their **libido**, or energy generated by the sexual instinct, becomes focused on sensitive parts of the body. A **fixation** occurs if a child is deprived of or receives too much pleasure from the part of the body that dominates one of the five developmental stages—**oral, anal, phallic, latency**, and **genital**. During the phallic stage, strong attachment to the parent of the opposite sex and jealousy of the parent of the same sex is termed the **Oedipus complex** in boys and the **Electra complex** in girls. Next the child enters the latency period, characterized by a lack of interest in sexual behavior. Finally, at puberty, the individual enters the genital stage of mature sexuality.

Carl Jung viewed the unconscious differently than Freud. Whereas Freud saw the id as a "cauldron of seething excitations," Jung viewed the unconscious as the ego's source of strength. Jung believed that the unconscious consisted of the **personal unconscious**, encompassing an individual's repressed thoughts, forgotten experiences, and undeveloped ideas; and the **collective unconscious**, a subterranean river of memories and behavior patterns flowing to us from previous generations. Certain universal thought forms, called **archetypes**, give rise to mental images or mythological representations and play a special role in shaping personality. Jung used the term **persona** to describe that part of personality by which we are known to other people, like a mask we put on to go out in public. Jung also divided people into two general attitude types—**extraverts** and **introverts**.

Alfred Adler believed that people possess innate positive motives and strive toward personal and social perfection. He originally proposed that the principal determinant of personality was the individual's attempt to **compensate** for actual physical weakness, but he later modified his theory to stress the importance of *feelings* of inferiority, whether or not those feelings are justified. Adler held that some people become so fixated on their feelings of inferiority that they become paralyzed and develop an **inferiority complex**. Adler concluded that strivings for superiority and perfection, both in one's own life and in the society in which one lives, are crucial to personality development.

For Karen Horney, *anxiety*—a person's reaction to real or imagined dangers or threats—is a stronger motivating force than the sexual drive, or libido. Overly anxious adults may adopt one of three maladaptive coping strategies—moving toward people (submission), moving against people (aggression), and moving away from people (detachment). By emphasizing that culture and not anatomy determines many of the personality traits that differentiate women from men and that culture can be changed, Horney became a forerunner of feminist psychology.

Erik Erikson argued that the quality of the parent–child relationship affects the development of personality because, out of this interaction, the child either feels competent and valuable and is able to form a secure sense of identity or feels incompetent and worthless and fails to build a secure identity. Erikson proposed that each person moves through eight stages of development, each involving a more successful versus a less successful adjustment.

Tying back to the opening story of Jaylene Smith, Freud would probably conclude that Jay had not successfully resolved her Electra complex. Erikson might suggest that Jay has problems achieving intimacy (Stage 6) because she had failed to develop satisfactory relations with other people earlier in her life.

Psychodynamic theories have had a profound impact on the way we view ourselves and others, but some of Freud's theories have been criticized as unscientific and culture bound, based on the anecdotal accounts of troubled individuals. As a therapy, **psychoanalysis** has been shown to be beneficial in some cases but no more so than are other therapies.

The chapter continues into a discussion of humanistic personality theories. Freud and many of his followers believed that personality grows out of the resolution of unconscious conflicts and developmental crises from the past. **Humanistic personality theory** emphasizes that we are positively motivated and progress toward higher levels of functioning; and it stresses people's potential for growth and change in the present.

Carl Rogers contended that every person is born with certain innate potentials and the **actualizing tendency** to realize our biological potential as well as our conscious sense of who we are. Rogers called the striving to fulfill our self-concept the **self-actualizing tendency**. A **fully functioning person** is one whose self-concept closely matches the person's inborn capabilities, and is encouraged when a child is raised in an atmosphere characterized by **unconditional positive regard**. By contrast, some parents and other adults offer children what Rogers called **conditional positive regard**: they value and accept only certain aspects of the child.

Regarding the example of Jaylene Smith, humanistic theorists would focus on the difference between Jay's self-concept and her actual capacities. Her inability to become what she "most truly is" would account for her anxiety, loneliness, and general dissatisfaction. Rogers would suspect that throughout Jay's life, acceptance and love came from satisfying other people's ideas of what she should become.

There is a lack of scientifically derived evidence for humanistic theories of personality. In addition, these theories are criticized for taking too rosy a view of human nature, for fostering self-centeredness, and for reflecting Western values of individual achievement.

The chapter next shifts its focus to the topic of trait theories. Trait theorists reject the notion that there are just a few distinct personality types. Instead, they insist that each person possesses a unique constellation of fundamental **personality traits**, which can be inferred from how the person behaves. Psychologist Raymond Cattell used **factor analysis** to find that personality traits cluster in groups.

Recent research suggests that there may be just five overarching and universal personality traits: extraversion, agreeableness, conscientiousness, emotional stability, and openness to experience (also called culture or intellect). Research shows these traits have some real world applications and are strongly influenced by heredity.

As it pertains to Jaylene Smith, trait theorists would probably ascribe Jaylene's high achievements to the traits of determination or persistence. Sincerity, motivation, intelligence, anxiety, and introversion would also describe Jay. In terms of Big Five factors, she would be considered high in conscientiousness, but low in emotional stability and extraversion.

Trait theories are primarily descriptive and provide a way of classifying personalities, but they do not explain why someone's personality developed as it did. Unlike psychodynamic and humanistic theories, however, trait theories are relatively easy to test experimentally, and research confirms the value of the five-factor model, referred to as the "**Big Five**," in pinpointing personality. Also, although most personality theories assume that behavior is consistent across situations and over a lifetime, a number of psychologists believe that situational variables have a significant effect on behavior.

The chapter continues by taking a look at cognitive–social learning theories. **Cognitive–social**

learning theories of personality view behavior as the product of the interaction of cognitions, learning and past experiences, and the immediate environment.

Albert Bandura maintains that certain internal **expectancies** determine how a person evaluates a situation and that this evaluation has an effect on the person's behavior. These expectancies prompt people to conduct themselves according to unique **performance standards**, individually determined measures of excellence by which they judge their behavior. According to Rotter, people with an internal **locus of control**—one type of expectancy—believe that they can control their own fate through their actions. Those who succeed in meeting their own internal performance standards develop an attitude that Bandura calls **self-efficacy**.

Regarding the factors that shaped Jaylene Smith's personality, these theorists would assert that Jaylene acquired extraordinarily high performance standards that almost inevitably left her with feelings of low self-efficacy, insecurity and uncertainty. She probably learned to be shy because she was rewarded for the many hours she spent alone studying. Reinforcement would also have shaped her self-discipline and high need to achieve. By watching her parents, Jay could have learned to respond to conflicts with aggressive outbursts.

Cognitive–social learning theories avoid the narrowness of trait theories, as well as the reliance on case studies and anecdotal evidence that weakens psychodynamic and humanistic theories. They also explain why people behave inconsistently, an area where the trait theories fall short. Cognitive–social learning theories have also spawned therapies that have been effectively used to treat depression.

The chapter concludes with an indepth section on personality assessment, beginning with how psychologists measure personality. Psychologists use four different methods to assess personality: the personal interview, direct observation of behavior, **objective tests**, and **projective tests**. Factors such as a desire to impress the examiner, fatigue, and fear of being tested can profoundly affect the reliability and validity of such tests.

During an unstructured interview, the interviewer asks questions about any issues that arise and poses follow-up questions where appropriate. In a structured interview, the order and the content of the questions are fixed, and the interviewer does not deviate from the format. Structured interviews are more likely to be used for systematic research on personality because they elicit comparable information from all interviewees.

Direct observation of a person over a period of time, which enables researchers to assess how situation and environment influence behavior, has the advantage of not relying on people's self-reported behavior. However, the observer runs the risk of misinterpreting the meaning of a given behavior.

Objective tests ask respondents to answer "yes–no" questions about their own behavior and thoughts. Cattell's **Sixteen Personality Factor Questionnaire (16PF)** provides scores on 16 basic personality traits, whereas the **NEO-PI-R** reports scores for each of the Big Five traits and their associated facets. The **Minnesota Multiphasic Personality Inventory (MMPI-2)**, originally developed as an aid to diagnose mental disorders, includes questions that measure the truthfulness of a person's response.

Psychodynamic theorists, who believe that much behavior is determined by unconscious processes, tend to discount tests that rely on self-reports. They are more likely to use projective tests consisting of ambiguous stimuli that can elicit an unlimited number of interpretations based on these unconscious processes. Two such tests are the **Rorschach Test** and the **Thematic Apperception Test** (**TAT**).

LEARNING OBJECTIVES EXERCISE

After you have read and studied the chapter, you should be able to answer the following learning objectives.

STUDYING PERSONALITY

- Define personality. Explain the difference between describing personality (in particular trait theory) and understanding the causes of personality (psychodynamic, humanistic, and cognitive–social learning theories).

PSYCHODYNAMIC THEORIES

- Describe the five propositions that are central to all psychodynamic personality theories.

- Describe Freud's theory of personality, including the concepts of *sexual instinct*, *libido*, *id*, *ego*, *superego*, and *pleasure principle* versus *reality principle*. Summarize Freud's stages of development and the consequences of *fixation* at a particular stage.

- Compare and contrast Freud's theory, Carl Jung's theory, Adler's theory, Horney's theory, and Erikson's theory of personality.

- Explain how contemporary psychologists view the contributions and limitations of the psychodynamic perspective.

HUMANISTIC PERSONALITY THEORIES

- Explain how humanistic personality theories differ from psychodynamic theories. Distinguish Rogers' concept of *actualizing tendency* and *self-actualizing tendency*, *conditional* versus *unconditional positive regard*, and what it means to be a *fully functioning person*.

- Summarize the contributions and limitations of the humanistic perspective.

TRAIT THEORIES

- Compare and contrast the trait theories of Cattell and Eysenck and the current five-factor model of personality. Briefly summarize the research evidence on the usefulness and universality of the five-factor model, the stability of personality traits over time and across situations, and the biological basis of personality traits.

- Summarize the contributions and limitations of the trait perspective.

COGNITIVE–SOCIAL LEARNING THEORIES

* Explain how cognitive–social learning theories of personality differ from other theories. Be sure to include *expectancies*, *performance standards*, *self-efficacy*, and *locus of control* in your explanation.

* Summarize the contributions and limitations of the cognitive–social learning perspective.

PERSONALITY ASSESSMENT

* Compare and contrast direct observation, structured and unstructured interviews, and objective and projective tests of personality. Indicate which approaches to personality assessment are preferred by psychodynamic, humanistic, trait, and cognitive–social learning theorists.

* Describe the three major objective tests of personality and the two major projective tests. Include a summary of their reliability and validity.

CHAPTER OUTLINE

I. Enduring Issues in Personality (page 335)

II. Studying Personality (page 335)
   - Unique Differences
   - Stable and Enduring

III. Psychodynamic Theories (page 336)
   A. Sigmund Freud
      i. How Personality is Structured
      ii. How Personality Develops
   B. Carl Jung
      - Personal Unconscious
      - Collective Unconscious
      - Archetypes
      - Persona
      - Introverts and Extraverts
   C. Alfred Adler
      - Inferiority Complex
      - Compensation
      - "Father of Humanistic Psychology"
   D. Karen Horney
      - Disagreed with Freud's Emphasis on Sexual Instincts
      - Focus on Anxiety
      - Childhood Relationships
   E. Erik Erikson
      - Eight Stages of Personality Development
   F. A Psychodynamic View of Jaylene Smith
   G. Evaluating Psychodynamic Theories
      - Freud's Ideas Have Had Lasting Impact
      - Criticisms of Theory:
         - Sexist View of Women
         - Lack Scientific Basis
      - Difficult to Test Experimentally

IV. Humanistic Personality Theories (page 344)
   A. Carl Rogers
      - Actualizing Tendency
      - Self-Actualizing Tendency
      - Fully-Functioning Person
      - Unconditional Positive Regard
      - Conditional Positive Regard
   B. A Humanistic View of Jaylene Smith
   C. Evaluating Humanistic Theories
      - Almost Impossible to Verify Central Tenets Scientifically
      - Criticisms Include Fostering of Self-Centeredness and Narcissism

V. Trait Theories (page 346)
   A. The Big Five
      i. Are the Big Five Personality Traits Universal?
      ii. Do the Big Five Have a Genetic Basis?
   B. A Trait View of Jaylene Smith
   C. Evaluating Trait Theories
      - Common-Sense Appeal
      - Easier to Test Scientifically
      - Criticisms:
         - Primarily Descriptive, Do Not Try to Explain Causes
         - Dangerous to Reduce Human Complexity to a Few Traits

VI. Cognitive–Social Learning Theories (page 351)
   A. Expectancies, Self-Efficacy, and Locus of Control
      i. How Consistent Are We?
   B. A Cognitive–Social Learning View of Jaylene Smith
   C. Evaluating Cognitive–Social Learning Theories
      - Seem to Have Great Potential
      - Put Mental Processes Back at Center of Personality
      - Focus on Conscious Behavior and Experience
      - Can Define and Scientifically Study Key Concepts
      - Too Early to Evaluate Fully

VII. Personality Assessment (page 353)
   A. The Personal Interview
      - Unstructured Interviews
      - Structured Interviews
   B. Direct Observation
      - Watch Behavior First-Hand
   C. Objective Tests
      - Sixteen Personality Factor Questionnaire
      - NEO-PI-R
   D. APPLYING PSYCHOLOGY: EVALUATING YOUR PERSONALITY
   E. Projective Tests
      - Minnesota Multiphasic Personality Inventory (MMPI-2)
      - Rorschach Test
      - Thematic Apperception Test (TAT)

Actualizing tendency	According to Rogers, the drive of every organism to fulfill its biological potential and become what it is inherently capable of becoming. (p. 345)
Anal stage	Second stage in Freud's theory of personality development, in which a child's erotic feelings center on the anus and on elimination. (p. 338)
Archetypes	In Jung's theory of personality, thought forms common to all human beings, stored in the collective unconscious. (p. 339)
Big Five	Five traits or basic dimensions currently considered to be of central importance in describing personality. (p. 347)
Cognitive–social learning theories	Personality theories that view behavior as the product of the interaction of cognitions, learning and past experiences, and the immediate environment. (p. 350)
Collective unconscious	In Jung's theory of personality, the level of the unconscious that is inherited and common to all members of a species. (p. 339)
Compensation	According to Adler, the person's effort to overcome imagined or real personal weaknesses. (p. 340)
Conditional positive regard	In Rogers's theory, acceptance and love that are dependent on another's behaving in certain ways and on fulfilling certain conditions. (p. 345)
Ego	Freud's term for the part of the personality that mediates between environmental demands (reality), conscience (superego), and instinctual needs (id); now often used as a synonym for "self." (p. 336)
Ego ideal	The part of the superego that consists of standards of what one would like to be. (p. 336)
Expectancies	In Bandura's view, what a person anticipates in a situation or as a result of behaving in certain ways. (p. 350)
Extraverts	According to Jung, people who usually focus on social life and the external world instead of on their internal experience. (p. 339)
Factor analysis	A statistical technique that identifies groups of related objects; it was used by Cattell to identify clusters of traits. (p. 347)
Fixation	According to Freud, a partial or complete halt at some point in the individual's psychosexual development. (p. 338)
Fully functioning person	According to Rogers, an individual whose self-concept closely resembles his or her inborn capacities or potentials. (p. 345)
Genital stage	In Freud's theory of personality development, the final stage of normal adult sexual development, which is usually marked by mature sexuality. (p. 338)
Humanistic personality theory	Any personality theory that asserts the fundamental goodness of people and their striving toward higher levels of functioning. (p. 344)
Id	In Freud's theory of personality, the collection of unconscious urges and desires that continually seek expression. (p. 336)
Inferiority complex	In Adler's theory, the fixation on feelings of personal inferiority that results in emotional and social paralysis. (p. 341)
Introverts	According to Jung, people who usually focus on their own thoughts and feelings. (p. 339)
Latency period	In Freud's theory of personality, a period in which the child appears to have no interest in the other sex; occurs after the phallic stage. (p. 338)
Libido	According to Freud, the energy generated by the sexual instinct. (p. 336)
Locus of control	According to Rotter, an expectancy about whether reinforcement is under internal or external control. (p. 350)

Minnesota Multiphasic Personality Inventory (MMPI-2)	The most widely used objective personality test, originally intended for psychiatric diagnosis. (p. 356)
NEO-PI-R	An objective personality test designed to assess the Big Five personality traits. (p. 355)
Objective tests	Personality tests that are administered and scored in a standard way. (p. 354)
Oedipus complex and Electra complex	According to Freud, a child's sexual attachment to the parent of the opposite sex and jealousy toward the parent of the same sex; generally occurs in the phallic stage. (p. 338)
Oral stage	First stage in Freud's theory of personality development, in which the infant's erotic feelings center on the mouth, lips, and tongue. (p. 338)
Performance standards	In Bandura's theory, standards that people develop to rate the adequacy of their own behavior in a variety of situations. (p. 350)
Persona	According to Jung, our public self, the mask we wear to represent ourselves to others. (p. 339)
Personal unconscious	In Jung's theory of personality, one of the two levels of the unconscious; it contains the individual's repressed thoughts, forgotten experiences, and undeveloped ideas. (p. 339)
Personality	An individual's unique pattern of thoughts, feelings, and behaviors that persists over time and across situations. (p. 335)
Personality traits	Dimensions or characteristics on which people differ in distinctive ways. (p. 346)
Phallic stage	Third stage in Freud's theory of personality development, in which erotic feelings center on the genitals. (p. 338)
Pleasure principle	According to Freud, the way in which the id seeks immediate gratification of an instinct. (p. 336)
Projective tests	Personality tests, such as the Rorschach inkblot test, consisting of ambiguous or unstructured material. (p. 356)
Psychoanalysis	The theory of personality Freud developed, as well as the form of therapy he invented. (p. 336)
Reality principle	According to Freud, the way in which the ego seeks to satisfy instinctual demands safely and effectively in the real world. (p. 336)
Rorschach test	A projective test composed of ambiguous inkblots; the way people interpret the blots is thought to reveal aspects of their personality. (p. 356)
Self-actualizing tendency	According to Rogers, the drive of human beings to fulfill their self-concepts, or the images they have of themselves. (p. 345)
Self-efficacy	According to Bandura, the expectancy that one's efforts will be successful. (p. 350)
Sixteen Personality Factor Questionnaire	Objective personality test created by Cattell that provides scores on the 16 traits he identified. (p. 355)
Superego	According to Freud, the social and parental standards the individual has internalized; the conscience and the ego ideal. (p. 336)
Thematic Apperception Test (TAT)	A projective test composed of ambiguous pictures about which a person is asked to write a complete story. (p. 356)
Unconditional positive regard	In Rogers's theory, the full acceptance and love of another person regardless of his or her behavior. (p. 345)
Unconscious	In Freud's theory, all the ideas, thoughts, and feelings of which we are not and normally cannot become aware. (p. 336)

POSTTEST

After studying the text and completing the Study Guide activities, answer these questions to determine if you need to review any areas before the course exam.

MULTIPLE CHOICE

1. Which of the following is NOT an aspect of personality?
   a. enduring
   b. unique
   c. stable
   d. unpredictable

2. For Freud, the term "sexual instinct" refers to _____.
   a. the personal unconscious
   b. erotic sexuality
   c. any form of pleasure
   d. childhood experiences

3. For Freud, the only personality structure present at birth is the ___.
   a. id
   b. ego
   c. superego
   d. ego ideal

4. The proper chronological order of Freud's psychosexual stages is _____.
   a. oral, anal, phallic, latency, genital
   b. anal, oral, phallic, latency, genital
   c. anal, oral, genital, latency, phallic
   d. oral, anal, genital, phallic, latency

5. According to Jung, the memories and behavior patterns inherited from past generations are part of the _____.
   a. persona
   b. alter-ego
   c. personal unconscious
   d. collective unconscious

6. Collective memories of experiences people have had in common since prehistoric times, such as mothers, heroes, or villains are called _____ by Carl Jung.
   a. personas
   b. celebrities' heroes
   c. archetypes
   d. collective

7. Marley is a joiner. She is interested in other people and events going on around her in the world. In Jung's view, she is an _____.
   a. archetype
   b. endomorph
   c. introvert
   d. extrovert

8. Adler's emphasis on people's positive social strivings has caused him to be labeled by many psychologists as the "father" of ____ psychology.
   a. humanistic
   b. Gestalt
   c. cognitive
   d. social

9. Erikson suggested that success in each of the eight life stages he outlined depends upon _____.
   a. resolution of the inferiority complex
   b. cognitive and moral development
   c. resolution of the Oedipus complex
   d. adjustment during the previous stage

10. Erikson's stage of autonomy versus shame and doubt corresponds approximately with Freud's ____ stage of psychosexual development.
    a. oral
    b. anal
    c. phallic
    d. latency

11. Erikson argues that for people to establish a sense of intimacy, they must feel secure in their _____.
    a. identity
    b. initiative
    c. persona
    d. integrity

12. Studies have found that the "Big Five" dimensions of personality _____.
    a. may only represent personality in Western industrial cultures
    b. may only represent personality in North American culture
    c. may only represent personality in non-Western, nonindustrial cultures
    d. may represent universal dimensions of personality across cultures

13. Each of the following is one of the "Big Five" dimensions of personality EXCEPT ____.
    a. neuroticism   c. emotional stability
    b. agreeableness   d. extroversion

14. The most widely used objective personality test is the ____.
    a. 16 PF
    b. TAT
    c. Rorschach
    d. MMPI

15. A behaviorist would prefer ____ when assessing someone's personality.
    a. objective tests
    b. observation
    c. interviews
    d. projective tests

16. The Rorschach test relies on the interpretation of ____ to understand personality.
    a. a 16-part questionnaire
    b. cards with human figures on them
    c. 10 cards containing ink blots
    d. sentence completion exercises

17. When explaining personality, cognitive-social learning theorists put ____ at the center of personality.
    a. unconscious processes   c. mental processes
    b. emotional stability   d. environmental cues

18. Bill believes he can control his own fate. He feels that by hard work, skill, and training it is possible to avoid punishments and find rewards. Rotter would say that Bill has a(n) ____ locus of control.
    a. internal   c. primary
    b. external   d. secondary

19. According to Bandura, the expectancy that one's efforts will be successful is called ____.
    a. self-esteem   c. self-actualizing tendency
    b. locus of control   d. self-efficacy

20. Which of the following is NOT one of the four basic types of tools used by psychologists to measure personality?
    a. personal interview   c. projective tests
    b. objective tests   d. aptitude tests

21. Which of the following is NOT related to expectancies as described by cognitive-social theory?
    a. performance standards
    b. actualizing tendency
    c. locus of control
    d. explanatory style

SHORT ESSAY QUESTIONS

1. Summarize the interaction of elements of personality according to Freud's theory: id, ego, and superego. Identify Freud's five stages of psychosexual development.

2. Differentiate among the theories of Jung, Adler, and Horney. Identify what these theories have in common.

3. Identify Erik Erikson's eight stages of personality development.

4. Contrast Carl Rogers's humanistic theory with Freudian theory.

5. Explain trait theory.

6. List the five basic traits that most describe differences in personality.

7. Compare cognitive social-learning theories to early views of personality.

8. Describe the four basic tools psychologists use to measure personality. List two objective tests, two projective tests, and their uses.

LABEL DRAWINGS

Fill in the Blanks

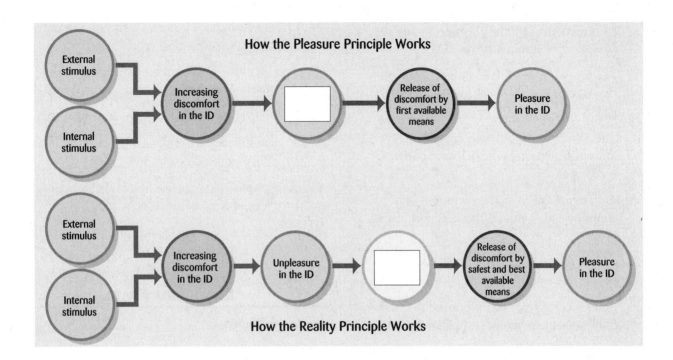

SUMMARY TABLE

Theories of Personality (Supply the roots of personality)

Theory	Roots of Personality	Methods of Assessing
_____ Psychodynamic	a. Relatively permanent dispositions within the individual that cause the person to think, feel, and act in characteristic ways.	Projective tests, personal interviews
_____ Humanistic	b. A drive toward personal growth and higher levels of functioning.	Objective tests and personal interviews
_____ Trait problem from early childhood	c. Unconscious thoughts, feelings, motives, and conflicts; repressed	Objective tests
_____ Social Learning Theories	d. Determined by past reinforcement and punishment as well as by observing what happens to other people.	Interviews, objective tests, observations

1. d. Unpredictability is not an aspect of personality. p. 336

2. c. For Freud, "sexual instinct" refers to any form of pleasure. p. 336

3. a. For Freud, the id is the only personality structure present at birth. p. 337

4. a. The proper order of Freud's psychosexual stages is: oral, anal, phallic, latency, genital. p. 338

5. d. The collective unconscious consists of inherited memories and behavior patterns. p. 339

6. c. Archetypes are collective memories of common types, such as mothers and heroes. p. 339

7. d. Extraverts are interested in being with other people and in the world. p. 339

8. a. Adler is considered by many to be the "father" of humanistic psychology. p. 340

9. d. Success in Erikson's eight life stages depends on adjustment during the previous stage. p. 341

10. b. Erikson's autonomy versus shame and doubt stage corresponds with Freud's anal stage. p. 342

11. a. For Erikson, people must feel secure in their identity to establish a sense of intimacy. p. 342

12. d. The "Big Five" dimensions of personality may represent universal dimensions across cultures. p. 347

13. a. Neuroticism is not one of the Big Five dimensions. p. 348

14. d. The MMPI is the most widely used objective personality test. p. 356

15. b. Behaviorists prefer observation when assessing personality. p. 354

16. c. The Rorschach test uses 10 cards containing inkblots. p. 357

17. c. Cognitive-social learning theorists put mental processes at the center of personality. p. 350

18. b. Bill has an external locus of control. p. 350

19. d. Self-efficacy is the expectancy that one's efforts will succeed. p. 350

20. d. Aptitude tests are not one of the four basic types of personality tests. p. 353

21. b. Actualizing tendency was proposed by Carl Rogers, a humanist. p. 345

Label Drawings

Fill In the Blanks

Fig. 10.2 p. 338

Pleasure Principle:	Unpleasure in the Id
Reality Principle:	Rational thought of Ego

Summary Table

Roots of Personality p. 354

___C.__ Psychodynamic
___B.__ Humanistic
___A.__ Trait
___D.__ Social Learning Theories

CHAPTER 11 Stress and Health Psychology

CHAPTER OVERVIEW

The chapter opens with the dramatic, life-altering experience of Greg Hughes, who tragically lost both of his legs during a series of fast-moving, completely unforeseen circumstances. Using the case study of Greg Hughes as a jump-off point, the chapter begins by looking at common sources of stress, and why some people are less vulnerable to stress than others.

We experience **stress** when we are faced with a tense or threatening situation that requires us to change or adapt our behavior (a **stressor**). Life-and-death situations, like war and natural disasters, are inherently stressful. Even events that are usually viewed as positive, like a wedding or a job promotion, can be stressful, because they require change, adaptation, and **adjustment**. How we adjust to the stress affects our health, since prolonged or severe stress can contribute to physical and psychological disorders.

Change is stressful for most people because we strongly desire order in our lives, any good or bad event involving change will be experienced as stressful. Day-to-day petty annoyances and irritations can be as stressful as major life events, because these seemingly minor incidents give rise to feelings of pressure, frustration, conflict, and anxiety.

When we experience **pressure** from either internal or external forces, we feel forced to intensify our efforts or to perform at higher levels. Internal forces include trying to live up to social and cultural norms as well as family and peer expectations.

We feel frustrated when someone or something stands between us and our goal. Five basic sources of **frustration** are delays, lack of resources, losses, failure, and discrimination.

Conflict arises when we are faced with two or more incompatible demands, opportunities, needs, or goals.

With **approach/approach conflict**, a person must either choose between two attractive but incompatible goals or opportunities, or modify them so as to take some advantage of both. With **avoidance/avoidance conflict**, a person must choose between two undesirable or threatening possibilities. If escape is impossible, the person may often vacillate between the two possibilities. With **approach/avoidance conflict**, a person is both attracted to and repelled by the same goal or opportunity. Because the desire to approach and the desire to avoid the goal both grow stronger as the person in this dilemma nears the goal, eventually the tendency to approach equals the tendency to avoid. The person then vacillates finally making a decision or until the situation changes.

Sometimes we subject ourselves to stress by internalizing a set of irrational, self-defeating beliefs that add unnecessarily to the normal stresses of living.

People who cope well with stress tend to be self-confident and optimistic. With their internal locus of control, they also see themselves as being able to affect their situations. Stress-resistant people share a trait called *hardiness*—a tendency to experience difficult demands as challenging rather than threatening. *Resilience*, the ability to bounce back after a stressful event, is also related to positive adjustment.

The chapter next takes a look at how we cope with stress. People generally adjust to stress in one of two ways: *Direct coping* describes any action people take to change an uncomfortable situation, whereas *defensive coping* denotes the various ways people convince themselves—through a form of self-deception—that they are not really threatened or do not really want something they cannot get.

When we confront a stressful situation and admit to ourselves that there is a problem that needs to be solved, we may learn new skills, enlist other people's aid, or try harder to reach our goal. **Confrontation** may also include expressions of anger. **Compromise** usually requires adjusting expectations or desires; the conflict is resolved by settling for less than what was originally sought. Sometimes the most effective way of coping with a stressful situation is to distance oneself from it. The danger of **withdrawal**, however, is that it may become a maladaptive habit.

When a stressful situation arises and there is little that can be done to deal with it directly, people often turn to **defense mechanisms** as a way of coping. Defense mechanisms are ways of deceiving ourselves about the causes of stressful events, thus reducing conflict, frustration, pressure, and anxiety. **Denial** is the refusal to acknowledge a painful or threatening reality. **Repression** is the blocking out of unacceptable thoughts or impulses from consciousness. When we cannot deny or repress a particular problem, we might resort to **projection**—attributing our repressed motives or feelings to others, thereby locating the source of our conflict outside ourselves. **Identification** may occur when people feel completely powerless. People who adopt this technique take on others' characteristics to gain a sense of control or adequacy. People under severe stress sometimes revert to childlike behavior, called **regression**. Because adults can't stand feeling helpless, becoming more childlike can make total dependency or helplessness more tolerable. A subtle form of denial is seen in **intellectualization**, when people emotionally distance themselves from a particularly disturbing situation. **Reaction formation** refers to a behavioral form of denial in which people express with exaggerated intensity ideas and emotions that are the opposite of their own. Through **displacement**, repressed motives and feelings are redirected from their original objects to substitute objects. **Sublimation** involves transforming repressed emotions into more socially accepted forms. Defensive coping can help us adjust to difficult circumstances, but it can also lead to maladaptive behavior if it interferes with our ability to deal constructively with a difficult situation.

How people handle stress is determined to a significant degree by the environment in which they live. People in low-income groups often experience more stress and have fewer personal and community resources to draw on for support as well as fewer coping strategies. Men and women may cope differently with stress.

Shifting gears, the chapter next examines how stress affects health. **Health psychologists** try to find ways to prevent stress from becoming debilitating and to promote healthy behaviors. Physiologist Hans Selye contended that people react to physical and psychological stress in three stages. In Stage 1 (*alarm reaction*) of the **general adaptation syndrome (GAS)**, the body recognizes that it must fight off some physical or psychological danger, resulting in quickened respiration and heart rate, increased sensitivity and alertness, and a highly charged emotional state—a physical adaptation that augments our coping resources and helps us to regain self-control. If direct or defensive coping mechanisms fail to reduce the stress, we progress to Stage 2 (*resistance stage*), during which physical symptoms of strain appear as we intensify our efforts to cope both directly and defensively. If these attempts to regain psychological equilibrium fail, psychological disorganization rages out of control until we reach Stage 3 (*exhaustion*). During this phase, we use increasingly ineffective defense mechanisms to bring the stress under control. At this point, some people lose touch with reality, whereas others show signs of "burnout," such as shorter attention spans, irritability, procrastination, and general apathy.

Stress is known to be an important factor in chemical changes in the body leading to the development of coronary heart disease (CHD). Research has demonstrated that the type A behavior pattern—characterized by impatience, hostility, urgency, competitiveness, and striving—predicts CHD.

Stress—such as that experienced by students during examination periods—can suppress the functioning of the immune system, the focus of the relatively new field of **psychoneuroimmunology (PNI)**. Stress can also increase one's susceptibility to the common cold, and it appears to be linked to the development of some forms of cancer.

The chapter next presents some solutions for staying healthy. We can reduce the negative impact of stress on our health by trying to reduce stress and by maintaining a healthy lifestyle, which equips the body to cope with stress that is unavoidable.

Exercising regularly and learning to relax reduce the body's responses to stress. Having a strong network of social support is also related to healthier adjustment. Religious and altruistic people also typically experience less stress, although the mechanism involved is not clear. Finally, people can take steps to minimize the impact of stressful events (proactive coping), by making the best of difficult situations (positive reappraisal), and by maintaining a sense of humor.

The *positive psychology* movement has prompted many psychologists to promote good health by adopting a healthier lifestyle. Eating a well-balanced diet, getting regular exercise, not smoking, and avoiding high-risk behaviors are all important to maintaining health.

The chapter takes a turn in a differenet direction by looking at "extreme stress," which differs significantly from everyday stress. People experiencing extreme stress cannot continue their everyday life as they did before the stress and, in some cases, they never fully recover.

Extreme stress derives from a number of sources, including unemployment, divorce and separation, bereavement, combat, and natural catastrophes. One of the impediments to effective coping occurs when a grieving person feels compelled to adjust in socially prescribed ways that do not provide effective relief.

Extreme traumas may result in **posttraumatic stress disorder (PTSD)**, a disabling emotional disorder whose symptoms include daytime flashbacks, social and occupational withdrawal, sleeplessness, and nightmares. Combat veterans and people with a history of emotional problems are especially vulnerable to PTSD. A few particularly stable individuals experience a *positive* form of personal growth following extreme trauma called **posttraumatic growth (PTG)**.

The chapter concludes by considering the qualities that describe a well-adjusted person. Psychologists disagree on what constitutes good adjustment. Some believe that well-adjusted people live according to social norms. Others disagree, arguing that well-adjusted people enjoy overcoming challenging situations and that this ability leads to growth and self-fulfillment. Finally, some psychologists use specific criteria to evaluate a person's ability to adjust, such as how well the adjustment solves the problem and satisfies both personal needs and the needs of others.

LEARNING OBJECTIVES EXERCISE

After you have read and studied the chapter, you should be able to answer the following learning objectives.

SOURCES OF STRESS

- Distinguish between *stressors* and *stress*. Identify the major sources of stress. Describe the three types of conflict. Explain what is meant by "self-imposed stress."

- Describe the role of optimism and pessimism, locus of control, hardiness, and resilience in affecting people's response to stress.

COPING WITH STRESS

- Compare and contrast direct coping and defensive coping. Describe and give an example of the three strategies for coping directly with stress. Describe and give an example of the major ways of coping defensively.

- Explain how socioeconomic status, culture, and gender affect levels of stress and ways of coping with stress.

HOW STRESS AFFECTS HEALTH

- Explain why "experiencing too much stress over too long a period can contribute to physical problems." In your explanation, include Cannon's theory of the fight-or-flight response and the several stages of Selye's general adaptation syndrome.

- Summarize the evidence that shows chronic stress can contribute to heart disease. Include Type A and Type D personalities in your summary.

- Summarize the research evidence that "stress also affects the functioning of the immune system."

STAYING HEALTHY

- Describe the four proven ways to reduce stress.

- Explain the role of proactive coping, positive reappraisal, and humor in reducing stress.

- Describe the four elements of a healthy lifestyle.

Extreme Stress

• Identify the five major sources of extreme stress and describe their impact.

The Well-Adjusted Person

• Describe the several standards for judging whether an individual is well-adjusted.

CHAPTER OUTLINE

Adjustment	Any effort to cope with stress. (p. 363)
Approach/approach conflict	According to Lewin, the result of simultaneous attraction to two appealing possibilities, neither of which has any negative qualities. (p. 366)
Approach/avoidance conflict	According to Lewin, the result of being simultaneously attracted to and repelled by the same goal. (p. 366)
Avoidance/avoidance conflict	According to Lewin, the result of facing a choice between two undesirable possibilities, neither of which has any positive qualities. (p. 366)
Compromise	Deciding on a more realistic solution or goal when an ideal solution or goal is not practical. (p. 369)
Conflict	Simultaneous existence of incompatible demands, opportunities, needs, or goals. (p. 365)
Confrontation	Acknowledging a stressful situation directly and attempting to find a solution to the problem or to attain the difficult goal. (p. 369)
Defense mechanisms	Self-deceptive techniques for reducing stress, including denial, repression, projection, identification, regression, intellectualization, reaction formation, displacement, and sublimation. (p. 370)
Denial	Refusal to acknowledge a painful or threatening reality. (p. 370)
Displacement	Shifting repressed motives and emotions from an original object to a substitute object. (p. 371)
Frustration	The feeling that occurs when a person is prevented from reaching a goal. (p. 364)
General adaptation syndrome (GAS)	According to Selye, the three stages the body passes through as it adapts to stress: alarm reaction, resistance, and exhaustion. (p. 374)
Health psychology	A subfield of psychology concerned with the relationship between psychological factors and physical health and illness. (p. 373)
Identification	Taking on the characteristics of someone else to avoid feeling incompetent. (p. 370)
Intellectualization	Thinking abstractly about stressful problems as a way of detaching oneself from them. (p. 371)
Posttraumatic growth (PTG)	Positive personal growth that may follow an extremely stressful event. (p. 384)
Posttraumatic stress disorder (PTSD)	Psychological disorder characterized by episodes of anxiety, sleeplessness, and nightmares resulting from some disturbing past event. (p. 383)
Pressure	A feeling that one must speed up, intensify, or change the direction of one's behavior or live up to a higher standard of performance. (p. 364)
Projection	Attributing one's repressed motives, feelings, or wishes to others. (p. 370)
Psychoneuroimmunology (PNI)	A new field that studies the interaction between stress on the one hand and immune, endocrine, and nervous system activity on the other. (p. 376)
Reaction formation	Expression of exaggerated ideas and emotions that are the opposite of one's repressed beliefs or feelings. (p. 371)
Regression	Reverting to childlike behavior and defenses. (p. 371)
Repression	Excluding uncomfortable thoughts, feelings, and desires from consciousness. (p. 370)
Stress	A state of psychological tension or strain. (p. 363)
Stressor	Any environmental demand that creates a state of tension or threat and requires change or adaptation. (p. 363)
Sublimation	Redirecting repressed motives and feelings into more socially acceptable channels. (p. 371)
Withdrawal	Avoiding a situation when other forms of coping are not practical. (p. 369)

POSTTEST

After studying the text and completing the Study Guide activities, answer these questions to determine if you need to review any areas before the course exam.

MULTIPLE CHOICE

1. The College Life Stress Inventory (CLSI) measures _____.
   a. how much stress and change a student has undergone in a given period
   b. how effective a student's coping mechanisms are
   c. the extent to which a student has resolved stress effectively
   d. the degree to which a student's stress reaction is genetically determined

2. Henry's term paper is due and he hasn't finished it. He can turn it in unfinished and receive a failing grade or he can hand it in later and lose so many points that he will also fail. Henry's dilemma is described by Lewin as a (n) _____ conflict.
   a. approach/approach
   b. approach/avoidance
   c. avoidance/avoidance
   d. multiple approach/avoidance

3. Ken wants to go to law school but he is concerned that he will be rejected if he applies or will fail if he is admitted. Ken is faced with what Lewin calls a (n) _____ conflict.
   a. approach/approach
   b. approach/avoidance
   c. avoidance/avoidance
   d. double approach/avoidance

4. Kobasa's work on hardiness and resilience has linked people's self-confidence to _____.
   a. their sense of having some control over events
   b. their levels of intelligence
   c. adopting and internalizing traditional sex roles
   d. the tendency to be extroverted

5. Acknowledging a stressful situation directly and attempting to find a solution to the problem or attain a difficult goal is called _____.
   a. sublimation
   b. compromise
   c. confrontation
   d. aggression

6. After weeks of being taunted by her so-called "friends" at school, Alyssa begins actively avoiding them whenever possible. Her coping style is best described as _____.
   a. confrontation
   b. withdrawal
   c. compromise
   d. rationalization

7. John refuses to admit he has a problem with procrastination, even though his procrastination is creating many problems in his life. John is using ____ to cope with his problem.
   a. denial
   b. sublimation
   c. repression
   d. intellectualization

8. A corporate executive who feels guilty about the way she rose to power accuses her colleagues of ruthless ambition. Her behavior typifies _____.
   a. sublimation
   b. projection
   c. displacement
   d. identification

9. A student, angry that he failed what he felt was an unfair test, goes back to his dormitory and slams the door violently. This student is using the defense mechanism of _____.
   a. sublimation
   b. reaction formation
   c. projection
   d. displacement

10. The proper order in which Selye's stages of the General Adaptation Syndrome (GAS) occur is _____.
    a. resistance, alarm stage, exhaustion
    b. exhaustion, resistance, alarm stage
    c. resistance, exhaustion, alarm stage
    d. alarm stage, resistance, exhaustion

11. People who respond to life events in an intense, time urgent manner are exhibiting a _____ behavior pattern.
    a. Type A
    b. Type B
    c. Type C
    d. hyperactive

12. Prolonged stress has _____ cancer.
    a. been shown to decrease vulnerability to
    b. been found to be unrelated to one's vulnerability to
    c. been shown to increase vulnerability to
    d. been shown to cause

13. When recent or past highly stressful events result in anxiety, sleeplessness, and nightmares, a psychological disorder called _____ might be occurring.
    a. generalized anxiety disorder
    b. panic disorder
    c. posttraumatic stress disorder
    d. panic disorder

14. Which of the following accurately lists in order the stages of reactions to natural catastrophes?
    a. suggestible stage, shock stage, recovery stage
    b. shock stage, suggestible stage, recovery stage
    c. rage, confusion, recovery
    d. confusion, rage, recovery

15. Kobasa described hardiness as a trait in which _____.
    a. our experience of stress is affected by heredity
    b. people adhere to rigid actions and won't compromise
    c. people react to conflict in a hard way
    d. people experience difficult environmental demands as challenging rather than threatening

16. When people are well-adjusted, they probably have _____.
    a. learned to get what they need regardless of what others want
    b. learned to balance conformity and nonconformity as well as self-control and spontaneity
    c. few problems
    d. none of the above

17. In addition to avoiding and coping better with stress, it is also important to _____ in order to maintain health.
    a. exercise regularly
    b. eat a well-balanced diet
    c. avoid high-risk behaviors
    d. quit smoking
    e. all of the above

18. According to Wortman, which of the following statements in NOT a myth about the bereavement process?
    a. People should recover from a loss within a year or so.
    b. People who do not seek greater understanding for their loss are the best adjusted and the least depressed.
    c. People should be intensely distressed when a loved one dies.
    d. People need to work through their grief
    e. All of the above are myths about bereavement.

19. A subfield of psychology concerned with the relationship between psychological factors and physical health and illness is called _____.
    a. positive psychology
    b. abnormal psychology
    c. health psychology
    d. physiological psychology

20. Which of the following statements is true regarding resistance to stress?
    a. Pessimists tend to cope better with stress than optimists.
    b. People with an external locus of control tend to cope better with stress than people with an internal locus of control.
    c. Self-confident people tend to feel less stress than people who lack self-assurance.
    d. There are little differences in the way individuals react to and cope with stress.

SHORT ESSAY QUESTIONS

1. Discuss the role of irrational thinking on stress and how some stress is self-imposed.

2. Identify and describe five sources of extreme stress and outline some of the physical and/or psychological problems caused by each source presented. Include the three myths of bereavement and the three reactions to natural catastrophes.

3. Summarize the article on why some people are happier than others.

4. List the four steps for staying healthy. Detail specific suggestions for improvement and include definitions of altruism, proactive coping, and positive reappraisal.

5. Define the psychological disorder, posttraumatic stress syndrome. Discuss possible causes, symptoms, and the 'normal' responses to a traumatic event. Include suggestions for recovery.

ANSWERS AND EXPLANATIONS TO MULTIPLE CHOICE POSTTEST

1. a. The CLSI measures how much stress and change a student has undergone in a given period. p. 364

2. c. Henry's dilemma is an avoidance/avoidance conflict because both outcomes are undesirable. p. 366

3. b. Ken is faced with an approach/avoidance conflict because he is both attracted to and repelled from his goals. p. 366

4. a. Kosaba links people's self-confidence to their sense of having some control over events. p. 367

5. c. Confrontation acknowledges a stressful situation directly and attempts to find a solution. p. 369

6. b. Alyssa is using the coping style of withdrawal by avoiding the situation. p. 369

7. a. John is using denial by refusing to acknowledge his problems with procrastination. p. 370

8. b. The female executive is using projection by attributing her repressed guilt about her success to her colleagues. p. 370

9. d. The student is using displacement by redirecting his anger to a substitute object. p. 371

10. d. The proper order in Seyle's stages of GAS are: alarm, resistance, exhaustion. p. 374

11. a. One characteristic of the Type A personality is intense time urgency. p. 375

12. c. Prolonged stress has been shown to increase vulnerability to cancer. p. 376

13. c. Posttraumatic stress disorder is characterized by episodes of anxiety, sleeplessness, and nightmares resulting from a disturbing past event. p. 383

14. b. The order of the states of reaction to natural catastrophes is: shock, suggestible, and recovery. p. 383

15. d. Hardiness is described as a trait in which people experience difficult environmental demands as challenging rather than threatening. p. 367

16. b. Well-adjusted people have learned to balance conformity and nonconformity as well as self-control and spontaneity. p. 385

17. e. Exercise, diet, avoiding smoking, and avoiding high risk behaviors are all elements of a healthy lifestyle. p. 379

18. b. It is a myth that people who find meaning in death cope better. In reality, people who do not seek greater understanding are the best adjusted and the least depressed. p. 382

19. c. Health psychology is a subfield of psychology concerned with the relationship between psychological factors and physical health and illness. p. 373

20. c. Self-confident people tend to feel less stress than people who lack self-assurance. p. 367

CHAPTER 12 Psychological Disorders

CHAPTER OVERVIEW

Vignettes featuring the unique cases of Jack, Claudia, and Jonathan open this chapter on psychological disorders. Mental health professionals define a psychological disorder as a condition that either seriously impairs a person's ability to function in life or creates a high level of inner distress, or both. This view does not mean that the category "disordered" is always easy to distinguish from the category "normal." In fact, it may be more accurate to view abnormal behavior as merely quantitatively different from normal behavior.

In early societies, abnormal behavior was often attributed to supernatural powers. As late as the 18th century, the mentally ill were thought to be witches or possessed by the devil. In modern times, three approaches have helped to advance our understanding of abnormal behavior: the biological, the psychoanalytic, and the cognitive behavioral.

The **biological model** holds that abnormal behavior is caused by physiological malfunction, especially of the brain.

Researchers assume the origin of these malfunctions is often hereditary. Although neuroscientists have demonstrated that genetic/biochemical factors are involved in some psychological disorders, biology alone cannot account for most mental illnesses.

The **psychoanalytic model** originating with Freud holds that abnormal behavior is a symbolic expression of unconscious conflicts that generally can be traced to childhood.

The **cognitive–behavior model** states that psychological disorders arise when people learn maladaptive ways of thinking and acting. What has been learned can be unlearned, however.

Cognitive–behavioral therapists strive to modify their patients' dysfunctional behaviors and distorted, self-defeating thought processes.

According to the **diathesis–stress model**, which integrates the biological and environmental perspectives, psychological disorders develop when a biological predisposition (known as a **diathesis**) is triggered by stressful circumstances. Another attempt at integrating causes is the **systems (biopsychosocial) approach**, which contends psychological disorders are "lifestyle diseases" arising from a combination of biological risk factors, psychological stresses, and societal pressures.

According to research, 15% of the population is suffering from one or more mental disorders at any given point in time.

The term **insanity** should be understood as a legal, not a psychological, one. It is typically applied to defendants who were so mentally disturbed when they committed their offense that they either did not know right from wrong or were unable to control their behavior.

The current fourth edition of the *Diagnostic and Statistical Manual of Mental Disorders (DSM-IV-TR)* provides careful descriptions of the symptoms of different disorders so that diagnoses based on them will be reliable and consistent among mental health professionals. The *DSM-IV-TR* includes little information on causes and treatments.

The chapter continues with a discussion of **mood disorders**, beginning with how they differ from ordinary mood changes. Most people have a wide emotional range, but in some people with mood disorders, this range is greatly restricted. They seem stuck at one or the other end of the emotional spectrum, or they may alternate back and forth between periods of mania and depression.

The most common mood disorder is **depression**, in which a person feels overwhelmed with sadness, loses interest in activities, and displays such other symptoms as excessive guilt, feelings of worthlessness, insomnia, and loss of appetite. **Major depressive disorder** is an episode of intense sadness that may last for several months; in contrast, **dysthymia** involves less intense sadness but persists with little relief for a period of 2 years or more.

Regarding the question of suicide, more women than men attempt suicide, but more men succeed. Suicide attempt rates among American adolescents and young adults have been rising. A common feeling associated with suicide is hopelessness, which is also typical of depression.

People suffering from **mania** become euphoric ("high"), extremely active, excessively talkative, and easily distracted. They typically have unlimited hopes and schemes, but little interest in realistically carrying them out. At the extreme, they may collapse from exhaustion. Manic episodes usually alternate with depression. Such a mood disorder, in which both mania and depression are alternately present and are sometimes interrupted by periods of normal mood, is known as **bipolar disorder**.

Mood disorders can result from a combination of biological, psychological, and social factors. Genetics and chemical imbalances in the brain seem to play an important role in the development of depression and, especially, bipolar disorder. **Cognitive distortions** (unrealistically negative views about the self) occur in many depressed people, although it is uncertain whether these cause the depression or are caused by it. Finally, social factors, such as troubled relationships, have also been linked with mood disorders.

Next, the chapter looks at anxiety disorders, whose effects extend beyond the experience of normal anxiety. Normal fear is caused by something identifiable and the fear subsides with time. With **anxiety disorder**, however, either the person doesn't know the source of the fear or the anxiety is inappropriate to the circumstances.

A **specific phobia** is an intense, paralyzing fear of something that it is unreasonable to fear so excessively. A **social phobia** is excessive, inappropriate fear connected with social situations or performances in front of other people. **Agoraphobia**, a less common and much more debilitating type of anxiety disorder, involves multiple, intense fears such as the fear of being alone, of being in public places, or of other situations involving separation from a source of security.

Panic disorder is characterized by recurring sudden, unpredictable, and overwhelming experiences of intense fear or terror without any reasonable cause.

Generalized anxiety disorder is defined by prolonged vague, but intense fears that, unlike phobias, are not attached to any particular object or circumstance. In contrast, **obsessive–compulsive disorder** involves either involuntary thoughts that recur despite the person's attempt to stop them or compulsive rituals that a person feels compelled to perform. Two other types of anxiety disorder are caused by highly stressful events. If the anxious reaction occurs soon after the event, the diagnosis is *acute stress disorder*; if it occurs long after the event is over, the diagnosis is *posttraumatic stress disorder*.

Psychologists with a biological perspective propose that a predisposition to anxiety disorders may be inherited because these types of disorders tend to run in families. Cognitive psychologists suggest that people who believe that they have no control over stressful events in their lives are more likely to suffer from anxiety disorders than other people are. Evolutionary psychologists hold that we are predisposed by evolution to associate certain stimuli with intense fears, serving as the origin of many phobias. Psychoanalytic thinkers focus on inner psychological conflicts and the defense mechanisms they trigger as the sources of anxiety disorders.

The chapter focuses next on psychosomatic and somatoform disorders, followed by a brief look at dissociative disorders. **Psychosomatic disorders** are illnesses that have a valid physical basis, but are largely caused by psychological factors such as excessive stress and anxiety. In contrast, **somatoform disorders** are characterized by physical symptoms without any identifiable physical cause. Examples are **somatization disorder**, characterized by recurrent vague somatic complaints without a physical cause, **conversion disorder** (a dramatic specific disability without organic cause), **hypochondriasis** (insistence that minor symptoms mean serious illness), and **body dysmorphic disorder** (imagined ugliness in some part of the body).

In **dissociative disorders**, some part of a person's personality or memory is separated from the rest. **Dissociative amnesia** involves the loss of at least some significant aspects of memory. When an amnesia victim leaves home and assumes an entirely new identity, the disorder is known as **dissociative fugue**. In **dissociative identity disorder** (*multiple personality disorder*), several distinct personalities emerge at different times. In **depersonalization disorder**, the person suddenly feels changed or different in a strange way.

Sexual and gender-identity disorders are explored next in the chapter. The *DSM-IV-TR* recognizes three main types of sexual disorders: sexual dysfunction, paraphilias, and gender-identity disorders.

Sexual dysfunction is the loss or impairment of the ability to function effectively during sex. In men, this may take the form of **erectile disorder (ED)**, the inability to achieve or keep an erection; in women, it often takes the form of **female sexual arousal disorder**, the inability to become sexually excited or to reach orgasm. **Sexual desire disorders** involve a lack of interest in or an active aversion to sex. People with **orgasmic disorders** experience both desire and arousal but are unable to reach orgasm. Other problems that can occur include **premature ejaculation**—the male's inability to inhibit orgasm as long as desired—and **vaginismus**—involuntary muscle spasms in the outer part of a woman's vagina during sexual excitement that make intercourse impossible.

Paraphilias involve the use of unconventional sex objects or situations. These disorders include **fetishism, voyeurism, exhibitionism, frotteurism, transvestic fetishism, sexual sadism**, and **sexual masochism**. One of the most serious paraphilias is **pedophilia**, the engaging in sexual relations with children.

Gender-identity disorders involve the desire to become, or the insistence that one really is, a member of the other sex. **Gender-identity disorder in children** is characterized by rejection of one's biological gender as well as the clothing and behavior society considers appropriate to that gender during childhood.

The chapter continues with sections on personality and schizophrenic disorders. **Personality disorders** are enduring, inflexible, and maladaptive ways of thinking and behaving that are so exaggerated and rigid that they cause serious inner distress or conflicts with others. One group of personality disorders is characterized by odd or eccentric behavior. People who exhibit **schizoid personality disorder** lack the ability or desire to form social relationships and have no warm feelings for other people; those with **paranoid personality disorder** are inappropriately suspicious, hypersensitive, and argumentative. Another cluster of personality disorders is characterized by anxious or fearful behavior. Examples are **dependent personality disorder** (the inability to

think or act independently) and **avoidant personality disorder** (social anxiety leading to isolation). A third group of personality disorders is characterized by dramatic, emotional, or erratic behavior. For instance, people with **narcissistic personality disorder** have a highly overblown sense of self-importance, whereas those with **borderline personality disorder** show much instability in self-image, mood, and interpersonal relationships. Finally, people with **antisocial personality disorder** chronically lie, steal, and cheat with little or no remorse. Because this disorder is responsible for a good deal of crime and violence, it creates the greatest problems for society.

In multiple-personality disorder, consciousness is split into two or more distinctive personalities, each of which is coherent and intact. This condition is different from **schizophrenic disorders**, which involve dramatic disruptions in thought and communication, inappropriate emotions, and bizarre behavior that lasts for years. People with schizophrenia are out of touch with reality (which is to say, **psychotic**) and usually cannot live a normal life unless successfully treated with medication. They often suffer from **hallucinations** (false sensory perceptions) and **delusions** (false beliefs about reality). Subtypes of schizophrenic disorders include **disorganized schizophrenia** (childish disregard for social conventions), **catatonic schizophrenia** (mute immobility or excessive excitement), **paranoid schizophrenia** (extreme suspiciousness related to complex delusions), and **undifferentiated schizophrenia** (characterized by a diversity of symptoms).

The chapter continues with material covering a spectrum of childhood disorders. *DSM-IV-TR* contains a long list of disorders usually first diagnosed in infancy, childhood, or adolescence. Children with **attention-deficit hyperactivity disorder (ADHD)** are highly distractible, often fidgety and impulsive, and almost constantly in motion. The **psychostimulants** frequently prescribed for ADHD appear to slow such children down because they increase the ability to focus attention on routine tasks. **Autistic disorder** is a profound developmental problem identified in the first few years of life. It is characterized by a failure to form normal social attachments, by severe speech impairment, and by strange motor behaviors. A much broader range of developmental disorders known as **autistic spectrum disorder (ASD)** is used to describe individuals with symptoms that are similar to those seen in autistic disorder, but may be less severe as is the case in *Asperger syndrome*.

Finally, the chapter concludes with a section on gender and cultural differences in psychological disorders. Although nearly all psychological disorders affect both men and women, there are some gender differences in the degree to which some disorders are found. Men are more likely to suffer from substance abuse and antisocial personality disorder; women show higher rates of depression, agoraphobia, simple phobia, obsessive–compulsive disorder, and somatization disorder. In general, gender differences are less likely to be seen in disorders that have a strong biological component. This tendency is also seen cross-culturally, where cultural differences are observed in disorders not heavily influenced by genetic and biological factors. These gender and cultural differences support the systems view that biological, psychological, and social forces interact as causes of abnormal behavior.

LEARNING OBJECTIVES EXERCISE

After you have read and studied the chapter, you should be able to answer the following learning objectives.

PERSPECTIVES ON PSYCHOLOGICAL DISORDERS

• Compare the three perspectives on what constitutes abnormal behavior. Explain what is meant by the statement "Identifying behavior as abnormal is also a matter of degree." Distinguish between the *prevalence* and *incidence* of psychological disorders, and between *mental illness* and *insanity*.

• Describe the key features of the biological, psychoanalytic, cognitive–behavioral, diathesis–stress, and systems models of psychological disorders.

• Explain what is meant by "*DSM-IV-TR*" and describe the basis on which it categorizes disorders.

MOOD DISORDERS

• Explain how mood disorders differ from ordinary mood changes. List the key symptoms that are used to diagnose major depression, dysthymia, mania, and bipolar disorder. Describe the causes of mood disorders.

• Describe the factors that are related to a person's likelihood of committing suicide. Contrast the three myths about suicide with the actual facts about suicide.

ANXIETY DISORDERS

• Explain how anxiety disorders differ from ordinary anxiety. Briefly describe the key features of phobias, panic disorders, generalized anxiety disorder, and obsessive–compulsive disorder.

• Describe the causes of anxiety disorders.

PSYCHOSOMATIC AND SOMATOFORM DISORDERS

• Distinguish between psychosomatic and somatoform disorders, somatization disorder, conversion disorders, hypochondriasis, and body dysmorphic disorder. Explain what is meant by the statement that "all physical ailments are to some extent psychosomatic."

DISSOCIATIVE DISORDERS

• Explain what is meant by *dissociation*. Briefly describe the key features of dissociative amnesia, dissociative fugue, dissociative identity disorder, and depersonalization disorder.

SEXUAL AND GENDER-IDENTITY DISORDERS

- Identify the three main types of sexual disorders that are recognized in the *DSM-IV-TR*.

PERSONALITY DISORDERS

- Identify the distinguishing characteristic of personality disorders. Briefly describe schizoid, paranoid, dependent, avoidant, narcissistic, borderline, and anti-social personality disorders.

SCHIZOPHRENIC DISORDERS

- Describe the common feature in all cases of schizophrenia. Explain the difference between hallucinations and delusions. Briefly describe the key features of disorganized, catatonic, paranoid, and undifferentiated schizophrenia.

- Describe the causes of schizophrenic disorders.

CHILDHOOD DISORDERS

- Describe the key features of attention-deficit hyperactivity disorder and autistic spectrum disorder including the difference between autism and Asperger syndrome.

GENDER AND CULTURAL DIFFERENCES IN PSYCHOLOGICAL DISORDERS

- Describe the differences between men and women in psychological disorders including the prevalence of disorders and the kinds of disorders they are likely to experience. Explain why these differences exist. Explain why "it is increasingly important for mental health professionals to be aware of cultural differences" in psychological disorders.

I.   Enduring Issues in Psychological Disorders (page 391)

II. Perspectives on Psychological Disorders (page 391)
     A. Historical Views of Psychological Disorders
     B. The Biological Model
     C. The Psychoanalytic Model
     D. The Cognitive–Behavioral Model
     E. The Diathesis–Stress Model and Systems Theory
     F. The Prevalence of Psychological Disorders
     G. Mental Illness and the Law
         • Insanity
     H. Classifying Abnormal Behavior
         • *DSM-IV-TR*

III. Mood Disorders (page 398)
     A. Depression
         • Major Depressive Disorder
         • Dysthymia
     B. APPLYING PSYCHOLOGY: RECOGNIZING DEPRESSION
     C. Suicide
         • Gender and Race Differences
         • Myths and Facts
     D. Mania and Bipolar Disorder
     E. Causes of Mood Disorders
         i.   Biological Factors
         ii.   Psychological Factors
         iii. Social Factors

IV. Anxiety Disorders (page 403)
     A. Specific Phobias
         • Social Phobias
         • Agoraphobia
     B. Panic Disorder
         • Recurrent Panic
     C. Other Anxiety Disorders
         • Generalized Anxiety Disorder
         • Obsessive–Compulsive Disorder
         • Acute Stress Disorder
         • Posttraumatic Stress Disorder
     D. Causes of Anxiety Disorders
         • Learned Behaviors
         • Biological Perspective
         • Internal Psychological Conflicts

V.   Psychosomatic and Somatoform Disorders (page 406)
     • Psychosomatic Disorder
     • Somatoform Disorder
     • Somatization Disorders
     • Conversion Disorder
     • Hypochondrias
     • Body Dysmorphic Disorder

VI. Dissociative Disorders (page 408)
     • Dissociative Amnesia
     • Dissociative Fugue
     • Dissociative Identity Disorder
     • Depersonalization Disorder

VII. Sexual and Gender-Identity Disorders (page 409)
     • Sexual Dysfunction
     • Sexual Disorders
     • Gender Identity Disorders

VIII. Personality Disorders (page 412)
     • Schizoid Personality Disorder
     • Paranoid Personality Disorder
     • Dependent Personality Disorder
     • Avoidant Personality Disorder
     • Narcissistic Personality Disorder
     • Borderline Personality Disorder
     • Antisocial Personality Disorder

IX. Schizophrenic Disorders (page 415)
     A. Types of Schizophrenic Disorders
         • Disorganized Schizophrenia
         • Catatonic Schizophrenia
         • Paranoid Schizophrenia
         • Undifferentiated Schizophrenia
     B. Causes of Schizophrenia
         • Biological Predisposition
         • Twins Studies

X.   Childhood Disorders (page 417)
     • Attention-deficit Disorder (ADHD)
     • Autistic Disorder
     • Autistic Spectrum Disorder (ASD)

XI. Gender and Cultural Differences in Psychological Disorders (page 419)
     A. Gender Differences
         • Differences Do Exist
     B. Cultural Differences
         • Some Disorders Occur Only in Particular Cultural Groups

KEY TERMS

Agoraphobia	An anxiety disorder that involves multiple, intense fears of crowds, public places, and other situations that require separation from a source of security such as the home. (p. 404)
Antisocial personality disorder	Personality disorder that involves a pattern of violent, criminal, or unethical and exploitative behavior and an inability to feel affection for others. (p. 413)
Anxiety disorders	Disorders in which anxiety is a characteristic feature or the avoidance of anxiety seems to motivate abnormal behavior. (p. 403)
Attention-deficit hyperactivity disorder (ADHD)	A childhood disorder characterized by inattention, impulsiveness, and hyperactivity. (p. 417)
Autistic disorder	A childhood disorder characterized by lack of social instincts and strange motor behavior. (p. 417)
Autistic spectrum disorder (ASD)	A range of disorders involving varying degrees of impairment in communication skills, social interactions, and restricted, repetitive, and stereotyped patterns of behavior. (p. 418)
Avoidant personality disorder	Personality disorder in which the person's fears of rejection by others lead to social isolation. (p. 413)
Biological model	View that psychological disorders have a biochemical or physiological basis. (p. 393)
Bipolar disorder	A mood disorder in which periods of mania and depression alternate, sometimes with periods of normal mood intervening. (p. 401)
Body dysmorphic disorder	A somatoform disorder in which a person becomes so preoccupied with his or her imagined ugliness that normal life is impossible. (p. 407)
Borderline personality disorder	Personality disorder characterized by marked instability in self-image, mood, and interpersonal relationships. (p. 413)
Catatonic schizophrenia	Schizophrenic disorder in which disturbed motor behavior is prominent. (p. 415)
Cognitive distortions	An illogical and maladaptive response to early negative life events that leads to feelings of incompetence and unworthiness that are reactivated whenever a new situation arises that resembles the original events. (p. 402)
Cognitive–behavioral model	View that psychological disorders result from learning maladaptive ways of thinking and behaving. (p. 394)
Conversion disorders	Somatoform disorders in which a dramatic specific disability has no physical cause but instead seems related to psychological problems. (p. 407)
Delusions	False beliefs about reality that have no basis in fact. (p. 415)
Dependent personality disorder	Personality disorder in which the person is unable to make choices and decisions independently and cannot tolerate being alone. (p. 413)
Depersonalization disorder	A dissociative disorder whose essential feature is that the person suddenly feels changed or different in a strange way. (p. 408)
Depression	A mood disorder characterized by overwhelming feelings of sadness, lack of interest in activities, and perhaps excessive guilt or feelings of worthlessness. (p. 398)
Diathesis	Biological predisposition. (p. 395)
Diathesis–stress model	View that people biologically predisposed to a mental disorder (those with a certain diathesis) will tend to exhibit that disorder when particularly affected by stress. (p. 394)
Disorganized schizophrenia	Schizophrenic disorder in which bizarre and childlike behaviors are common. (p. 415)

Dissociative amnesia	A disorder characterized by loss of memory for past events without organic cause. (p. 408)
Dissociative disorders	Disorders in which some aspect of the personality seems separated from the rest. (p. 408)
Dissociative fugue	A disorder that involves flight from home and the assumption of a new identity with amnesia for past identity and events. (p. 408)
Dissociative identity disorder	(Also called multiple personality disorder.) Disorder characterized by the separation of the personality into two or more distinct personalities. (p. 408)
Dysthymia	A depressive disorder where the symptoms are generally less severe than for major depressive disorder, but are present most days and persist for at least 2 years. (p. 398)
Erectile disorder (or erectile dysfunction) (ED)	The inability of a man to achieve or maintain an erection. (p. 409)
Exhibitionism	Compulsion to expose one's genitals in public to achieve sexual arousal. (p. 411)
Female sexual arousal disorder	The inability of a woman to become sexually aroused or to reach orgasm. (p. 409)
Fetishism	A paraphilia in which a nonhuman object is the preferred or exclusive method of achieving sexual excitement. (p. 411)
Frotteurism	Compulsion to achieve sexual arousal by touching or rubbing against a nonconsenting person in public situations. (p. 411)
Gender-identity disorder in children	Rejection of one's biological gender in childhood, along with the clothing and behavior that society considers appropriate to that gender. (p. 412)
Gender-identity disorders	Disorders that involve the desire to become, or the insistence that one really is, a member of the other biological sex. (p. 412)
Generalized anxiety disorder	An anxiety disorder characterized by prolonged vague but intense fears that are not attached to any particular object or circumstance. (p. 404)
Hallucinations	Sensory experiences in the absence of external stimulation. (p. 415)
Hypochondriasis	A somatoform disorder in which a person interprets insignificant symptoms as signs of serious illness in the absence of any organic evidence of such illness. (p. 407)
Insanity	Legal term applied to defendants who do not know right from wrong or are unable to control their behavior. (p. 396)
Major depressive disorder	A depressive disorder characterized by an episode of intense sadness, depressed mood, or marked loss of interest or pleasure in nearly all activities. (p. 398)
Mania	A mood disorder characterized by euphoric states, extreme physical activity, excessive talkativeness, distractedness, and sometimes grandiosity. (p. 401)
Mood disorders	Disturbances in mood or prolonged emotional state. (p. 398)
Narcissistic personality disorder	Personality disorder in which the person has an exaggerated sense of self-importance and needs constant admiration. (p. 413)
Obsessive–compulsive disorder (OCD)	An anxiety disorder in which a person feels driven to think disturbing thoughts or to perform senseless rituals. (p. 405)
Orgasmic disorders	Inability to reach orgasm in a person able to experience sexual desire and maintain arousal. (p. 410)
Panic disorder	An anxiety disorder characterized by recurrent panic attacks in which the person suddenly experiences intense fear or terror without any reasonable cause. (p. 404)
Paranoid personality disorder	Personality disorder in which the person is inappropriately suspicious and mistrustful of others. (p. 413)
Paranoid schizophrenia	Schizophrenic disorder marked by extreme suspiciousness and complex, bizarre delusions. (p. 415)

Paraphilias	Sexual disorders in which unconventional objects or situations cause sexual arousal. (p. 411)
Pedophilia	Desire to have sexual relations with children as the preferred or exclusive method of achieving sexual excitement. (p. 411)
Personality disorders	Disorders in which inflexible and maladaptive ways of thinking and behaving learned early in life cause distress to the person or conflicts with others. (p. 412)
Premature ejaculation	Inability of man to inhibit orgasm as long as desired. (p. 411)
Psychoanalytic model	View that psychological disorders result from unconscious internal conflicts. (p. 394)
Psychosomatic disorder	A disorder in which there is real physical illness that is largely caused by psychological factors such as stress and anxiety. (p. 406)
Psychostimulants	Drugs that increase ability to focus attention in people with ADHD. (p. 417)
Psychotic (psychosis)	Behavior characterized by a loss of touch with reality. (p. 415)
Schizoid personality disorder	Personality disorder in which a person is withdrawn and lacks feelings for others. (p. 412)
Schizophrenic disorders	Severe disorders in which there are disturbances of thoughts, communications, and emotions, including delusions and hallucinations. (p. 415)
Sexual desire disorders	Disorders in which the person lacks sexual interest or has an active distaste for sex. (p. 410)
Sexual dysfunction	Loss or impairment of the ordinary physical responses of sexual function. (p. 409)
Sexual masochism	Inability to enjoy sex without accompanying emotional or physical pain. (p. 411)
Sexual sadism	Obtaining sexual gratification from humiliating or physically harming a sex partner. (p. 411)
Social phobias	Anxiety disorders characterized by excessive, inappropriate fears connected with social situations or performances in front of other people. (p. 403)
Somatization disorder	A somatoform disorder characterized by recurrent vague somatic complaints without a physical cause. (p. 406)
Somatoform disorders	Disorders in which there is an apparent physical illness for which there is no organic basis. (p. 406)
Specific phobia	Anxiety disorder characterized by an intense, paralyzing fear of something. (p. 403)
Systems approach	View that biological, psychological, and social risk factors combine to produce psychological disorders. Also known as the biopsychosocial model of psychological disorders. (p. 395)
Transvestic fetishism	Wearing the clothes of the opposite sex to achieve sexual gratification. (p. 411)
Undifferentiated schizophrenia	Schizophrenic disorder in which there are clear schizophrenic symptoms that do not meet the criteria for another subtype of the disorder. (p. 415)
Vaginismus	Involuntary muscle spasms in the outer part of the vagina that make intercourse impossible. (p. 411)
Voyeurism	Desire to watch others having sexual relations or to spy on nude people. (p. 411)

Vocabulary Flashcards

Cut out each term and use as study cards. The definition is on the back side of each term.

Biological model	**Systems approach**
Psychoanalytic model	**Insanity**
Cognitive–behavioral model	**Mood disorders**
Diathesis–stress model	**Depression**
Diathesis	**Major depressive disorder**

View that biological, psychological, and social risk factors combine to produce psychological disorders. Also known as the biopsychosocial model of psychological disorders.	View that psychological disorders have a biochemical or physiological basis.
Legal term applied to defendants who do not know right from wrong or are unable to control their behavior.	View that psychological disorders result from unconscious internal conflicts.
Disturbances in mood or prolonged emotional state.	View that psychological disorders result from learning maladaptive ways of thinking and behaving.
A mood disorder characterized by overwhelming feelings of sadness, lack of interest in activities, and perhaps excessive guilt or feelings of worthlessness.	View that people biologically predisposed to a mental disorder (those with a certain diathesis) will tend to exhibit that disorder when particularly affected by stress.
A depressive disorder characterized by an episode of intense sadness, depressed mood, or marked loss of interest or pleasure in nearly all activities.	Biological predisposition.

Dysthymia	Specific phobia
Mania	Social phobias
Bipolar disorder	Agoraphobia
Cognitive distortions	Panic disorder
Anxiety disorders	Generalized anxiety disorder

Anxiety disorder characterized by an intense, paralyzing fear of something.

A depressive disorder where the symptoms are generally less severe than for major depressive disorder, but are present most days and persist for at least 2 years.

Anxiety disorders characterized by excessive, inappropriate fears connected with social situations or performances in front of other people.

A mood disorder characterized by euphoric states, extreme physical activity, excessive talkativeness, distractedness, and sometimes grandiosity.

An anxiety disorder that involves multiple, intense fears of crowds, public places, and other situations that require separation from a source of security such as the home.

A mood disorder in which periods of mania and depression alternate, sometimes with periods of normal mood intervening.

An anxiety disorder characterized by recurrent panic attacks in which the person suddenly experiences intense fear or terror without any reasonable cause.

An illogical and maladaptive response to early negative life events that leads to feelings of incompetence and unworthiness that are reactivated whenever a new situation arises that resembles the original events.

An anxiety disorder characterized by prolonged vague but intense fears that are not attached to any particular object or circumstance.

Disorders in which anxiety is a characteristic feature or the avoidance of anxiety seems to motivate abnormal behavior.

Obsessive–compulsive disorder (OCD)	**Hypochondriasis**
Psychosomatic disorder	**Body dysmorphic disorder**
Somatoform disorders	**Dissociative disorders**
Somatization disorder	**Dissociative amnesia**
Conversion disorders	**Dissociative fugue**

A somatoform disorder in which a person interprets insignificant symptoms as signs of serious illness in the absence of any organic evidence of such illness.

An anxiety disorder in which a person feels driven to think disturbing thoughts or to perform senseless rituals.

A somatoform disorder in which a person becomes so preoccupied with his or her imagined ugliness that normal life is impossible.

A disorder in which there is real physical illness that is largely caused by psychological factors such as stress and anxiety.

Disorders in which some aspect of the personality seems separated from the rest.

Disorders in which there is an apparent physical illness for which there is no organic basis.

A disorder characterized by loss of memory for past events without organic cause.

A somatoform disorder characterized by recurrent vague somatic complaints without a physical cause.

A disorder that involves flight from home and the assumption of a new identity with amnesia for past identity and events.

Somatoform disorders in which a dramatic specific disability has no physical cause but instead seems related to psychological problems.

Dissociative identity disorder	**Sexual desire disorders**
Depersonalization disorder	**Orgasmic disorders**
Sexual dysfunction	**Premature ejaculation**
Erectile disorder (or erectile dysfunction) (ED)	**Vaginismus**
Female sexual arousal disorder	**Paraphilias**

Disorders in which the person lacks sexual interest or has an active distaste for sex.	(Also called multiple personality disorder.) Disorder characterized by the separation of the personality into two or more distinct personalities.
Inability to reach orgasm in a person able to experience sexual desire and maintain arousal.	A dissociative disorder whose essential feature is that the person suddenly feels changed or different in a strange way.
Inability of man to inhibit orgasm as long as desired.	Loss or impairment of the ordinary physical responses of sexual function.
Involuntary muscle spasms in the outer part of the vagina that make intercourse impossible.	The inability of a man to achieve or maintain an erection.
Sexual disorders in which unconventional objects or situations cause sexual arousal.	The inability of a woman to become sexually aroused or to reach orgasm.

Fetishism	Sexual sadism
Voyeurism	Sexual masochism
Exhibitionism	Pedophilia
Frotteurism	Gender-identity disorders
Transvestic fetishism	Gender-identity disorder in children

Obtaining sexual gratification from humiliating or physically harming a sex partner.

A paraphilia in which a nonhuman object is the preferred or exclusive method of achieving sexual excitement.

Inability to enjoy sex without accompanying emotional or physical pain.

Desire to watch others having sexual relations or to spy on nude people.

Desire to have sexual relations with children as the preferred or exclusive method of achieving sexual excitement.

Compulsion to expose one's genitals in public to achieve sexual arousal.

Disorders that involve the desire to become, or the insistence that one really is, a member of the other biological sex.

Compulsion to achieve sexual arousal by touching or rubbing against a nonconsenting person in public situations.

Rejection of one's biological gender in childhood, along with the clothing and behavior that society considers appropriate to that gender.

Wearing the clothes of the opposite sex to achieve sexual gratification.

Personality disorders	**Narcissistic personality disorder**
Schizoid personality disorder	**Borderline personality disorder**
Paranoid personality disorder	**Antisocial personality disorder**
Dependent personality disorder	**Schizophrenic disorders**
Avoidant personality disorder	**Psychotic (psychosis)**

Personality disorder in which the person has an exaggerated sense of self-importance and needs constant admiration.

Disorders in which inflexible and maladaptive ways of thinking and behaving learned early in life cause distress to the person or conflicts with others.

Personality disorder characterized by marked instability in self-image, mood, and interpersonal relationships.

Personality disorder in which a person is withdrawn and lacks feelings for others.

Personality disorder that involves a pattern of violent, criminal, or unethical and exploitative behavior and an inability to feel affection for others.

Personality disorder in which the person is inappropriately suspicious and mistrustful of others.

Severe disorders in which there are disturbances of thoughts, communications, and emotions, including delusions and hallucinations.

Personality disorder in which the person is unable to make choices and decisions independently and cannot tolerate being alone.

Behavior characterized by a loss of touch with reality.

Personality disorder in which the person's fears of rejection by others lead to social isolation.

Hallucinations	**Undifferentiated schizophrenia**
Delusions	**Attention-deficit hyperactivity disorder (ADHD)**
Disorganized schizophrenia	**Psychostimulants**
Catatonic schizophrenia	**Autistic disorder**
Paranoid schizophrenia	**Autistic spectrum disorder (ASD)**

Schizophrenic disorder in which there are clear schizophrenic symptoms that do not meet the criteria for another subtype of the disorder.

Sensory experiences in the absence of external stimulation.

A childhood disorder characterized by inattention, impulsiveness, and hyperactivity.

False beliefs about reality that have no basis in fact.

Drugs that increase ability to focus attention in people with ADHD.

Schizophrenic disorder in which bizarre and childlike behaviors are common.

A childhood disorder characterized by lack of social instincts and strange motor behavior.

Schizophrenic disorder in which disturbed motor behavior is prominent.

A range of disorders involving varying degrees of impairment in communication skills, social interactions, and restricted, repetitive, and stereotyped patterns of behavior.

Schizophrenic disorder marked by extreme suspiciousness and complex, bizarre delusions.

After studying the text and completing the Study Guide activities, answer these questions to determine if you need to review any areas before the course exam.

MULTIPLE CHOICE

1. The turning point year in the history of treatment of the mentally ill was _____, when Phillipe Pinel became director of the Bicetre Hospital in Paris and argued for pleasant living conditions for the patients.
   a. 1379
   b. 1793
   c. 1894
   d. 1937

2. The basic reason for the failed, and sometimes abusive, treatment of mentally disturbed people throughout history has been _____.
   a. fear of retribution by supernatural forces
   b. a lack of understanding of the causes and treatments of psychological disorders
   c. political and legal restrictions placed on treatment by insensitive authorities
   d. lack of money to provide adequate care for disturbed people

3. The _____ model of mental illness holds that abnormal behavior is caused by physiological malfunction that is often attributable to hereditary factors.
   a. biological
   b. cognitive-behavioral
   c. psycho-dynamic
   d. naturalistic

4. The view that people biologically predisposed to a mental disorder will tend to exhibit that acute stress disorder when particularly affected by stress is known as the _____ model of abnormal behavior.
   a. multimodal
   b. pluralistic
   c. psychoneuro-immunological
   d. diathesis-stress

5. An affective/mood disorder that includes both depression and mania is known as _____.
   a. histrionic
   b. bipolar
   c. obsessive-compulsive
   d. diathesis-stress

6. An intense, paralyzing fear of a specific situation, object, person, or thing in the absence of any real danger is a _____.
   a. histrionic
   b. phobic disorder
   c. dual process
   d. obsessive-compulsive

7. An anxiety disorder in which a person feels driven to think disturbing thoughts and/or to perform senseless rituals is _____ disorder.
   a. panic
   b. phobic
   c. conversion
   d. obsessive-compulsive

8. Mental disorders are categorized according to ___ in the DSM-IV.
   a. family histories
   b. biological causes of disruptive behavior
   c. significant behavior patterns
   d. specific theoretical approaches

9. The disorder previously known as "multiple personality disorder" is now known as _____.
   a. dissociative amnesia
   b. dissociative identity disorder
   c. dissociative fugue
   d. depersonal-ization disorder

10. The most widely accepted explanation for dissociative identity disorder is that it is a response to _____.
    a. neurotransmitter imbalances
    b. childhood abuse
    c. role diffusion
    d. extreme loneliness

11. Sexual arousal as a result of fantasizing about or engaging in sexual activity with prepubescent children is _____.
    a. infantile sexual regression
    b. sadomasochistic immaturity
    c. pedophilia
    d. transvestism

12. Rejection of one's biological gender and persistently desiring to become a member of the opposite sex is known as _____.
    a. sexual orientation disorder
    b. bisexuality
    c. gender identity disorder
    d. hermaphroditism

13. John is a pathological liar. He takes things from others, takes advantage of them, and never exhibits any remorse after he is done. John has _____ personality disorder.
    a. paranoid
    b. narcissistic
    c. antisocial
    d. borderline

14. _____ disorders are marked by disordered communication and thoughts, inappropriate emotions, and bizarre behaviors.
    a. Psychosexual
    b. Neurotic
    c. Somatoform
    d. Schizophrenic

15. The psychological term for someone who is mentally disturbed to the point of not being in contact with reality and not being legally responsible for his or her actions is _____.
    a. schizophrenia
    b. split personality
    c. insanity
    d. psycho-pathology

16. Research suggests that a biological vulnerability to schizophrenia may lie in excess amounts of _____.
    a. thyroxin
    b. epinephrine
    c. vasopressin
    d. dopamine

17. Currently the cause of attention deficit/hyperactivity disorder and autism is thought to be _____.
    a. arrested emotional development
    b. biological and/or genetic abnormalities
    c. over-demanding and emotionally detached parents
    d. prenatal maternal alcohol use

18. Women are more likely to suffer from _____ than men, and men are more likely to suffer from _____ than women.
    a. depression; substance abuse disorders
    b. antisocial personality; anxiety disorder
    c. substance abuse disorders; depression
    d. paranoid disorders; histrionic disorders

SHORT ESSAY QUESTIONS

1. Distinguish among the standards for defining abnormal behavior from the view of society, the individual, and the mental health professional.

2. Summarize historical attitudes toward abnormal behavior.

3. State the four current models of abnormal behavior and explain the diathesis-stress model. Explain how the DSM-IV classifies mental disorders.

4. Distinguish between the two basic kinds of mood disorders and how they may interact with each other.

5. Describe the differences between depression and a normal reaction to negative life events.

6. Discuss the possible causes of mood disorders including biological and psychological factors.

7. Describe the characteristics of the psychophysiological disorders and the somatoform disorders.

8. Define and give examples of the sexual disorders.

9. Describe four types of schizophrenic disorders and identify possible causes of the disorder.

10. Discuss the complex factors that contribute to different rates of abnormal behavior in men and women.

ANSWERS AND EXPLANATIONS TO MULTIPLE CHOICE POSTTEST

1. b.   In 1793, Philippe Pinel was made Director of the Bicetre Hospital in Paris and drastically reorganized the care and treatment for the mentally ill. p. 393

2. b.   Lack of understanding of the nature and causes of psychological disorders is the basic reason for the failed and sometimes abusive treatment of the mentally ill. p. 393

3. a.   The biological model holds that psychological disorders have a biochemical or physiological basis. p. 393

4. d.   The diathesis-stress model sees people who are biologically predisposed to a mental disorder will exhibit that disorder when affected by extreme stress. p. 394

5. b.   Bipolar disorder alternates between periods of mania and depression, along with period of normal moods. p. 401

6. b.   Phobic disorders are characterized by an intense, paralyzing, and irrational fear of something. p. 403

7. d.   A person with obsessive/compulsive disorder feels driven to think disturbing thoughts or to perform senseless rituals to reduce anxiety. p. 405

8. c.   The DSM-IV lists mental disorders in terms of significant behavior patterns. p. 397

9. b.   Dissociative identity disorder was formerly called multiple personality disorder. p. 408

10. b.   Clinicians report a history of child abuse in more than three-fourths of their dissociative identity disorder cases. p. 408

11. c.   Pedophilia is the desire to have sexual relationships with children. p. 411

12. c.   Gender identity disorder is the desire to become a member of the other biological sex. p. 411

13. c.   Some individual with antisocial personality disorder lie, steal, cheat, and show little or no sense of responsibility or remorse. p. 413

14. d.   Schizophrenia is marked by disordered communications and thoughts and inappropriate emotions and bizarre behavior. p. 415

15. c.   Insanity is a legal term for mentally disturbed people not considered responsible for their criminal actions. p. 396

16. d.   Recent research suggests that schizophrenia may be related to excessive amounts of dopamine in the central nervous system. p. 416

17. b.   We don't yet know the cause of either ADHD or autism, but most theorists believe that they result almost entirely from biological or genetic factors. p. 417

18. a.   Men drink or abuse drugs more when they have psychological problems, and women are more likely to become depressed and helpless. p. 419

CHAPTER 13   Therapies

CHAPTER OVERVIEW

Beginning with the story of Brooke Shields' postpartum depression and her subsequent treatment (a combination of medication and **psychotherapy**), this chapter sets out to describe a variety of treatments that mental health professionals provide. The first of these is insight therapy.

The various types of **insight therapy** share the common goal of providing people with better awareness and understanding of their feelings, motivations, and actions to foster better adjustment. Among these are psychoanalysis, client-centered therapy, and Gestalt therapy.

Psychoanalysis is based on the belief that psychological problems stem from feelings and conflicts repressed during childhood. These repressed feelings can be revealed through **free association**, a process in which the client discloses whatever thoughts or fantasies come to mind without inhibition. As therapy progresses, the analyst takes a more active interpretive role, with the goal being to help the client gain **insight**—to become aware of what was formerly outside of their awareness. **Transference** is the client's carrying over to the analyst feelings held toward childhood authority figures.

Carl Rogers believed treatment for psychological problems should be based on the client's view of the world rather than that of the therapist. The therapist's most important task in his approach, called **client-centered** or **person-centered therapy**, is to provide unconditional positive regard for clients so they will learn to accept themselves.

Gestalt therapy helps people become more aware of their feelings and thus, more genuine. Unlike Freud, who sat quietly out of sight while his clients recalled past memories, the Gestalt therapist confronts the patient, emphasizes the present, and focuses on the *whole* person.

Contemporary insight therapists are more actively involved than traditional psychoanalysts, offering clients direct guidance and feedback. An especially significant development is the trend toward **short-term psychodynamic therapy**, in which treatment time is limited and oriented toward current life situations and relationships, rather than childhood traumas.

The chapter focuses next on **behavior therapies**, which are based on the belief that all behavior is learned and that people can be taught more satisfying ways of behaving. Maladaptive behaviors are the focus of behavioral psychotherapy, rather than the deeper underlying conflicts that presumably are causing them.

When new conditioned responses are evoked to old stimuli, classical conditioning principles are being used as a basis for treatment. One therapeutic example is **systematic desensitization**, in which people learn to remain in a deeply relaxed state while confronting feared situations. *Flooding*, which exposes phobic people to feared situations at full intensity for a prolonged period, is a harsh but effective method of desensitization. In **aversive conditioning**, the goal is to eliminate undesirable behavior by associating it with pain and discomfort.

Therapies based on operant conditioning encourage or discourage behaviors by reinforcing or punishing them. In **behavior contracting,** client and therapist agree on certain behavioral goals and on the reinforcement that the client will receive on reaching them. In the **token economy** technique, tokens that can be exchanged for rewards are used for positive reinforcement of adaptive behaviors.

In **modeling**, a person learns new behaviors by watching others perform them. Modeling has been used to teach fearless behaviors to phobic people and job skills to mentally retarded people.

The chapter progresses with a look at cognitive therapies. **Cognitive therapies** focus not so much on maladaptive behaviors as on maladaptive ways of thinking. By changing people's distorted, self-defeating ideas about themselves and the world, cognitive therapies help to encourage better coping skills and adjustment.

The things we say to ourselves as we go about our daily lives can encourage success or failure, a self-confidence or anxiety. With **stress-inoculation therapy**, clients learn how to use self-talk to "coach" themselves through stressful situations.

Rational–emotive therapy (RET) is based on the idea that emotional problems derive from a set of irrational and self-defeating beliefs that people hold about themselves and the world. They must be liked by *everyone*, competent at *everything*, *always* be treated fairly, *never* be stymied by a problem. The therapist vigorously challenges these beliefs, enabling clients to reinterpret their experiences in a more positive light.

Aaron Beck believes that depression results from thought patterns that are strongly and inappropriately self-critical. Like RET but in a less confrontational manner, Beck's **cognitive therapy** tries to help such people think more objectively and positively about themselves and their life situations.

The chapter moves next into a discussion of group therapies. **Group therapies** are based on the idea that psychological problems are partly interpersonal and therefore, best approached in a group. Group therapies offer a circle of support and shared insight, as well as psychotherapy at a lower cost. Examples include self-help groups, family therapy, and couple therapy.

Family therapy is based on the belief that a person's psychological problems often signal family problems. Therefore, the therapist treats the entire family, rather than just the troubled individual, with the primary goals of improving communication and empathy and reducing family conflict.

Couple therapy concentrates on improving patterns of communication and interaction between partners. It attempts to change relationships, rather than individuals. Empathy training and scheduled exchanges of rewards are two techniques used to improve relationships.

Owing to the high cost of private psychotherapy, low-cost self-help groups have become increasingly popular. In groups like Alcoholics Anonymous, people share their concerns and feelings with others who are experiencing similar problems.

The chapter raises the question of psychotherapy's effectiveness. Formal psychotherapy helps about two-thirds of people treated. Although there is some debate over how many untreated people recover, the consensus is that those who get therapy are generally better off than those who don't.

Although each kind of therapy works better for some problems than for others, most treatment benefits derive from the therapeutic experience, regardless of the therapist's particular perspective. All therapies provide an explanation of problems, hope, and an alliance with a caring, supportive person. The general trend in psychotherapy is toward **eclecticism**, the use of whatever treatment works best for a particular problem.

The chapter shifts focus to cover a different area of treatment: biological treatments. **Biological treatments**—including medication, electroconvulsive therapy, and psychosurgery—are sometimes used when people are too agitated or disoriented to respond to psychotherapy, when there is a strong biological component to the psychological disorder, and when people are dangerous to themselves and others. Medication is often used in conjunction with psychotherapy. Traditionally, psychiatrists were the only mental health professionals licensed to offer biological treatments. However, some states now extend that privilege to specially trained clinical psychologists.

Drugs are the most common form of biological therapy. **Antipsychotic drugs** are valuable in treating schizophrenia. They do not cure the disorder, but they reduce its symptoms, though side effects can be severe. Many types of medications are used to treat psychological disorders, including antidepressants, antimanic and antianxiety drugs, sedatives, and psychostimulants.

Electroconvulsive therapy (ECT) is used for cases of severe depression that do not respond to other treatments. An electric current is briefly passed through a patient's brain. Newer forms of ECT are given to only one side of the brain.

Psychosurgery is brain surgery performed to change a person's behavior and emotional state. Rarely used today, it is a final, desperate measure on people who have severe and intractable problems and don't respond to any other form of treatment.

The chapter next examines the subject of institutionalization and its alternatives. For 150 years, institutionalization in large mental hospitals was the most common approach. Patients with serious mental disorders were given shelter and some degree of treatment, but a many never recovered enough to be released. With the advent of antipsychotic drugs in the 1950s, a trend began toward **deinstitutionalization**.

Poorly funded community mental health centers and other support services have proved inadequate in caring for previously institutionalized patients with mental disorders. Many patients stopped taking their medication, became psychotic, and ended up homeless on the streets. Although the concept of deinstitutionalization may have been good in principle, in practice it has failed for many patients and for society.

Alternatives to rehospitalization include living at home with adequate supports provided to all family members; living in small, homelike facilities in which residents and staff share responsibilities; living in hostels with therapy and crisis intervention provided; and receiving intensive outpatient counseling or frequent visits from public health nurses. Most alternative treatments involve daily professional contact and skillful preparation of the family and community. Most studies have found more positive outcomes for alternative treatments than for hospitalization.

Prevention refers to efforts to reduce the incidence of mental illness before it arises. **Primary prevention** consists of improving the social environment through assistance to parents, education, and family planning. **Secondary prevention** involves identifying high-risk groups and intervention thereof. **Tertiary prevention** involves helping hospitalized patients return to the community and community education.

The chapter concludes with a section on client diversity and treatment. Given that humans differ as much as they do, it isn't surprising that a one-size-fits-all concept isn't always appropriate in the treatment of psychological problems. In recent years, the special needs of women and people from other cultures have particularly occupied the attention of mental health professionals.

Women are more likely than men to be in psychotherapy, and are more likely prescribed psychoactive medication. Because, in traditional therapy, women are often expected to conform to gender stereotypes in order to be pronounced "well," many women have turned to "feminist therapists." The American Psychological Association has issued guidelines to ensure that women receive treatment that is not tied to traditional ideas about appropriate behavior for the sexes.

When a client and therapist come from different cultural backgrounds or belong to different racial or ethnic groups, misunderstandings can arise in therapy. Therapists must recognize that cultural differences exist in the nature of the psychological disorders that affect people. Treatment and prevention must be tailored to the beliefs and cultural practices of the person's ethnic group.

LEARNING OBJECTIVES EXERCISE

After you have read and studied the chapter, you should be able to answer the following learning objectives.

INSIGHT THERAPIES

- Describe the common goal of all insight therapies. Compare and contrast psychoanalysis, client-centered therapy, and Gestalt therapy.

- Explain how short-term psychodynamic therapy and virtual therapy differ from the more traditional forms of insight therapy.

BEHAVIOR THERAPIES

- Explain the statement that "Behavior therapies sharply contrast with insight-oriented approaches."

- Describe the processes of desensitization, extinction, flooding, aversive conditioning, behavior contracting, token economies, and modeling.

COGNITIVE THERAPIES

- Describe the common beliefs that underlie all cognitive therapies.

- Compare and contrast stress-inoculation therapy, rational–emotive therapy, and Beck's cognitive therapy.

GROUP THERAPIES

- Describe the potential advantages of group therapy compared to individual therapy.

- Compare and contrast family therapy, couple therapy, and self-help groups.

EFFECTIVENESS OF PSYCHOTHERAPY

- Summarize the research evidence that psychotherapy is, in fact, more effective than no therapy at all. Briefly describe the five major results of the *Consumer Reports* study.

- Describe the common features shared by all forms of psychotherapy that may account for the fact that there is little or no overall difference in their effectiveness. Explain the statement that "Some kinds of psychotherapy seem to be particularly appropriate for certain people and problems"; include examples.

BIOLOGICAL TREATMENTS

- Explain why some clients and therapists opt for biological treatment instead of psychotherapy.

- Describe the major antipsychotic and antidepressant drugs including their significant side effects.

- Describe electroconvulsive therapy and psychosurgery, their effectiveness in treating specific disorders, and their potential side effects. Explain why these are "last resort treatments" that are normally used only other treatments have failed.

INSTITUTIONALIZATION AND ITS ALTERNATIVES

- Describe the process of deinstitutionalization and the problems that have resulted from it. Identify alternatives to deinstitutionalization including the three forms of prevention.

CLIENT DIVERSITY AND TREATMENT

- Explain how gender and cultural differences can affect the treatment of psychological problems and the training of therapists.

CHAPTER OUTLINE

I. Enduring Issues in Therapies (page 425)

II. Insight Therapies (page 425)
   A. Psychoanalysis
      • Free Association
      • Transference
      • Insight
   B. Client-Centered Therapy
      • Nondirective Approach
   C. Gestalt Therapy
      • Fritz Perls
      • Emphasis on Whole Person
   D. Recent Developments
      • Short-term Psychodynamic Therapy

III. Behavior Therapies (page 431)
   A. Therapies Based on Classical Conditioning
      i. Desensitization, Extinction, And Flooding
      ii. Aversive Conditioning
   B. Therapies Based on Operant Conditioning
      • Behavior Contracting
      • Token Economy
   C. Therapies Based on Modeling
      • Bandura's Snake Phobia Cure

IV. Cognitive Therapies (page 434)
   A. Stress-Inoculation Therapy
      • Self-talk
   B. Rational–Emotive Therapy
      • Confrontation of Dysfunctional Beliefs with Variety of Techniques
   C. Beck's Cognitive Therapy
      • Focus on Debugging Self-Criticism

V. Group Therapies (page 436)
   A. Family Therapy
      • Involves Entire Family
   B. Couple Therapy
      • Empathy Training
   C. Self-Help Groups
      • Alchoholics Anonymous
   D. APPLYING PSYCHOLOGY: HOW TO FIND HELP

VI. Effectiveness of Psychotherapy (page 439)
   A. Which Type of Therapy Is Best for Which Disorder?
      • Different Therapies More Successful in Certain Contexts
      • Trend Toward Eclecticism

VII. Biological Treatments (page 441)
   A. Drug Therapies
      i. Antipsychotic Drugs
      ii. Antidepressant Drugs
      iii. Lithium
      iv. Other Medications
   B. Electroconvulsive Therapy
      • Prolonged, Severe Depression Not Responding to Other Treatments
   C. Psychosurgery
      • Drastic Step
      • Prefrontal Lobotomy
      • Rarely Performed Today

VIII. Institutionalization and its Alternatives (page 446)
   A. Deinstitutionalization
      • Has Created Serious Challenges
   B. Alternative Forms of Treatment
      • More Positive Outcomes Than Expensive Hospitalization
   C. Prevention
      • Primary Prevention
      • Secondary Prevention
      • Tertiary Prevention

IX. Client Diversity and Treatment (page 449)
   A. Gender and Treatment
      • Significant Gender Differences in Disorders
      • However, Treatments Mostly the Same for Men and Women
      • Critics of "Equal Treatment"
   B. Culture and Treatment
      • Clients/Therapists Tend to Share Racial and Ethnic Background
      • New Challenge of Treating Immigrants

KEY TERMS

Antipsychotic drugs	Drugs used to treat very severe psychological disorders, particularly schizophrenia. (p. 442)
Aversive conditioning	Behavioral therapy techniques aimed at eliminating undesirable behavior patterns by teaching the person to associate them with pain and discomfort. (p. 432)
Behavior contracting	Form of operant conditioning therapy in which the client and therapist set behavioral goals and agree on reinforcements that the client will receive on reaching those goals. (p. 432)
Behavior therapies	Therapeutic approaches that are based on the belief that all behavior, normal and abnormal, is learned, and that the objective of therapy is to teach people new, more satisfying ways of behaving. (p. 431)
Biological treatments	A group of approaches, including medication, electroconvulsive therapy, and psychosurgery, that are sometimes used to treat psychological disorders in conjunction with, or instead of, psychotherapy. (p. 441)
Client-centered (or person-centered) therapy	Nondirectional form of therapy developed by Carl Rogers that calls for unconditional positive regard of the client by the therapist with the goal of helping the client become fully functioning. (p. 427)
Cognitive therapies	Psychotherapies that emphasize changing clients' perceptions of their life situation as a way of modifying their behavior. (p. 434)
Cognitive therapy	Therapy that depends on identifying and changing inappropriately negative and self-critical patterns of thought. (p. 435)
Couple therapy	A form of group therapy intended to help troubled partners improve their problems of communication and interaction. (p. 436)
Deinstitutionalization	Policy of treating people with severe psychological disorders in the larger community or in small residential centers such as halfway houses, rather than in large public hospitals. (p. 446)
Eclecticism	Psychotherapeutic approach that recognizes the value of a broad treatment package over a rigid commitment to one particular form of therapy. (p. 441)
Electroconvulsive therapy (ECT)	Biological therapy in which a mild electrical current is passed through the brain for a short period, often producing convulsions and temporary coma; used to treat severe, prolonged depression. (p. 444)
Family therapy	A form of group therapy that sees the family as at least partly responsible for the individual's problems and that seeks to change all family members' behaviors to the benefit of the family unit as well as the troubled individual. (p. 436)
Free association	A psychoanalytic technique that encourages the person to talk without inhibition about whatever thoughts or fantasies come to mind. (p. 426)
Gestalt therapy	An insight therapy that emphasizes the wholeness of the personality and attempts to reawaken people to their emotions and sensations in the present. (p. 428)
Group therapy	Type of psychotherapy in which clients meet regularly to interact and help one another achieve insight into their feelings and behavior. (p. 436)
Insight	Learning that occurs rapidly as a result of understanding all the elements of a problem. (p. 426)
Insight therapies	A variety of individual psychotherapies designed to give people a better awareness and understanding of their feelings, motivations, and actions in the hope that this will help them to adjust. (p. 425)
Modeling	A behavior therapy in which the person learns desired behaviors by watching others perform those behaviors. (p. 433)

Primary prevention	Techniques and programs to improve the social environment so that new cases of mental disorders do not develop. (p. 447)
Psychoanalysis	The theory of personality Freud developed, as well as the form of therapy he invented. (p. 426)
Psychosurgery	Brain surgery performed to change a person's behavior and emotional state; a biological therapy rarely used today. (p. 444)
Psychotherapy	The use of psychological techniques to treat personality and behavior disorders. (p. 425)
Rational–emotive therapy (RET)	A directive cognitive therapy based on the idea that clients' psychological distress is caused by irrational and self-defeating beliefs and that the therapist's job is to challenge such dysfunctional beliefs. (p. 434)
Secondary prevention	Programs to identify groups that are at high risk for mental disorders and to detect maladaptive behavior in these groups and treat it promptly. (p. 448)
Short-term psychodynamic therapy	Insight therapy that is time limited and focused on trying to help clients correct the immediate problems in their lives. (p. 430)
Stress-inoculation therapy	A type of cognitive therapy that trains clients to cope with stressful situations by learning a more useful pattern of self-talk. (p. 434)
Systematic desensitization	A behavioral technique for reducing a person's fear and anxiety by gradually associating a new response (relaxation) with stimuli that have been causing the fear and anxiety. (p. 431)
Tertiary prevention	Programs to help people adjust to community life after release from a mental hospital. (p. 448)
Token economy	An operant conditioning therapy in which people earn tokens (reinforcers) for desired behaviors and exchange them for desired items or privileges. (p. 433)
Transference	The client's carrying over to the analyst feelings held toward childhood authority figures. (p. 426)

Vocabulary Flashcards

Cut out each term and use as study cards. The definition is on the back side of each term.

Psychotherapy	**Insight**
Insight therapies	**Client-centered (or person-centered) therapy**
Psychoanalysis	**Gestalt therapy**
Free association	**Short-term psychodynamic therapy**
Transference	**Behavior therapies**

Learning that occurs rapidly as a result of understanding all the elements of a problem.

The use of psychological techniques to treat personality and behavior disorders.

Nondirectional form of therapy developed by Carl Rogers that calls for unconditional positive regard of the client by the therapist with the goal of helping the client become fully functioning.

A variety of individual psychotherapies designed to give people a better awareness and understanding of their feelings, motivations, and actions in the hope that this will help them to adjust.

An insight therapy that emphasizes the wholeness of the personality and attempts to reawaken people to their emotions and sensations in the present.

The theory of personality Freud developed, as well as the form of therapy he invented.

Insight therapy that is time limited and focused on trying to help clients correct the immediate problems in their lives.

A psychoanalytic technique that encourages the person to talk without inhibition about whatever thoughts or fantasies come to mind.

Therapeutic approaches that are based on the belief that all behavior, normal and abnormal, is learned, and that the objective of therapy is to teach people new, more satisfying ways of behaving.

The client's carrying over to the analyst feelings held toward childhood authority figures.

Systematic desensitization	**Cognitive therapies**
Aversive conditioning	**Stress-inoculation therapy**
Behavior contracting	**Rational–emotive therapy (RET)**
Token economy	**Cognitive therapy**
Modeling	**Group therapy**

Psychotherapies that emphasize changing clients' perceptions of their life situation as a way of modifying their behavior.

A behavioral technique for reducing a person's fear and anxiety by gradually associating a new response (relaxation) with stimuli that have been causing the fear and anxiety.

A type of cognitive therapy that trains clients to cope with stressful situations by learning a more useful pattern of self-talk.

Behavioral therapy techniques aimed at eliminating undesirable behavior patterns by teaching the person to associate them with pain and discomfort.

A directive cognitive therapy based on the idea that clients' psychological distress is caused by irrational and self-defeating beliefs and that the therapist's job is to challenge such dysfunctional beliefs.

Form of operant conditioning therapy in which the client and therapist set behavioral goals and agree on reinforcements that the client will receive on reaching those goals.

Therapy that depends on identifying and changing inappropriately negative and self-critical patterns of thought.

An operant conditioning therapy in which people earn tokens (reinforcers) for desired behaviors and exchange them for desired items or privileges.

Type of psychotherapy in which clients meet regularly to interact and help one another achieve insight into their feelings and behavior.

A behavior therapy in which the person learns desired behaviors by watching others perform those behaviors.

Family therapy	**Electroconvulsive therapy (ECT)**
Couple therapy	**Psychosurgery**
Eclecticism	**Deinstitution-alization**
Biological treatments	**Primary prevention**
Antipsychotic drugs	**Secondary prevention**

Biological therapy in which a mild electrical current is passed through the brain for a short period, often producing convulsions and temporary coma; used to treat severe, prolonged depression.

A form of group therapy that sees the family as at least partly responsible for the individual's problems and that seeks to change all family members' behaviors to the benefit of the family unit as well as the troubled individual.

Brain surgery performed to change a person's behavior and emotional state; a biological therapy rarely used today.

A form of group therapy intended to help troubled partners improve their problems of communication and interaction.

Policy of treating people with severe psychological disorders in the larger community or in small residential centers such as halfway houses, rather than in large public hospitals.

Psychotherapeutic approach that recognizes the value of a broad treatment package over a rigid commitment to one particular form of therapy.

Techniques and programs to improve the social environment so that new cases of mental disorders do not develop.

A group of approaches, including medication, electroconvulsive therapy, and psychosurgery, that are sometimes used to treat psychological disorders in conjunction with, or instead of, psychotherapy.

Programs to identify groups that are at high risk for mental disorders and to detect maladaptive behavior in these groups and treat it promptly.

Drugs used to treat very severe psychological disorders, particularly schizophrenia.

Tertiary
prevention

Programs to help people adjust to community life after release from a mental hospital.

After studying the text and completing the Study Guide activities, answer these questions to determine if you need to review any areas before the course exam.

MULTIPLE CHOICE

1. Insight therapies focus on giving people _____.
   a. skills to change their behaviors
   b. clearer understanding of their feelings, motives, and actions
   c. an understanding of perceptual processes
   d. an understanding of biological influences on behavior

2. Neo-Freudians differ from traditional Freudian approaches to therapy in that they encourage clients to focus on the _____ and they favor _____ their clients.
   a. past; face-to-face discussions with
   b. present; face-to-face discussions with
   c. past; sitting behind and passively listening to
   d. present; sitting behind and passively listening to

3. The cardinal rule in client-centered therapy is for the therapist to express _____ for the client.
   a. unconditional positive regard
   b. conditional positive regard
   c. positive transference
   d. psychological congruence

4. Gestalt therapy emphasizes _____.
   a. the here and now
   b. face-to-face confrontations
   c. becoming more genuine in daily interactions
   d. all of the above

5. The main task of behavioral therapy is to _____.
   a. get the patient to look past the problem
   b. provide a warm atmosphere for discussing problems
   c. teach clients to behave in more effective ways
   d. provide insight into the causes of problems

6. The technique of _____ trains a client to remain relaxed and calm in the presence of a stimulus that he or she formerly feared.
   a. reciprocal inhibition
   b. free association
   c. systematic desensitization
   d. operant conditioning

7. Making someone who is afraid of snakes handle dozens of snakes in an effort to get him to overcome his fear is called _____.
   a. systematic desensitization
   b. flooding
   c. paradoxical intent
   d. aversive conditioning

8. In what type of therapy is a contract drawn up, binding both client and therapist as if they were involved in a legal agreement?
   a. behavioral contracting
   b. reciprocal inhibition
   c. transactional analysis
   d. a token economy

9. Showing a client how his or her irrational and self-defeating beliefs are causing problems is MOST characteristic of _____ therapy.
   a. psychoanalytic
   b. behavioral
   c. stress-inoculation
   d. rational-emotive

10. Alcoholics Anonymous is an example of a (n)_____ group.
    a. encounter
    b. desensitization
    c. self-help
    d. structured behavior therapy

11. The psychotherapeutic approach that recognizes the value of a broad treatment package over a rigid commitment to one particular form of therapy is _____.
    a. situationalism
    c. interactionism
    b. existentialism
    d. eclecticism

12. In 1988, the new drug ___ was put on the market as the first of a new class of antidepressant drugs.
    a. Ecstasy
    c. Prozac
    b. Lithium
    d. Thorazine

13. Drugs that combat depression work by ____.
    a. increasing the amount of serotonin in the brain
    b. blocking dopamine receptors in the brain
    c. inhibiting the function of the hypothalamus
    d. increasing acetylcholine in the brain

14. Most antipsychotic drugs work by _____.
    a. increasing acetylcholine in the brain
    b. increasing the amount of serotonin in the brain
    c. blocking dopamine receptors in the brain
    d. inhibiting the function of the hypothalamus

15. Electroconvulsive therapy is most often used to alleviate ____.
    a. anxiety
    c. schizophrenia
    b. somatoform disorders
    d. severe depression

16. Which of the following treatments is LEAST likely to be used today?
    a. electroconvulsive therapy
    c. prefrontal lobotomy
    b. drug treatment
    d. behavioral therapy

17. Educating young people about AIDS through TV ad campaigns is a form of ___ prevention.
    a. basic
    c. tertiary
    b. primary
    d. secondary

18. Suicide hot lines and crisis intervention centers are all involved in ___ prevention.
    a. basic
    c. tertiary
    b. primary
    d. secondary

19. Halfway houses and other places where ex-patients can be supported in their efforts to return to normal life after release from institutions are forms of _____ prevention.
    a. basic
    c. tertiary
    b. primary
    d. secondary

20. Which of the following is NOT a type of group therapy?
    a. couple therapy
    b. family therapy
    c. cognitive therapy
    d. self-help group

21. Which of the following statements does NOT describe aspects that are common in the various forms of psychotherapy?
    a. Clients are provided with explanations for their problems.
    b. Most psychotherapies offer people hope.
    c. Clients are engaged in a therapeutic alliance.
    d. Clients are treated with medication.

SHORT ESSAY QUESTIONS

1. Differentiate among insight therapies, behavior therapies, cognitive therapies, and group therapies.

2. Discuss the criticisms of psychoanalysis.

3. Explain how client-centered and rational-emotive therapists interpret causes of emotional problems. Describe the therapeutic techniques of these approaches.

4. Summarize the behavioral therapist's interpretation of disorders. Describe aversive conditioning, desensitization, and modeling.

5. Describe stress-inoculation therapy, Beck's cognitive therapy, and Gestalt therapy.

6. List the advantages and disadvantages of group therapies. Identify five current approaches to group therapy.

7. Discuss the effectiveness of insight therapy and behavior therapy.

8. Outline the available biological treatments and discuss the advantages and disadvantages of each.

9. Summarize the inadequacies of institutionalization. List the alternative to institutionalization.

10. Explain the differences among primary, secondary, and tertiary prevention.

11. Discuss gender and cultural differences in relationship to treatment of psychological problems.

ANSWERS AND EXPLANATIONS TO MULTIPLE CHOICE POSTTEST

1. b. Insight therapies are designed to give people better awareness and clearer understandings of their feelings, motivations, and actions. p. 425

2. b. Many Neo-Freudian therapists encourage dealing with current situations and having face-to-face discussions. p. 427

3. a. The cardinal rule in client-centered therapy is for the therapist to express unconditional positive regard or true acceptance. p. 428

4. d. Gestalt therapy emphasizes the here and now, face-to-face confrontations and becoming more genuine in the client's daily life. p. 428

5. c. Behavior therapy's main task is to teach clients new and more satisfying ways of behaving. p. 431

6. c. Systematic desensitization gradually reduces fear and anxiety by association relaxation with the fearful stimuli. p. 431

7. b. Flooding involves full intensity exposure to a feared stimulus. p. 432

8. a. Behavioral contracting is a signed agreement between client and therapist regarding therapeutic goals and reinforcements. p. 432

9. d. Rational-emotive therapy (RET) is based on the idea that irrational and self-defeating beliefs cause psychological problems. p. 434

10. c. AA is the best-known self-help group. p. 437

11. d. Eclecticism recognizes the value of a broad treatment package over one form of therapy. p. 441

12. c. In 1988, Prozac was the first antidepressant drug to be introduced. p. 443

13. a. Antidepressant drugs, like Prozac, work by increasing the amount of serotonin in the brain. p. 443

14. c. Most antipsychotic drugs work by blocking dopamine receptors in the brain. p. 442

15. d. ECT is most often used for prolonged and severe depression when no other treatment is effective. p. 444

16. c. Prefrontal lobotomies are rarely performed today. p. 444

17. b. Programs that educate people about illness are forms of primary prevention. p. 447

18. d. Suicide hotlines and crisis intervention are forms of secondary prevention. p. 448

19. c. Halfway houses are a form of tertiary prevention. p. 448

20. c. Couple therapy, family therapy, and self-help groups are all types of group therapies. Cognitive therapy is not a type of group therapy. p. 436

21. d. Medications may be used to treat a number of different psychological problems, but their prescription is not common to all psychotherapies. p. 442

CHAPTER

14 Social Psychology

CHAPTER OVERVIEW

The chapter opens with a harrowing case of mistaken identity involving Sher Singh, accused by police of being a fugitive terrorist on September 12, 2001. The incident raises the kind of questions that researchers who specialize in the field of social psychology aim to find answers to. **Social psychology** is the scientific study of ways in which the thoughts, feelings, and behaviors of one individual are influenced by the real, imagined, or inferred behavior or characteristics of other people.

The chapter first looks at the subject of social cognition. Forming impressions, explaining others' behavior, and experiencing interpersonal attraction are all examples of **social cognition**, the process of taking in and assessing information about other people. It is one way in which we are influenced by others' thoughts, feelings, and behaviors.

When forming impressions of others, we rely on *schemata*, or sets of expectations and beliefs about categories of people. Impressions are also affected by the order in which information is acquired. First impressions are the strongest (the **primacy effect**), probably because we prefer not to subsequently expend more cognitive effort to analyze or change them. This same preference also encourages us to form impressions by using simplistic, but strongly held schemata called **stereotypes**. First impressions can also bring about the behavior we expect from other people, a process known as **self-fulfilling prophecy**.

Attribution theory holds that people seek to understand human behavior by attributing it either to internal or external causes. Perceptual biases can lead to the **fundamental attribution error**, in which we overemphasize others' personal traits in attributing causes to their behavior. **Defensive attribution** motivates us to explain our own actions in ways that

protect our self-esteem. *Self-serving bias* refers to our tendency to attribute our successes to internal factors and our failures to external ones. The **just-world hypothesis** may lead us to blame the victim when bad things happen to other people.

People who are similar in attitudes, interests, backgrounds, and values tend to like one another. **Proximity** also promotes liking. The more we are in contact with certain people, the more we tend to like them. We also tend to like people who make us feel appreciated and rewarded, an idea based on the concept of **exchange**. Exchanges work only insofar as they are fair or equitable. A relationship is based on **equity** when both individuals receive equally from each other. Most people also tend to like physically attractive people, as well as attributing to them, correctly or not, many positive personal characteristics.

The topic of attitudes is featured next in the chapter. An **attitude** is a relatively stable organization of beliefs, feelings, and tendencies toward an *attitude object*. Attitudes are important because they often influence behavior. **Self-monitoring** is the tendency for an individual to observe a situation for cues about how to react.

The three major components of attitudes are (1) evaluative beliefs about the attitude object, (2) feelings about that object, and (3) behavioral tendencies toward it. These three components are very often (but not always) consistent with one another.

Prejudice is an unfair negative attitude directed toward a group and its members, whereas **discrimination** is unfair behavior based on prejudice. One explanation of prejudice is the **frustration–aggression theory**, which states that people who feel exploited and oppressed displace their hostility toward the powerful onto *scapegoats*—people who are "lower" on the social scale than they are. Another theory links prejudice to the **authoritarian**

personality, a rigidly conventional and bigoted type marked by exaggerated respect for authority and hostility toward those who defy society's norms. A third theory proposes a cognitive source of prejudice—oversimplified or stereotyped thinking about categories of people (an example would be **racism**). Finally, conformity to the prejudices of one's social group can help to explain prejudice. Three strategies for reducing prejudice appear to be especially promising: recategorization (expanding our schema of a particular group), controlled processing (training ourselves to be mindful of people who differ from us), and improving contact between groups.

Attitudes may be changed when new actions, beliefs, or perceptions contradict preexisting attitudes, called **cognitive dissonance**. Attitudes can also change in response to efforts at persuasion. The first step in persuasion is to get the audience's attention. Then the task is to get the audience to comprehend and accept the message. According to the *communication model*, persuasion is a function of the source, the message itself, the medium of communication, and the characteristics of the audience. The most effective means of changing attitudes—especially important attitudes, behaviors, or lifestyle choices—may be *self-persuasion*.

The chapter next turns to examine the role of social influence. **Social influence** is the process by which people's perceptions, attitudes, and actions are affected by others' behavior and characteristics. The power of social influence is especially apparent in the study of cultural influences and of conformity, compliance, and obedience.

The culture in which you are immersed has an enormous influence on your thoughts and actions. Culture dictates differences in diet, dress, and personal space. One result of this is the unquestioning acceptance of **cultural truisms**—beliefs or values that most members of a society accept as self-evident. Eating pizza, shunning rattlesnake meat, dressing in jeans instead of a loincloth, and feeling uncomfortable when others stand very close to you when they speak are all results of culture. As we adapt our behavior to that of others, we learn the **norms** of our culture, as well as its beliefs and values.

Voluntarily yielding one's preferences, beliefs, or judgments to those of a larger group is called **conformity**. Research by Solomon Asch and others has shown that characteristics of both the situation and the person influence the likelihood of conforming. Cultural influences on the tendency to conform also exist, with people in collectivist cultures often being more prone to conformity than those in noncollectivist ones.

Compliance is a change in behavior in response to someone's explicit request. One technique to encourage compliance is the *foot-in-the-door approach*, or getting people to go along with a small request to make them more likely to comply with a larger one. Another technique is the *lowball procedure*: initially offering a low price to win commitment, and then gradually escalating the cost. Also effective is the *door-in-the-face tactic*, or initially making an unreasonable request that is bound to be turned down but will perhaps generate enough guilt to foster compliance with another request.

Classic research by Stanley Milgram showed that many people were willing to obey orders to administer harmful shocks to other people. This **obedience** to an authority figure was more likely when certain situational factors were present. For example, people found it harder to disobey when the authority figure issuing the order was nearby. They were also more likely to obey the command when the person being given the shock was some distance from them. According to Milgram, obedience is brought on by the constraints of the situation.

The chapter concludes with a section on social action, raising the question of whether we behave differently when other people are present. Conformity, compliance, and obedience may take place even when no one else is physically present, but other processes of social influence depend on the presence of others.

Immersion in a large, anonymous group may lead to **deindividuation**, the loss of a sense of personal responsibility for one's actions. Deindividuation can sometimes lead to violence or other forms of irresponsible behavior. The greater the sense of anonymity, the more this effect occurs.

Helping someone in need without expectation of a reward is called **altruistic behavior**. Altruism is influenced by situational factors such as the presence of other people. According to the **bystander effect**, a person is less apt to offer assistance when other potential helpers are present. Conversely, being the only person to spot someone in trouble tends to encourage helping. Also encouraging helping are an unambiguous emergency situation and certain personal characteristics, such as empathy for the victim and being in a good mood.

Research on the **risky shift** and the broader phenomenon of group **polarization** shows that group decision making actually increases tendencies toward extreme solutions, encouraging members to lean toward either greater risk or greater caution. People deliberating in groups may also display *social loafing*, or a tendency to exert less effort on the assumption that others will do most of the work. And in very cohesive groups and isolated groups, there is a tendency toward **groupthink**, an unwillingness to criticize the emerging group consensus even when it seems misguided.

According to the **great-person theory**, leadership is a function of personal traits that qualify one to lead others. An alternative theory attributes leadership to being in the right place at the right time. According to the transactional view, traits of the leader and traits of the group interact with certain aspects of the situation to determine what kind of leader will come to the fore. Fred Fiedler's *contingency theory* focused on two contrasting leadership styles: task oriented and relationship oriented. The effectiveness of each style depends on the nature of the task, the relationship of the leader with group members, and the leader's power over the group.

The task-oriented leadership style typical of American businesses is being transformed through the introduction of a management style that emphasizes small work teams and input from all members of the group. Recent research indicates that women in leadership positions tend to have a more democratic, collaborative, and interpersonally oriented style of managing employees than do men in similar positions.

LEARNING OBJECTIVES EXERCISE

After you have read and studied the chapter, you should be able to answer the following learning objectives.

SOCIAL COGNITION

- Describe the role of schemata, stereotypes, and the primacy effect in impression formation. Explain how impressions of others can become self-fulfilling prophecies.

- Summarize the way in which *distinctiveness*, *consistency*, and *consensus* affect our judgment about whether a given behavior is due to internal or external causes.

- Explain what is meant by the statement "the causal attributions we make are often vulnerable to *biases*." In your answer, include the *actor-observer bias*, the *fundamental attribution error*, and *defensive attribution* (including the self-serving bias and the just-world hypothesis).

- Briefly summarize the five factors that influence attraction and the tendency to like another person.

ATTITUDES

- Describe the three major components of attitudes and the variables that determine whether an attitude will be reflected in behavior.

- Distinguish between prejudice, racism, and discrimination. Explain the role of stereotypes and the *ultimate attribution error* in prejudicial attitudes. Compare and contrast the following potential sources of prejudice: frustration-aggression, authoritarian personality, "cognitive misers," and conformity. Describe the three strategies that appear promising as ways to reduce prejudice and discrimination.

- Describe the three steps in the use of persuasion to change attitudes: attention, comprehension, and acceptance. In your description, include the source (credibility and the sleeper effect), the message itself (one-sided vs. two-sided, fear), the medium of communication, and characteristics of the audience.

- Explain what is meant by "cognitive dissonance" and how that can be used to change attitudes.

SOCIAL INFLUENCE

- Explain what is meant by the statement that "culture is a major form of social influence." In your explanation, include cultural truisms and norms.

- Compare and contrast conformity, compliance, and obedience. Describe the factors that influence conforming behavior. Distinguish between the foot-in-the-door technique, lowball procedure, and the door-in-the-face effect as ways to get compliance. Describe the factors that influence obedience.

- Explain how deindividuation and the snowball effect can contribute to mob behavior.

- Explain the role of the following factors in influencing helping behavior: altruism, the bystander effect, the ambiguity of the situation, and the personal characteristics of bystanders.

- Describe the process of polarization in group discussion. Identify the factors that affect whether a group is likely to be more or less effective than individuals acting alone.

- Compare and contrast the following theories of leadership: the great-person theory, the right-place-at-the-right-time theory, and contingency theory.

- Briefly summarize cultural and gender differences in leadership.

KEY TERMS

Altruistic behavior	Helping behavior that is not linked to personal gain. (p. 477)
Attitude	Relatively stable organization of beliefs, feelings, and behavior tendencies directed toward something or someone—the attitude object. (p. 463)
Attribution theory	The theory that addresses the question of how people make judgments about the causes of behavior. (p. 458)
Authoritarian personality	A personality pattern characterized by rigid conventionality, exaggerated respect for authority, and hostility toward those who defy society's norms. (p. 465)
Bystander effect	The tendency for an individual's helpfulness in an emergency to decrease as the number of passive bystanders increases. (p. 477)
Cognitive dissonance	Perceived inconsistency between two cognitions. (p. 469)
Compliance	Change of behavior in response to an explicit request from another person or group. (p. 474)
Conformity	Voluntarily yielding to social norms, even at the expense of one's preferences. (p. 472)
Cultural truisms	Beliefs that most members of a society accept as self-evidently true. (p. 472)
Defensive attribution	The tendency to attribute our successes to our own efforts or qualities and our failures to external factors. (p. 459)
Deindividuation	A loss of personal sense of responsibility in a group. (p. 476)
Discrimination	An unfair act or series of acts taken toward an entire group of people or individual members of that group. (p. 464)
Equity	Fairness of exchange achieved when each partner in the relationship receives the same proportion of outcomes to investments. (p. 461)
Exchange	The concept that relationships are based on trading rewards among partners. (p. 461)
Frustration–aggression theory	The theory that, under certain circumstances, people who are frustrated in their goals turn their anger away from the proper, powerful target and toward another, less powerful target that is safer to attack. (p. 464)
Fundamental attribution error	The tendency of people to overemphasize personal causes for other people's behavior and to underemphasize personal causes for their own behavior. (p. 458)
Great-person theory	The theory that leadership is a result of personal qualities and traits that qualify one to lead others. (p. 479)
Groupthink	A process that occurs when the members of a group like one another, have similar goals and are isolated, leading them to ignore alternatives and not criticize group consensus. (p. 479)
Just-world hypothesis	Attribution error based on the assumption that bad things happen to bad people and good things happen to good people. (p. 459)
Norm	A shared idea or expectation about how to behave. (p. 472)
Obedience	Change of behavior in response to a command from another person, typically an authority figure. (p. 474)
Polarization	The condition of a neuron when the inside is negatively charged relative to the outside; for example, when the neuron is at rest. (p. 478)
Prejudice	An unfair, intolerant, or unfavorable attitude toward a group of people. (p. 464)
Primacy effect	The fact that early information about someone weighs more heavily than later information in influencing one's impression of that person. (p. 456)
Proximity	How close two people live to each other. (p. 460)
Racism	Prejudice and discrimination directed at a particular racial group. (p. 465)
Risky shift	Greater willingness of a group than an individual to take substantial risks. (p. 478)

Self-fulfilling prophecy	The process in which a person's expectation about another elicits behavior from the second person that confirms the expectation. (p. 457)
Self-monitoring	The tendency for an individual to observe the situation for cues about how to react. (p. 463)
Social cognition	Knowledge and understanding concerning the social world and the people in it (including oneself). (p. 456)
Social influence	The process by which others individually or collectively affect one's perceptions, attitudes, and actions. (p. 471)
Social psychology	The scientific study of the ways in which the thoughts, feelings, and behaviors of one individual are influenced by the real, imagined, or inferred behavior or characteristics of other people. (p. 455)
Stereotype	A set of characteristics presumed to be shared by all members of a social category. (p. 457)

Social psychology	**Attribution theory**
Social cognition	**Fundamental attribution error**
Primacy effect	**Defensive attribution**
Self-fulfilling prophecy	**Just-world hypothesis**
Stereotype	**Proximity**

The theory that addresses the question of how people make judgments about the causes of behavior.	The scientific study of the ways in which the thoughts, feelings, and behaviors of one individual are influenced by the real, imagined, or inferred behavior or characteristics of other people.
The tendency of people to overemphasize personal causes for other people's behavior and to underemphasize personal causes for their own behavior.	Knowledge and understanding concerning the social world and the people in it (including oneself).
The tendency to attribute our successes to our own efforts or qualities and our failures to external factors.	The fact that early information about someone weighs more heavily than later information in influencing one's impression of that person.
Attribution error based on the assumption that bad things happen to bad people and good things happen to good people.	The process in which a person's expectation about another elicits behavior from the second person that confirms the expectation.
How close two people live to each other.	A set of characteristics presumed to be shared by all members of a social category.

Exchange	Discrimination
Equity	Frustration–aggression theory
Attitude	Authoritarian personality
Self-monitoring	Racism
Prejudice	Cognitive dissonance

An unfair act or series of acts taken toward an entire group of people or individual members of that group.

The concept that relationships are based on trading rewards among partners.

The theory that, under certain circumstances, people who are frustrated in their goals turn their anger away from the proper, powerful target and toward another, less powerful target that is safer to attack.

Fairness of exchange achieved when each partner in the relationship receives the same proportion of outcomes to investments.

A personality pattern characterized by rigid conventionality, exaggerated respect for authority, and hostility toward those who defy society's norms.

Relatively stable organization of beliefs, feelings, and behavior tendencies directed toward something or someone—the attitude object.

Prejudice and discrimination directed at a particular racial group.

The tendency for an individual to observe the situation for cues about how to react.

Perceived inconsistency between two cognitions.

An unfair, intolerant, or unfavorable attitude toward a group of people.

Social influence	Obedience
Cultural truisms	Deindividuation
Norm	Altruistic behavior
Conformity	Bystander effect
Compliance	Risky shift

Change of behavior in response to a command from another person, typically an authority figure.	The process by which others individually or collectively affect one's perceptions, attitudes, and actions.
A loss of personal sense of responsibility in a group.	Beliefs that most members of a society accept as self-evidently true.
Helping behavior that is not linked to personal gain.	A shared idea or expectation about how to behave.
The tendency for an individual's helpfulness in an emergency to decrease as the number of passive bystanders increases.	Voluntarily yielding to social norms, even at the expense of one's preferences.
Greater willingness of a group than an individual to take substantial risks.	Change of behavior in response to an explicit request from another person or group.

Polarization

Groupthink

Great-person theory

	The condition of a neuron when the inside is negatively charged relative to the outside; for example, when the neuron is at rest.
	A process that occurs when the members of a group like one another, have similar goals and are isolated, leading them to ignore alternatives and not criticize group consensus.
	The theory that leadership is a result of personal qualities and traits that qualify one to lead others.

POSTTEST

After studying the text and completing the Study Guide activities, answer these questions to determine if you need to review any areas before the course exam.

MULTIPLE CHOICE

1. The process by which others individually or collectively affect one's perceptions, attitudes, and actions.
   a. group dynamics
   b. social influence
   c. conformity
   d. culture

2. Whenever a person has two contradictory cognitions at the same time, a state of _____ exists.
   a. cognitive congruence
   b. nonreciprocity
   c. cognitive dissonance
   d. creative conflict

3. The person who conducted the most well-known research on obedience is _____.
   a. Asch
   b. Milgram
   c. Luchens
   d. Kelley

4. _____ behavior is helping other people with no expectation of personal gain.
   a. Reciprocal
   b. Deindividuated
   c. Diffused
   d. Altruistic

5. The _____ effect is that people are more likely to comply with a second, larger request after complying with a first, small request.
   a. response cue
   b. bait and switch
   c. foot-in-the-door
   d. primacy

6. _____ is a process by which people feel anonymous in a large group.
   a. Deindividuation
   b. Identity moratorium
   c. Identity diffusion
   d. Groupthink

7. The tendency for an individual's helpfulness in an emergency to decrease as the number of bystanders increases is called _____.
   a. the risky shift phenomenon
   b. groupthink
   c. the bystander effect
   d. social loafing

8. In a mob, one dominant person can often convince people to act due to the _____ effect.
   a. lowball
   b. snowball
   c. primacy
   d. door-in-the-face

9. The poor decisions made in the Watergate cover-up, the Challenger disaster, and the Bay of Pigs invasion were due primarily to _____.
   a. groupthink
   b. deindividuation
   c. risky shift
   d. polarization

10. Most of us associate _____ with good personality traits, intelligence, and happiness.
    a. youth
    b. attractiveness
    c. old age
    d. wealth

11. The most important factor in interpersonal attraction is _____.
    a. proximity
    b. similarity
    c. attractiveness
    d. reciprocity

12. Rebecca consistently expresses her beliefs with a little regard for the constraints imposed by the situation. She is probably a _____ self-monitor.
    a. reactive
    b. nonreactive
    c. low
    d. high

13. According to attribution theory, people ___ for good situations and ____ for bad ones.
    a. take credit; take credit
    b. deny responsibility; deny responsibility
    c. take credit; deny responsibility
    d. deny responsibility; take credit

14. Bad things happen to bad people and good things happen to good people, according to _____.
    a. the self-serving bias
    c. the self-fulfilling prophecy
    b. the just-world hypothesis
    d. the reciprocity model

15. Each of the following is a promising strategy for reducing prejudice and discrimination EXCEPT _____.
    a. recategorization
    b. controlled processing
    c. improving contact between groups
    d. increased competition between groups

16. If a man is wearing a blue uniform with a badge and gun holster, we might categorize him as a policeman. We may also have expectations that he will enforce the law and be helpful to people. This process plays a role in impression formation and refers to _____.
    a. creating norms
    b. applying schema
    c. the primacy effect
    d. stereotyping

17. Which of the following statements is NOT true about attitudes?
    a. Attitudes about objects can be changed.
    b. Attitudes may not accurately predict behavior.
    c. Discrimination is a type of unfavorable attitude.
    d. All of the above are true.

SHORT ESSAY QUESTIONS

1. Describe the process by which we form first impressions of other people. Identify three factors that influence personal perception.

2. Explain three aspects of attribution and explain attribution errors.

3. Explain the dynamics of interpersonal attraction.

4. Identify the components of attitudes. Explain how attitudes are acquired and how they change.

5. Explain the origin of prejudice and discrimination and how prejudice can be reduced.

6. Discuss the dynamics of attitude change and the process of persuasion.

7. Explain the theory of cognitive dissonance.

8. Explain how culture, conformity, compliance, and obedience exert social influence.

9. Define risky shift and polarization. Summarize the conditions under which groups are effective and ineffective in solving problems.

ANSWERS AND EXPLANATIONS TO MULTIPLE CHOICE POSTTEST

1. b.   Social influence is the process by which others individually or collectively affect one's perceptions, attitudes, and actions. p. 471

2. c.   Cognitive dissonance occurs when a person has two contradictory cognitions at the same time. p. 469

3. b.   Milgram has conducted the most well-known research on obedience. p. 474

4. d.   Altruistic behavior seeks no personal gain. p. 477

5. c.   The foot-in-the-door effect occurs when people comply with a second larger request after complying first with a small request. p. 474

6. a.   Deindividuation is the process by which people feel anonymous in a large group. p. 476

7. c.   The bystander effect occurs when an increase in the number of bystanders decreases the likelihood than an individual in the group will be helpful. p. 477

8. b.   The snowball effect occurs when a dominant person in a mob is able to convince people to act. p. 476

9. a.   Groupthink occurs when there is so much pressure from the group to conform that people don't feel free to express critical ideas. p. 479

10. b.   Most people associate attractiveness with good personality traits, intelligence, and happiness. p. 460

11. a.   Proximity, or how close people live to each other, is the most important factor in interpersonal attraction. p. 460

12. c.   Rebecca is a low self-monitor. p. 463

13. c.   People take credit for good situations and deny responsibility for bad ones, according to attribution theory. p. 458

14. b.   The just-world hypothesis holds that bad things happen to bad people and good things happen to good people. p. 459

15. d.   Increased competition between groups is not a promising strategy for reducing prejudice and discrimination. p. 466

16. b.   Schema refers to a set of beliefs and expectations based on past experience that is presumed to apply to all members of that category. p. 456

17. c.   Discrimination is a behavior, not an attitude. p. 464